D1674002

France in the Hollande Presidency

French Politics, Society and Culture

General Editor: Jocelyn Evans, Professor of Politics, University of Leeds, UK.

France has always fascinated outside observers. Now, the country is undergoing a period of profound transformation. France is faced with a rapidly changing international and European environment and it is having to rethink some of its most basic social, political and economic orthodoxies. As elsewhere, there is pressure to conform. And yet, while France is responding in ways that are no doubt familiar to people in other European countries, it is also managing to maintain elements of its long-standing distinctiveness. Overall, it remains a place that is not exactly *comme les autres*.

This new series examines all aspects of French politics, society and culture. In so doing it focuses on the changing nature of the French system as well as the established patterns of political, social and cultural life. Contributors to the series are encouraged to present new and innovative arguments so that the informed reader can learn and understand more about one of the most beguiling and compelling of all European countries.

Titles include:

David S. Bell, John Gaffney (*editors*)
THE PRESIDENTS OF THE FRENCH FIFTH REPUBLIC

Jocelyn Evans, Gilles Ivaldi
THE 2012 FRENCH PRESIDENTIAL ELECTIONS
The Inevitable Alternative

John Gaffney
POLITICAL LEADERSHIP IN FRANCE
From Charles de Gaulle to Nicolas Sarkozy

Imogen Long
WOMEN INTELLECTUALS IN POST-68 FRANCE
Petitions and Polemics

Gino G. Raymond (*editor*)
THE SARKOZY PRESIDENCY
Breaking the Mould?

David S. Bell and Byron Criddle
EXCEPTIONAL SOCIALISTS
The Case of the French Socialist Party

Jeremy Ahearne
GOVERNMENT THROUGH CULTURE IN CONTEMPORARY FRANCE

French Politics, Society and Culture
Series Standing Order ISBN 978–0–333–80440–7 hardcover
Series Standing Order ISBN 978–0–333–80441–4 paperback
(*outside North America only*)

You can receive future titles in this series as they are published by placing a standing order. Please contact your bookseller or, in case of difficulty, write to us at the address below with your name and address, the title of the series and the ISBNs quoted above.

Customer Services Department, Macmillan Distribution Ltd, Houndmills, Basingstoke, Hampshire RG21 6XS, England

France in the Hollande Presidency

The Unhappy Republic

John Gaffney
Professor of Politics, Aston University, Birmingham, UK

palgrave
macmillan

First published 2015 by
PALGRAVE MACMILLAN

Palgrave Macmillan in the UK is an imprint of Macmillan Publishers Limited, registered in England, company number 785998, of Houndmills, Basingstoke, Hampshire, RG21 6XS.

Palgrave Macmillan in the US is a division of St Martin's Press LLC, 175 Fifth Avenue, New York, NY 10010.

Palgrave is the global academic imprint of the above companies and has companies and representatives throughout the world.

Palgrave® and Macmillan® are registered trademarks in the United States, the United Kingdom, Europe and other countries.

ISBN: 978-1-137-45390-7

This book is printed on paper suitable for recycling and made from fully managed and sustained forest sources. Logging, pulping and manufacturing processes are expected to conform to the environmental regulations of the country of origin.

A catalogue record for this book is available from the British Library.

A catalog record for this book is available from the Library of Congress.

For Eva

Contents

Acknowledgements

I have a debt of gratitude to two people in particular: Graeme Hayes who read and commented – with varying degrees of severity and approval – the whole manuscript; and Evelyne Descause with whom it has been a delight to share insights and observations and often differing perspectives on French politics over the period of researching and writing this book. The final text has also profited from support and exchanges with colleagues in the Politics and International Relations Department at Aston University, UK, in particular Nat Copsey, and from colleagues at Sciences-Po, Lille and at Sciences-Po, Rennes, in particular Dominique Maliesky and Gilles Richard. Students on my Political Leaders courses at Aston and at Sciences-Po Lille and Rennes have been such fun to work with and have all helped me develop and criticise my own ideas. The School of Languages and Social Sciences at Aston granted me a sabbatical term in 2014–15 which helped greatly with finishing the manuscript. I spent the term as a Professorial Visiting Fellow at Sciences-Po, Paris, and am grateful to Florence Faucher and Colin Hay for their support, and to Silvia Duerich-Morandi and the Paris library staff for all their help. Catherine Fieschi and Cressida Gaffney have been extremely helpful with ideas, disagreements, and suggestions throughout. Jocelyn Evans, The French Politics and Society Series Editor, has been very supportive, as have the editorial team at Palgrave and Shirley Tan, my copy editor. There was also a newspaper vendor near the Place de la Madeleine in Paris who put me right on several points for over two hours, demonstrating how politically interested and interesting so many French people are. My thanks go to everyone. All the mistakes are mine and François Hollande's alone.

List of Abbreviations

CDU	Christlich Demokratische Union Deutschlands
CERES	Centre d'études et de recherches socialistes
CFDT	Confédération française démocratique du travail
CGT	Confédération générale du travail
CICE	Crédit d'impôt pour la compétitivité et l'emploi
CIR	Convention des institutions républicaines
EELV	Europe Écologie Les Verts
ENA	Ecole normale d'administration
EP	European Parliament
EU	European Union
FDS	Fédération démocrate et socialiste
FGDS	Fédération de la gauche démocrate et socialiste
FN	Front national
G8	Group of Eight (France, United Kingdom, United States, Japan, Germany, Italy, Canada (Russia suspended 2014), and European Union)
G20	Group of Twenty (G8 plus Argentina, Australia, Brazil, China, India, Indonesia, Mexico, Saudi Arabia, South Africa, South Korea, Turkey, and central banks and invited countries and organisations)
GDP	Gross Domestic Product
IMF	International Monetary Fund
IVF	In vitro fertilisation
MEP	Member of the European Parliament
MP	Member of Parliament
MRG	Mouvement des radicaux de gauche
NATO	North Atlantic Treaty Organization
ORTF	Office de la radiodiffusion télévision française
PCF	Parti communiste français
Pcm	Per calendar month
PRG	Parti radical de gauche
PS	Parti socialiste
PSA	Parti socialiste autonome
PSU	Parti socialiste unifié
RI	Républicains indépendants
RPF	Rassemblement du peuple français

RPR   Rassemblement pour la république
SFIO   Section française de l'internationale ouvrière (Socialist Party
          1905–1969)
SMIC   Salaire minimum interprofessionel de croissance
SPD   Sozialdemokratische Partei Deutschlands
TGV   Train à grande vitesse (high-speed train)
UDF   Union pour la démocratie française
UDI   Union des démocrates et indépendants
UDR   Union des démocrates pour la république
UDT   Union démocratique du travail
UK   United Kingdom
UKIP   United Kingdom Independence Party
UMP   Union pour un mouvement populaire
UNR   Union pour la nouvelle république

1
Understanding the French Presidency

The aim of this book is, through an analysis of the first half of François Hollande's five-year presidential term, to grasp the strengths and weaknesses of presidential politics following the left's return to power in 2012 and, further, to understand the underlying nature of contemporary French politics, and the Fifth Republic itself. A consequent subtheme to our analysis is to demonstrate that the Fifth Republic is 'dysfunctional'; this in great part because of the manner in which political observers and actors have understood this singular republic and its 'performative requirements'. We shall analyse how François Hollande, as President, acted 'out of category'.

Our study is not focused upon a chronology of events nor upon power relations within the presidential and party political system. What we are concerned with is what the first half of the five-year term – up until the creation of the Valls government, the European elections, the publication of Valérie Trierweiler's book (2014), and the return to frontline politics of Nicolas Sarkozy – tells us about the nature of the republic, and the way in which the left and François Hollande understood or failed to understand the politics of the Fifth Republic, in particular the notions of time, character, and what we call 'sequencing the self'. From a theoretical point of view, therefore, we are concerned with structure and agency, context and performance: to appraise the political performance of an individual and his/her entourage within a particular configuration of institutions and expectations. Our concern is not to chronicle the fortunes and misfortunes of the Hollande presidency (Amar 2013; Baumel 2013; Bercoff 2013) but to understand them within the framework of the Fifth Republic. François Hollande won the presidential election against the incumbent President, Nicolas Sarkozy (Estier 2012; Malouines 2012); but within

1

two-and-a-half years of his election was the most unpopular President of the Republic's seven Presidents. By May 2014, 86% of respondents had a very negative view of Hollande's first two years (BFMTV 5/5/14). In some polls only 1% expressed full confidence in him by this time. Our analysis aims to show how and why this happened. It is almost unavoidable being critical of Hollande himself and his team. We are not, however, concerned with his real character except in as much as it informs us about his 'performative character'; it is the relationship of this to the configuration of institutions and to public opinion that is the central focus of this study.

We are also interested in the long-term historical success and fortunes, the 'health' one might say of the Fifth Republic, and the way in which – historically, culturally, institutionally, rhetorically, and performatively – its evolution has been path-dependent, while not being 'determined'. We shall examine this in Chapter 3 when we examine how presidential 'character' helps us understand from the theoretical perspective how the Fifth Republic has developed. Conversely, lack of political success, misfortune, and 'dysfunction' raise questions of the regime's 'appropriateness', of the imperatives behind the legacy of the republic itself, and how the institutions function today. Does the Fifth Republic's presidentialism still work? And if once it did, how was this so, and what has changed? Our focus is, therefore, on the presidency in the context of its historical, cultural, and institutional conditions of performance. We shall also, perhaps paradoxically, be particularly concerned with presidential politics at the daily political level, because this is where the presidency as a perceived and symbolic institution and one that is 'active' in political life actually 'performs'. It is also our conviction that, for reasons we shall discuss below, the 'trivial', the incidental, the apparently unimportant, and the 'trivial unexpected' in French politics are now in a systematic and often dysfunctional relationship to 'real politics', and this to the point where the trivial has become unpredictable in its effects and potentially of major political consequence. We, therefore, set our study of the presidency at the daily political level in terms of what these developments tell us about France and the presidency at an historical and theoretical level.

What is crucial to yet missing from the myriad of accounts of the 'Mitterrand years', the 'Sarkozy presidency', and so on (*inter alia* Berstein and Rioux 2000; Becker 1998; Favier and Martin-Roland 1990–99; Frears 1981; Frerejean 2007; Jeudy and Vigogne 2007; Lacouture 1984–86, 1998; Viansson-Ponté 1970–71), and which limits the explanatory value of these rich accounts, is a theory of the Fifth

Republic and in particular a theory of the presidency and leadership within it and, more specifically, how longer-term evolutions of presidential character and contingent daily actions and developments interrelate and determine the thrust of politics in a path-dependent manner.

We have elsewhere set out a framework for the analysis of presidential performance (Gaffney 2012). It is part of our argument here or at least a contention that the Hollande presidency is an acute – although by no means the only – illustration of the *dysfunction* of the presidency in the Fifth Republic. The recession, the role of EU, the future of the euro, unemployment, and the developments within the political parties and public opinion are crucial to an understanding of how the Fifth Republic functions (or dysfunctions), but our analysis will be concerned with the way in which central political actors (President, government, contenders for the presidency, political leaders) address these issues, and why they address them in the way they do, and how these 'addressings', that is to say the 'style' of political action and presidential 'image' in the Fifth Republic, impact upon issues in turn, and influence events; how all these affect other political actors and the political parties, and the way these actions and reactions are perceived by the media and wider public, and how the latter responds to this activity, and what these interactions tell us about how French presidential politics functions. Functionally, these actions, reactions, and responses all take place within a symbolic or ideational framework (Edelman 1964, 1988), in large part related to how the Fifth Republic is perceived, and has been historically perceived, 'imagined' and 'constructed' since 1958. We shall, therefore, focus upon how the republic – for us and for the actors – functions and acts symbolically, how it 'enacts itself'. We shall demonstrate, moreover, that for a range of historical and cultural reasons we shall identify and discuss, the Fifth Republic is one in which 'symbolic politics' and its related manifestations – myths, leadership, image, discourse, rhetoric, and the President as the 'embodiment' of politics, have taken on inordinate if not determining political significance.

Understanding and explaining politics is generally effected through an understanding of power relations, and perhaps a theory of power; by calculating the role and effects of governance through understanding how and how successfully interests compete for power and resources; how the economy and the polity interact, how goods are distributed and interests mediated; and how parties compete for power and office and for control of the legislative agenda. Understanding these issues by actors, academics, journalists, or other observers is as necessary in this regime as in all others but, in the case of France, it is necessary but not adequate. The received view is not a complete explanation of how France works for, as we shall demonstrate in this book, all of these processes are steeped – for historical and cultural reasons – in an inordinately consequent matrix of symbolic politics. This means, for example, that the ostentatious deployment not only of presidential pre-eminence but also the trivial, the *fait divers*, are more complex than each purports to be; their interaction has become one of the motors driving the republic. A scandal here, an act of *lèse majesté* there, a poor speech, a failure to return from holiday to address a crisis, these issues in other regimes give journalists something to write about in the summer recess, the 'silly season'. We shall examine systemically how and why France is as if in a permanent but consequential relationship between presidential pretention and a kind of 'silly season' silliness where the incidental can have dramatic political consequences. This means that understanding France means taking all of the above into consideration while recognising that symbolic politics at a bewildering range of levels has acquired heightened status as a 'driver' of politics, and must be incorporated into a theory of the Fifth Republic.

Without claiming that the French presidency is a 'French Exception' (Chafer and Godin 2006), the history of acute personalisation in French politics, the institution of the presidency, created to solve 'crises', and the subsequent advent of a politically consequential 'celebrity politics' and '*peopolisation*' (Charaudeau 2008; Corner 2000; Street 2004, 2012; Wheeler 2012) now characterise the French presidency, and mean that the daily, the 'trivial', interact with more traditional rhythms in the political process in a dynamic, consequential way, so that the clash of 'political time' (e.g. the elaboration of the budget) and 'mediatic time' (the pace and exigencies of the 24/7 media) (Pingaud 2013) or what we might call 'performative time' create stress within the functioning of the presidency and of politics more generally.

Much of this collision and collusion of the 'serious political' and the 'trivial symbolic' has, since 1958, focused – in an evolving variety of ways – upon the presidency of the republic, and upon leadership more generally. We shall elaborate upon this in Chapter 3. Here we can simply state that such colliding has brought to the fore the consequent significance of gesture, political image, and rhetoric, through which the President 'displays' his character, and with it the formative influence of presidential popularity (and unpopularity), and with that the role of 'opinion', and the perceived relationship between the President and opinion; 'opinion', in fact, does not simply reflect publicly held views but is itself a political actor. We have argued elsewhere that in the Fifth Republic 'opinion' has itself become a major political actor, even though at a certain level of analysis one could argue that it does not even exist in that it is an abstraction from sampled views (Gaffney 2012); but it holds a place in the political process, in particular as regards presidential popularity.

As regards the trivial symbolic, we can make an analogy here between our approach and the methodology of classical psychoanalysis. This is not to say that our approach to politics here is psychoanalytical, but the very special circumstances of French politics make the method a rewarding one to consider for its insights, for although not psychological, a central thrust of our approach is semiological in that we are concerned with eliciting the meaning of signs and signifiers, and the inordinate influence of the former on the latter, i.e. the 'performance' of the sign as well as what the sign signifies. In Freud's 1901 path-breaking research (Freud 2002), deeper psychic processes can be inferred and demonstrated from the interrogative interactions of the daily and trivial between the psychoanalyst and the analysand. In French politics, because of historical and cultural circumstances and the dramatic reconfiguration of political institutions in 1958, what we might call 'the gestures of leadership' (Messenger 2006) in 'everyday life' whether skilful or clumsy, effective or inadequate, become revealing of an influential symbolism which leads us back to the fundamental structures of the republic. Our purpose here, in part, is to build a semiological understanding of presidential performance (Barthes 1957; Mayaffre 2012; Bertrand *et al.* 2007), and its relationship to or role within the overall political process.

Revealing the Republic

In spite of Hollande's deep unpopularity, the first part of his presidency was not accompanied by a resurgence of the mainstream right opposition because the latter was caught in its own series of political setbacks – as with Hollande, some performative, some systemic, which we shall analyse in Chapter 5 – as it struggled with the aftermath of the 2012 presidential and parliamentary defeat, trying to come to terms with the post-Sarkozy period, and the question of succession, or of Sarkozy's 'return', which took place in September 2014 when he decided to run for the leadership of the UMP. The right's inability to respond effectively offers us semiological clues as to how the right had also not adapted properly to the Fifth Republic, how the exigencies of leadership within the republic made it dysfunctional, and that in leadership terms the Fifth Republic posed real challenges to all political parties.

The post-Sarkozy period on the right (2012–) offers insights of major theoretical significance. In the prevailing climate, along with an acute public disillusionment, with the left in particular but also with the whole established political class generally, and in a deteriorating social atmosphere, rising unemployment, and almost zero growth, only the extremes, in particular the well-organised far right National Front, seemed to profit, as its popularity, and especially that of its leader, Marine Le Pen, increased dramatically (see Chapter 5). In the period we are examining, the FN's membership tripled, By late 2014 it stood at over 80,000, while those of the UMP and PS were falling dramatically. This phenomenon, moreover, is not simply like the appearance or resurgence of the hard right as has occurred across Europe in a variety of forms over the last 20 years (Wodak *et al.* 2013; Carter 2011). The specific conditions of political activity in the Fifth Republic create a complex 'theatre' for the playing out of political competition, the development of public policies, and so on. The 'Marine' phenomenon, for example (she gained over 18% in the 2012 presidential election and by 2014 was seen as a likely round two contender in 2017), is an integral feature of the Fifth Republic, whereby the personalisation of politics – in particular the myth of the politics of *recours*, or return of the 'saviour', a feature of French politics for two centuries – has been given an institutional platform by the Fifth Republic. The presidentialisation of French politics in 1958 and the constitutional reform of 1962 whereby the President would be elected by direct universal suffrage transformed French politics (Viansson-Ponté 1970–71). One of the consequences has been that the myth of *recours* has become a feature of French politics, culturally and historically, and is strengthened institutionally by the Fifth Republic; and hostility to personalised politics breeds another very personalised alternative politics rather than militates against it, which sends the republic stumbling from one (institutionally framed) personalised crisis to another, so that a crisis of personalised leadership does not call into question the notion itself but rather encourages the emergence of yet another contender.

How do we measure what we might call these 'deeper structures' of political symbolism, their political effects and evolution? How do we '*apprécier*', appraise, and analyse this republic? From the practical point of view, we can ask a series of 'normal' political questions about Hollande's presidency and his government/s: Why were they so unpopular? How do we account for the rise of all the negative indices of the regime barely four months into office? How do we account for the extremes, the surges of opinion, such as the widespread *Manif pour tous* or *Bonnets rouges* protests in 2013 (see Chapters 4 and 5)? More widely, how do we account for the general, almost clinical, depression of the whole population, the political demobilisation of the electorate, and a growing disdain for politics throughout the first two years of Hollande's presidency? Was all of this inevitable? What should Hollande have been doing? What should he have not been doing? And an even wider question: how do we understand this profusion of surface phenomena in terms of the deeper structures? To return to our psychoanalytical analogy: gestures and actions at a daily level 'betray' and 'reveal' the fundamentals of the Fifth Republic. Extending the analogy, we can characterise, for example, the storm of trivial activity through the spring and summer of 2013 at the beginning of 'Year II', of gestures, actions, interventions, short holidays, media saturation of presidential and prime ministerial '*déplacements*' during July and August 2013 as surface expressions of a kind of neurotic attempt to 'cope with' the barely understood exigencies of the republic which had led to the swift collapse of popularity of the executive at the beginning of 'Year I'. We do not mean that these gestures were unconscious but that, beyond the grasp of their authors, they demonstrate, perform even, the dilemmas of the Fifth Republic, in particular the highly problematic nature of the presidency.

This raises again our puzzle or question, from the theoretical point of view: what is this regime? What might it require for the unfortunate developments that happened under François Hollande not to have happened; even for the opposite to have happened, and the Fifth Republic thrive? We shall elaborate upon all of these points in Chapters 2 and 3, from both an empirical and theoretical perspective. We place great analytical stress upon the nature of the presidency itself and its importance, for this is the way to an understanding of both the role of 'popularity' and the role of leadership authority in the Fifth Republic. Crucial to understanding Hollande's presidency, for example, is the idea of knowing what was the symbolic – but very consequential – legacy of the earlier holders of the presidential office from de Gaulle to Sarkozy: what did they do to the republic for it to be as it is? How did they contribute to the 'fashioning' of the presidency? We shall look at this in greater detail in Chapter 3, but can say here that de Gaulle created, brought to the fore, a very singular republic based inordinately upon 1) the role of the persona of the President, the role of discourse and of personal image and gesture, and the 'character' of the President; and 2) the constructed, 'imagined' relationship between the President and people on the one hand, and the President and 'France' on the other (Gaffney in Gaffney and Holmes 2011). These two facets of the new republic in 1958 would have a dramatic and complex effect upon the nature of political competition, the influence of the political culture (later the role of the celebrity culture), the role of the symbolic, and the role and configuration of the institutions, in particular, the presidency, the parties, the media, and 'opinion'.

Today, partly because so much of it chronicles politics and/or political lives, and in spite of the brilliance of many of these studies, there is a general failure in the literature to calculate these issues, the actual norms and the exigencies of this republic, and its comportmental framework (Becker 1998; Berstein 1989; Berstein 2001; Berstein and Milza 1991, 1994; Berstein *et al.* 2003; Berstein and Rioux 2000; Berstein and Sirinelli 2007; Chapsal and Lancelot 1975; Chevrier and Gusse 2010; Donegani and Sadoun 1998; Johnson 1981; Rioux 1983; Sirinelli 1992); and in the Hollande presidency there was a series of such fundamental and on-going miscalculations that they raise the question of whether the political actors understand the republic. Such miscalculation is itself striking, given that François Hollande had been 'close to power' since 1980; an advisor to Jacques Attali and Max Gallo, deeply involved with PS politics for 30 plus years, and a politician involved directly in several semi-secret 'missions' on behalf of President Mitterrand (1981–95). For ten years he was leader of the Socialist Party (1997–2008), and his former partner, Ségolène Royal, had been a Minister and, in 2007, the party's presidential candidate (Amar and Hassoux 2005; Bartolone 2007; Malouines and Meeus 2006). And yet, as we shall see, simple things like an appropriate way to 'be' the President – how to talk, not constantly to joke, control the public comportment of his partner, and so on – betrayed a lack of sensitivity to both the exigencies of the office and the nature of the republic, even though, as we shall see in Chapter 4, he held strong views on what the presidency meant in protocolary terms.

After every interview, announcement, and press conference in his first two years, Hollande's popularity fell significantly. In 2012, 2013, and 2014 as we shall show – and this brings us back to our earlier point about his moving 'out of category' – virtually no gesture, speech, or action had traction on opinion. At times, indifference seemed even to replace hostility, as if the President had become an irrelevance, as if he barely existed. In the spring and summer of 2013 (the beginning of 'Year II'), as we have mentioned, there was a belated recognition by the presidential team of the miscalculations and, in response, a series of frantic activities around attempts at 'spin' and political communication. We shall identify and analyse these in Chapter 5.

Political and constitutional theory and their theorists are partly to blame for our misperceptions: many French scholars and outside observers have discoursed upon what they thought constituted the institutional and constitutional Fifth Republic (Chagnollaud and Quermonne 1996; Charlot 1994; Duhamel 1993; Portelli 1987; Quermonne 1980), generally adopting a received view of politics, often contrasting France to other republics – elsewhere or in France since the Revolution of 1789 (identifying a 'French Exception' of poor heuristic value). This emphasis upon personal v. public power was understandable given French republican history, and in particular that of the previous 50 or so years throughout Europe. The personal v. public thesis was paradigmatic during the Fourth Republic, as if this view offered definitive explanation, almost invariably referring to the inadequate yet widespread notion of what constituted 'personal power', contrasting it with parliamentary power (Andrews 1982; Chandernagor 1967; Defferre 1965; Duverger 1961, 1974, 1978; Pickles 1958, 1962). We shall look at this issue in Chapter 3. We are not saying that such an approach is wrong; comparative constitutionalism and institutional approaches are essential in the analysis of the Fifth Republic (Bell 2000; Cole 1998, 2008; Cole *et al.* 2005; Hayward 1983, 1993; Knapp 2006; Williams and Harrison 1960), but there is another dimension to the presidential phenomenon, namely, its performative evolution and symbolic enactment, and analysis here has been more restricted. We might venture here that inadequately understanding the republic was Hollande's own first mistake. Not that Sarkozy had understood things much better. Sarkozy's style might or might not have been appropriate, but Hollande's own was in large part based upon his being simply and concertedly the negation of Sarkozy, operationally, stylistically, politically, and – which would come to be highly problematic – ethically. Hollande had faced only half the issue (i.e. what unwanted features Nicolas Sarkozy had brought to the republic); what was not developed was an understanding of what he was going to replace them with, and why, and how. We shall come back to these points below, and develop them further in Chapter 2 but can say here that all previous Presidents – even Pompidou and Giscard – had traits that contrasted with and aligned with their predecessors, but they also projected the notion of themselves as 'a future'. For Hollande, 'the future' would be/would return the republic to 'Normal'. The fundamental difference between the mutually exclusive nature of 'would be' and 'would return the republic to' was never understood by the Hollande team, either in its anticipation of the future or its interpretation of the past or the interrelationship between the two.

The upshot of these various misapprehensions of the republic is that everything informs the functioning of the republic in a way few understand or few polities before have functioned or been seen as functioning. And it is understandable that the Fifth Republic is misunderstood because it has not been properly theorised; to paraphrase – at the risk of misquoting – Durkheim on contract: all that is in the constitution of this republic is not constitutional.

Generally, traditionally, Nicolas Sarkozy's fate as respected new President in 2007 was seen as being sealed the night of his victory by an ostentatious 'bling' celebration meal in the Champs Elysées restaurant *Fouquet's* (Jaigu 2009). Very badly received by the media and the public, this perceived, somewhat common, expression of conspicuous consumption and celebration inserted fragility into his presidential status, and then a relentless decline in the new President's popularity. This was the first time in the Fifth Republic such an 'event' had had such a crystallising effect. In 2012, Hollande's going off on holiday (almost immediately after election, and while unemployment burned) in July–August was his equivalent to Sarkozy's defining miscalculation. Each of these events tells us a great deal about the 'nature' of this republic today: a single trivial act, given oxygen, as it were, by the media, can throw a presidency out of kilter. In some respects, this is now a new and perhaps normative feature of governance or malgovernance (Helms 2012) in France. In another respect, it is not new at all, or is rather the singular new expression of a fundamental feature as old as the Fifth Republic, namely, the dramatically consequent phenomenon of personal popularity, or more accurately in these cases, unpopularity, themselves the product of a complex 'imagined' relationship between President and public. By creating the operational conditions of the Fifth Republic, namely, the imagined relationship of leader and public, itself very complex as we shall see in Chapter 3, notions of dependency become central to the republic's functioning. Charles de Gaulle brought to the Fifth Republic a very volatile emotional political relationship. Today, de Gaulle approaches sainthood in public memory, but that was not the lived reality.

Although the volatility of the relationship was displayed by him as appeasing of conflict, he was viscerally liked and disliked (one might venture to say loved and hated, admired and feared) in almost equal and varying measure; and this relationship saw his ultimate undoing in 1969 (and, ironically, established the conditions for the perenniality of both the republic itself and his mythical status). Beyond popularity, moreover, was the question of political and emotional need, what was 'required' of the presidency and how this fitted into the rapidly established parameters of the new republic between 1958 and 1962. De Gaulle responded to this need by developing all the dramatic aspects of his character, lending to the new French republic the 'character' of its new President: grand, visionary, imperial – in manner if not always in policies – interventionist, dramatic, in a word, larger than life. And presidential character was in a relationship to public approval – hence the triumphs of 1958 and 1962 but also defeat such as 1969. The same was less true of Pompidou, who acted as a kind of dramatic relief from such imperium and such intimacy (besides, any attempt to 'follow de Gaulle', as it were, would have looked farcical); but Valéry Giscard d'Estaing, François Mitterrand and Jacques Chirac's presidencies each displayed enormous swings in ratings of popularity-unpopularity in the polls, ratings utterly alien to, for example, UK political culture (with the possible exception of Margaret Thatcher, and briefly, in terms of popularity, the first three years of Tony Blair's premiership). All of this suggests an emotional volatility between the public and the Presidents. With the celebrity culture from circa 2000, a new feature does not simply emerge in France but *merges with* this deeper structural phenomenon of the Fifth Republic, changing the problematic 'intimacy' in leader-public relations. In spite of pretending to exploit it, neither Sarkozy nor Hollande seemed fully to grasp this aspect of the regime, the emotional intensity and complexity of an, albeit 'imagined', relationship, and the fact that with the new celebrity politics the President would be in the public eye on a daily basis.

Today (since circa 2000) this relational trait within presidential politics has been dramatically affected in that the 'ordinary' political, the deeper symbolic, and the utterly trivial have begun to interact and affect politics in new and unexpected ways, and with equal intensity and mutual interdependence. The development of 'celebrity culture' and what the French call *'peopolisation'* has had particular effects because of the presidency and the nature of personalisation in the Fifth Republic. The trivial is consequential now to the point where it has begun to precipitate major political consequences; and this to the point where we need to track changes in this area as much as the 'underlying' or 'overarching' issues of the economy, unemployment, party competition, social protest, and so on. It can be negative e.g. the 'tweet' of Valérie Trierweiler – because of its 'fallout' upon François Hollande (see Chapter 4); or positive e.g. Nicolas Sarkozy's momentary 'return' to politics in July 2013 – a dress rehearsal for his actual return in September 2014 (see Chapter 5), triggering, on the right at least, the idea once again of the political saviour in the Fifth Republic (itself compromised by the surge in popularity of Alain Juppé and Bruno Le Maire's good showing in the UMP leadership elections in November 2014). We shall return to these issues and their significance in the body of our analysis; let us here probe the consequences of the 'fallout' from celebrity politics.

Scandals, trivia, and 'opinion'

The role of scandal has a special place. Throughout the Fifth Republic (throughout the post-Revolutionary period, in fact), scandals have had great political influence; and the new circumstances of the post-2000 'celebrity politics' period are no exception: they rumble along, they then surface, and can have enormous effects (Montoya and Anger 2004; Robert 1997; Faligot and Guisnel 2007; Williams 1970a), e.g. the Cahuzac scandal in 2013, which we shall analyse in Chapter 4, where the Budget Minister had to resign because of personal financial misdoing: on the surface, it was just a political cliché, as in the Third Republic where these were commonplace (e.g. the 1934 Stavisky scandal); but what simply seemed like (an echo of) a very French problem of financial corruption, now had the capacity to destabilise the presidential relationship; and this compounded by the fact that the principal actors – having used rectitude as fundamental to their claims to legitimacy – did not know what to do, other than express prudish yet noisy outrage and rail against bad practice, and therefore make matters worse, drawing the regime into that most dangerous of political phenomena, ridicule. Since forever in France, but since the digital age with great intensity, hearsay and gossip have added further virulence to the role of scandal (*inter alia* Mascret and Jeanvoine 2007; Sinclair 1997; Weber 2010). Trivia, scandals, gossip, and so on become integral to questions of the President's status and the regime's stability. This raises the question that we shall come back to throughout this book, of where the 'fault' lies. Is it within the republic which cannot function properly and therefore dysfunctions repeatedly at the 'lower', daily level of activity because of its emphasis upon concentrated power (and, therefore, lack of accountability); or is it that – at all levels – the republic is 'being performed' badly? It is our view that it is both, and we hope that our overall analysis will demonstrate this.

From this, a further phenomenon of great consequence in Fifth Republic politics emerges: the role in the regime of 'opinion' that we referred to earlier. With a regime based upon the 'character' of the President and his relationship with 'the French' which existed both in de Gaulle's imagination and in enacted form via the plebiscite, referendum, and elections, and high-drama press conferences and TV/radio broadcasts, the idea of the French as a kind of single character, with a single set of character traits and strong emotions, became a very strong element in the functioning of the republic. This is a complex phenomenon because, as the republic develops, this entity becomes a major 'actor' within the regime – appealed to, expressed democratically, 'measured' in polls, and 'imagined' in political rhetoric and discourse. Because the regime is so personalised and imagined, not just the presidency but 'opinion' too becomes a major political actor. This is not like 'public opinion' as it is usually depicted in the UK, US, or Germany, for example, but a major discursive element implying a strong emotional relationship within the republic, driving the comportment of political actors, and with a dual presence in both the political *imaginaire* and in reality.

From the political perspective of the 'surface' of French politics, the first half of the 2012–17 presidential term saw a vertiginous fall in the popularity and standing of the President and his government, a fall that set new records for the collapse of political authority vis-à-vis both opinion and the presidential majority itself, as Hollande's growing lack of popularity made it more and more difficult to assert his control over parts of his government, his party, and his allies; and this to the point where his popularity and his perceived relationship to the presidency itself made a qualitative move *out of category* as we have called it, that is to say, that the presidential relationship with the public began to collapse into not simply disapproval but also a kind of exasperated indifference, as if he was almost not the President, a development with very serious potential consequences for the republic. Let us look at the context of his 2012 victory, and then the calamitous first year, followed by the second year in which the President and government desperately tried to remedy the situation.

Chapter 2 will set the scene for François Hollande's presidency, by setting it within the context of his perception of Nicolas Sarkozy, his own projected image, and the nature of the 2012 presidential campaign; a contest between 'appropriate' presidential personalities. In order to give our analysis of Hollande's presidency a wider historical and theoretical context, in Chapter 3 we shall develop a theory of leadership and of the presidency in the Fifth Republic. We shall be concerned, in particular, with how the presidency reflects and interpolates ideas about how France is 'imagined' and how presidential character relates to this. We shall look at 'presidential comportment' and image, and at presidential attitudes and discourse, and their crucial importance in the evolution of the Fifth Republic. We will also discuss how presidential style and its importance developed from Charles de Gaulle onwards. We need to bear in mind in this context the arguably 'diminishing returns' of *grandeur* and their relationship to the personalisation of power, and how each of the Presidents responded to this and to the accumulated 'character' of the presidency. Chapter 4 will examine 'Year I' of François Hollande's presidency (May 2012–summer 2013). A first remark we can make here is how unprepared everyone was for government; second, as we have mentioned, how striking the fact that the first 'moments' of a presidency today are defining and formative (e.g. for Sarkozy, *Fouquet's*, the yacht, Cécilia and Carla etc.); how, for Hollande, the prolonged soaking at his inaugural, his disrespectful attitude to his opponent at the *passage des pouvoirs*, his not responding immediately to 'the crisis' while his partner ordered expensive cushions for their holiday, and indeed his going on holiday almost immediately after his election; how these, the presidency's first moments, led to such catastrophic results in the polls. Chapter 5, Year II or *'L'An II'* (summer 2013–summer–autumn 2014) was very different from Year I. As a response to Year I, politically and symbolically, it was a concerted attempt to rectify a deleterious situation, but which had still been, and was still, poorly grasped. *L'An II* (even the expression in the press lampooned the presidency because it referred to the 1789 revolutionary calendar) became a concerted effort at making all the President's efforts in public relations attempts to try and reverse the situation. We shall take our analysis of these developments through the Municipal and European elections of March and May 2014, and the virtual destruction of Hollande's presidential persona by the revelations of his former partner, Valérie Trierweiler, in September 2014.

As we have mentioned, this study is not a chronology of the five-year term but an analysis, in part designed to demonstrate how initial perceptions and actions defined the five-year term and our understanding of it. Chapter 6 will examine the way in which Hollande 'performed' the French presidency in his first two and a half years by appraising it against the analytical framework elaborated in Chapter 3. Taking our analysis up to the *rentrée* 2014 facilitates an analytical appraisal of the first half of the Hollande presidency, his exercise of the presidency up until his near-eclipse by September 2014, and the unofficial beginnings of the campaign for 2017.

2

The Normal President v. the Hyper President: Self-definition as Antithesis

In the immediate aftermath of his presidential victory in May 2012, the dominant media cliché and general public reaction was that François Hollande did not win the presidential election in May 2012, Nicolas Sarkozy lost it. It was a cliché but no less true for that. This commonplace of electoral politics would define Hollande's presidency, in part because Hollande allowed this 'accidental' victory to dictate the character of his presidency, initially and concertedly by taking what was seen (by himself and his team) as a winning electoral deployment of a 'normal' character, and imposing it upon the presidency as a comportmental and rhetorical recasting of the Sarkozy presidency; namely, himself and all he was bringing to the presidency as the antithesis of the Sarkozy presidency. With the exception of Giscard in 1981, this was the first presidential election that was essentially a referendum on the outgoing President (Maarek 2013).

Whatever the conditions of his election, Hollande could have begun his presidency with great confidence. Instead, for at least a year after his election, as we shall see, his own self-definition was to be, in all the ways he thought the case – which was as often as not, not the case – a kind of fetishised antithesis of Nicolas Sarkozy: moral as opposed to amoral, modest as opposed to bling and brash, reserved as opposed to omnipresent, '(self) satisfied' as opposed to 'driven', 'concertative' as opposed to confrontational; undoing of Sarkozy's legislation, and with a government that would slow the tempo of activity, through its size (Ayrault II 39 ministers) and, unintentionally, its inexperience, and its emphasis upon involving the 'social partners' (business and the unions) in grand processes of deliberation – launched by the President – designed to give the impression of a non-conflictual, unhurried 'concert' of legislative action. In practice, however, both his and the government's actions became synonymous with little action at all, and few results. None of this overall approach – normality, bringing the 'social partners' into long deliberations on what were arguably very pressing measures, relative inaction, and significantly reduced tempo and 'tension' – addressed the demands of the hour or public expectations of Hollande's presidency but were, rather, a concerted rejection of what he perceived as his predecessor's imprint.

A damaging accumulation of mistaken actions and inactions, undertakings, gestures, and interventions was the result almost from the beginning, throwing into relief the developing sense of the inappropriateness and the inadequacies of Hollande's claims to a new kind of sober presidency. Not only had Sarkozy's popularity declined throughout his presidency, the intensity of ill feeling as measured in polls (*très mécontents*) had grown steadily. During the campaign, the only real issue had been whether the French were exasperated enough with Nicolas Sarkozy to allow Hollande into the presidency, someone who, up until – and including – his election, they had little true enthusiasm for, and until a few months before, had been relatively unknown, and before the Dominique Strauss-Kahn (DSK) affair, never considered as a likely President.

Hollande's defining his presidency as the antithesis of Sarkozy's may have been a mistake, but was perhaps an understandable one. The preoccupation with Sarkozy between 2007 and 2012 by not only the general public but also the media and the academic world was acute. These three 'estates', as it were, obsessed about Sarkozy throughout his presidency, the latter two reflecting in part their own preoccupation, in part the intensity of the emotional response of the French themselves. It was an intensity of response that was lived almost as a personal antipathy. Would this disappear with the arrival of the 'modest' François Hollande? We shall come back to this idea of the acute focus upon personality politics and upon emotion in politics again and again, for it is one of the drivers of the Fifth Republic, and a little understood one at that, both outside France, but by large swathes of the academic community and the media inside France too. The problem that Hollande would have to face but had assumed being 'normal' would overcome, was that the acutely personal quality of presidential politics which Sarkozy had exploited and perhaps abused was elemental to the Fifth Republic, not something that would disappear with a different presidential 'character'. Sarkozy had brought celebrity politics to the presidency – not without its contradictions – but he was able to exploit the phenomenon, for better and worse, because of the pre-eminence of the Fifth Republic's focus upon the deployment of character.

Until 6 May 2012, the focus of all attention was on the outgoing President. During the campaign, before round one of the presidential elections on 22 May, there had been some interest in what was something of a *Grand Guignol* knockabout side show between Jean-Luc Mélenchon and Marine Le Pen on the far left and right, respectively (they would repeat this at even closer quarters in the legislative elections in June). Here, Mélenchon stole Hollande's thunder, although not, as it turned out, his votes. It was Mélenchon's high profile (a near-revolutionary rhetoric and opinion polls in the mid-teens (he received only 11% on polling day), as if out-flanking Hollande on his left) that made Hollande propose both the 75% tax on very high incomes, and the raising of the minimum wage, both relatively inconsequential in their actual effects but arguably effective electorally against Mélenchon (Delapierre 2012). They were not 'successful' politically: the first was thrown out by the Constitutional Council, and the second was derisory – an increase of 14 centimes per hour after deductions (an estimated 24 million working people are on the minimum wage, ar. 1,500 euros, and an estimated nine million live on less than 1,000 euros per month). During the election campaign the Centrist candidate, François Bayrou, was almost completely ignored, as were all the others, except, of course, Marine Le Pen, and the Ecologist candidate, Eva Joly, who drew media attention for downplaying environmental issues, and for being, according to the media, oddly dressed, including outsized bright red, sometimes green, spectacle frames, and having such a strong Norwegian accent (in spite of or because of the wide but shallow media coverage, she gained only 2.3% of the vote). In round two, because of the presidential rules, Hollande was the only candidate against Sarkozy, but still there was little sense of a rally around him. The passion was still all directed at Sarkozy, both in a growing, belated, positive sense but mainly, still, a negative one, the culmination of five years of public exasperation. It was both negative and personal; the election continued to be, right up until the end, a referendum on Sarkozy's five-year unpopularity; positive, in that there were the beginnings of a revival of enthusiasm which, if the campaign had lasted two or three days more, might just have seen him retain the crown. But the continued and intense hostility to him saw a sufficient swathe of those who had voted Sarkozy in 2007 offer their suffrage to the quiet, perhaps even uninspiring, François Hollande; and this to a sufficient extent to propel him to victory, and Sarkozy to unexpected defeat, almost the shortest serving President of the Fifth Republic (Georges Pompidou, who died in office, served as President for four years, nine months and 12 days).

The new President

And yet on 7 May, as Sarkozy's (dark) star fell from the sky on the evening of the run-off, the concern of everyone was suddenly with Hollande who had stressed first throughout the PS primaries that he was the '*candidat normal*', then throughout the campaign that he would be a '*Président normal*', in contrast to the hyperactive Sarkozy. What would he do: *how* would he do in his immediate meeting with Angela Merkel, then to the US for a meeting with President Barack Obama, then to Chicago (G8), then NATO, then the G20, then an EU summit in Brussels? All within a few days of taking office. How would he cope? Indeed, who was he? Who would be his Prime Minister? Who would be an appropriate Prime Minister to a 'normal' President? How would he organise for the legislative elections (given that he had said he would not take part in party politics) and, of course, what was the new President's style? Could it be defined? The public realised he was the somewhat ordinary former partner of the captivating 2007 candidate, Ségolène Royal (Dély 2008). And now the partner of the attractive, somewhat enigmatic, Valérie Trierweiler (Cabana and Rosencher 2012), the new 'First Lady'. Perhaps personality politics was not over, after all, at least at the superficial level of the new '*peopolisation*'; we shall see, however, it was not over at all, either at this level or down to the roots of the Fifth Republic.

The public had had some indication of who François Hollande was before, but not much (Hollande 2006, 2009). In the Autumn of 2011, the French Socialist Party, in order to try to minimise internal rivalries and help create a smoother passage of accession to the party's nomination for the former Finance Minister, current Director of the IMF, and biggest party 'baron', Dominique Strauss-Kahn, the PS had decided on internal primaries (partially open to non-PS candidates, with voting rights open to the wider public). DSK never made it, his career, his life, turned upside down by a charge of attempted rape in a New York hotel in May 2011, followed by an unending series of stories and rumours of other sexual misdemeanours. The only candidate left with a credible chance of winning the presidency was the relatively unknown François Hollande, former leader of the party (1997–2008), who had overseen in relative obscurity two party defeats at presidential level – Lionel Jospin in 2002 and Ségolène Royal in 2007 – (although not at other local and regional elections). Hollande had not been central to those campaigns; in Jospin's it was Jospin and his team who were at the heart of the defeat, and in 2007, other party barons (Fabius and Strauss-Kahn in particular) were irresponsibly hostile to Royal. Hollande, however, had exercised little authority as party leader. He also failed after 2002 to stop the internal rivalries from turning the party away from any doctrinal purpose or potential for policy renewal it may have had (Bachelay 2007; Baumel 2007; Blier 2008; Bourmaud 2010; Noir 2007; Revault d'Allonnes 2012). This too would create serious challenges for the new Socialist government, essentially devoid of policy perspectives or an approach adapted to a Europe in crisis from 2008 onwards.

There were five other candidates for the primaries: Ségolène Royal, party candidate in 2007, but something of a spent force in 2011 (her fortunes would revive later); Jean-Michel Baylet, a Left Radical (and therefore without hope of nomination), Arnaud Montebourg (too far to the left); and Manuel Valls (too far to the right). The only real competition for the suddenly luckiest person in French politics was the party leader, Martine Aubry (Lucas and Mourgue 2011), who was indeed a serious candidate, but who, outside the party, generated very mixed feelings (she was seen as too doctrinaire and old-fashioned left-wing in the wider national community – '*Madame 35 heures*'; Aubry had introduced the controversial 35-hour week in 1998 when Employment Minister in Lionel Jospin's government). Even inside the party she was seen as divisive and 'cleaving' (Delais 2012). In October 2011, Hollande won the primaries with 56.5% of the vote (39% in round one), and went on to be the 'quiet' candidate for the presidency, supported by the whole, suddenly united party, who sensed as imminent, given Sarkozy's flat-lining popularity, the prospect of its first presidential victory since 1988.

Hollande then went on to win the presidential election itself on 6 May 2012 (Binet 2012; Centre de Recherches Politiques de Sciences Po 2013; Evans and Ivaldi 2013; Gauvin 2012; Jouan 2012; Lafay 2012; Michel 2011; Perrineau 2013). During the campaign, the public got to know him better. Three top-selling books on him and his election came out in less than three weeks of his becoming President (André and Rissouli 2012; Dupin 2012; Neumann 2012). Such 'instant' studies are now a market trend in French publishing. The 'persona' he constructed was, as we have seen, the opposite of Sarkozy's: ordinary, down-to-Earth, 'normal' ('Am I normal? Yes, and let me say I think the time for a normal President has come'; '*Est-ce que je suis normal? Oui. Et je vais vous dire: je pense que le temps d'un Président normal est venu'*, he said in December 2010 (*Le Magazine du Monde* 18/8/12)). Then the 'summiting' of May 2012 – Berlin, Chicago, NATO, etc. saw him a great deal in the media. His inauguration on 15 May saw him (legally and symbolically) 'become' the seventh President of the Fifth Republic; although he looked a sorry figure without a brolly or raincoat, utterly drenched in the pouring rain with his glasses steamed up; normal in the pouring rain would be a recurring problem.

We shall come back to the effects of the flurry of international activity in Chapter 4 but can mention here that in the first few days of his presidency he did actually make an impression. Hollande had to act immediately to address the problem of the financial markets' disapproval of a 'tax and spend' socialist, and to address the Eurozone crisis. He had immediately to go and see Angela Merkel to revise, if he could, the Eurozone fiscal package and stability pact which she (and Sarkozy) had managed, at enormous effort, to put together. They, together and with others, had to sort out or create a firewall against the Greek crisis. Hollande then had to fly to Washington to tell Obama he was pulling French troops out of Afghanistan ahead of time; then it was NATO, then the G20. Before all this he had to form a government, and after all this he had to win the legislative elections. Hollande had no government experience at all; and not a nano-second of foreign policy experience. The 'Normal' President was hit by a tsunami of issues, both domestic and international. He might need his own firewall of Gaullian grandeur just to face the challenges, although all his persona and demeanour militated against him drawing upon any such characteristics. He did generally well in all these meetings, however, downplaying any claims to *grandeur* and ostentation; and his approval ratings were – though not stratospheric – 'good'... normal.

The government he formed with his new Prime Minister, Jean-Marc Ayrault, also had good approval ratings. Initially, Hollande was clearly making sure his new Prime Minister received as much publicity as he had himself. Ayrault was not widely known but had been a well-considered mayor of Nantes, and had been the leader of the PS group in the National Assembly. Ayrault's rating in the polls was 65%, the highest for any incoming Prime Minister in the Fifth Republic (Cotta 2012). The government enacted a series of measures immediately – reduction in government salaries, encouraging ministers to take trains instead of planes, a promise to raise the minimum wage, and a series of other minor but popular measures. What was also being put into place, as it were, were the elements of Hollande's presidential 'character':

normal and unassuming, sharing of the limelight, moral, discreet in his private life, frugal; in a word, quietly exemplary as a 'character' who would display a new kind of presidential being. As we shall see, the exigencies of such a change are highly complex, and the elements Hollande chose to foreground – normal, moral, discreet etc. – would not simply be hostages to fortune but presidential 'qualities' that would – were bound to – escape Hollande's control, and undermine his image and popularity very quickly indeed. It was also the case that presidential activity on these two fronts, the international and the mildly 'domestic symbolic', meant that there was no bold simultaneous practical and symbolic activity on the domestic economic front (this was crucial); clearly nothing substantial would be introduced for months as part of the budgetary cycle. Not establishing an immediate symbolic association – in the initial moments – with this area of policy and concern would find Hollande trying to create a symbolic and presidential authority over both economic and foreign policy issues and, after September 2014 and his virtual eclipse, over any area, culture, and the environment for example, for the rest of his five-year term until with macabre irony, the Charlie Hebdo massacre in January 2015 revived his fortunes somewhat.

The accidental candidate

Hollande said he did not want to live in the Elysée Palace, but in his ordinary flat in the 15th arrondissement with his partner, the journalist, Valérie Trierweiler. He celebrated his victory on 6 May, not immediately in Paris but in the little town of Tulle, in rural Corrèze where he had been mayor. The symbolism of 'leaving' is strong in leadership mythology. He said to Tulle constituents on 6 May 'We will always be together. I'll be back!' (*Nous ne nous séparerons jamais. Je reviendrai!*), and on 10 June when voting in the legislative elections there was widespread coverage of the dozens and dozens of '*bisous*' between the President and the women of Tulle, as he went to the polling station before returning to Paris, like Lincoln going from Springfield to Washington. Hollande had been variously Mayor, President of the Regional Council, and an MP for the area for more than two decades. He stated during the campaign that he wanted to be a 'normal' President and so, quite deliberately, began to behave in a way that reinforced this image. He did, indeed, look rather like one's friendly local bank manager or estate agent. He was a politician of committee rooms, of consensus, compromise, and muddling through. As a younger man he had been a bright young thing, committed to the party, undertaking a series of tasks for people in President Mitterrand's immediate entourage. But he was never of the inner circle, although his then partner, Ségolène Royal, was favoured. She became a junior minister three times. Hollande was never appointed a minister either by Mitterrand or by Lionel Jospin. He had been made party spokesperson by Jospin in 1995 as a kind of 'safe pair of hands', and became – for precisely the same reason – leader of the Party in 1997 when Jospin became Prime Minister.

As party leader, he had for a decade simply managed or tried to manage the 'stars', as it were; finding interminable compromises between the factions led by figures such as Laurent Fabius and Martine Aubry (both of whom disparaged him), while maintaining his own kind of 'caretaker'-style leadership, even though he remained leader for a decade. Might one run a country successfully like this? The 'balance-sheet' of the French Socialist Party between 1997 and 2008 under Hollande's leadership was seen as very poor. The left had had gains in local, regional, and senatorial elections, especially from 2002 as the main opposition party. But there was little enthusiasm for the party, no 'panache' as there had been in the 1970s and '80s under Mitterrand, and again under Jospin in the 1990s, and it is arguable that poor leadership by Hollande contributed to failure in two consecutive presidential elections (2002 and 2007), both of which the PS could have won. At the national level, the PS was without real direction. The party had also backed the 2005 European Treaty referendum which was lost (Mergier *et al.* 2005) – Fabius, Valls, and Montebourg had been isolated 'no' voices. It effectively ended Jacques Chirac's presidential authority (President 1995–2007), but it seriously damaged the credibility of the Socialist Party too (and, in fact, Hollande's secret hopes for 2007). One more failure and it was generally felt that the party would just fold. In 2008, Hollande stepped down from the leadership in near-disgrace. So, in 2012, Hollande went from relative obscurity to fame and a place in the history books. This historical irony would not be without consequences; in fact, the irony – of a more than lucky guy elected to presidential office as if by chance – would haunt his presidency.

More significant as regards Hollande's presidency itself was the fact that under Hollande's 1997–2008 party leadership – in part because he was just trying to manage the several strong factions within the party and achieve *'synthèse'* at party conferences and agreed conference resolutions that would help avoid party strife – there was no policy, doctrinal, or organisational renewal throughout the whole period. The French Socialist Party remained the least modernised of European

Socialist and Social Democratic parties. In part because of the acute personalisation of factions in the PS (ironically, this did not include himself; he was the only PS leader ever who had had no faction, this also militating against internal exchange and dialogue), there was no doctrinal renewal, nor any deep policy rethinks, as there had been in, say, the British Labour Party, the German SPD, the Spanish Socialists, the Dutch, and the Scandinavian parties. There was some 'think tank' activity (e.g. Olivier Ferrand's Terra Nova), but it was marginal to the party, and the PS's official think tank, the Jean Jaurès Institute, gave no intellectual lead. Issues that would have been of enormous help once power and office were regained could have been addressed fruitfully: such as the PS's relation to various social classes and the socially *'exclus'*, a constituency which formerly 'belonged' to the left and now belonged to the far right or else to no one; the deprived suburbs, an issue of deep significance for the fabric of French life, but forgotten by the left (there were over 120,000 homeless, 25,000 of whom were children – the PS had no policy on what to do); the left's relationship to the state and to the Market, to European integration (to Germany particularly), to the Eurozone crisis, the health system, globalisation, the education system in the twenty-first century; to the regime itself and – especially – to the presidency. None of these issues was addressed in the ten years of the left's opposition, and every single one would become major issues for the Socialist government in 2012.

When Aubry took the leadership of the party in 2008 (Hollande was rather unceremoniously pushed out of the leadership), she took the party organisation in hand, often critically commenting on the mess that had been left (she is reported to have said even the toilets didn't work); and tried to develop a kind of discourse of ideological renewal which became the party's *'Projet'* of 2009 which, in turn – with rather a lot of imaginative dexterity – was argued as forming the basis of Hollande's 60-point presidential election programme in 2012. To a certain extent, these developments, in the context of Hollande's subsequent electoral success, throw into relief the question of their value: Hollande, relatively ineffective (1997–2008), the party taken in hand by a more 'traditional' left-winger, the development of a more 'fundamental' party programme (2009), the primaries and the triumph of the abandoned leader, a 60-point manifesto based upon the 2009 *Projet*, but both, by and large, ignored before, during, and after the campaign, then the success of the party's almost accidental candidate through the defeat of the outgoing President. All these issues raise fundamental questions about the role of the party, and the possibilities for its effectiveness as a government in the post-2012 period. It appeared to need the *Projet*, but only for internal purposes of solidarity and direction. The *Projet* was pitched to the left, and all its premises predicated on economic growth, so it would not be implemented in reality. During the 2012 campaign, the First Secretary (Aubry) claimed the presidential campaign was based upon 'her' *Projet*.

This dichotomy (a presidential candidate who ignores a text that the party thinks it must have) has existed since Mitterrand in the 1981 elections (he commissioned a several-hundred page *Projet socialiste* just before the presidential elections of 1981, and then completely ignored it (Chevènement 1980)). He did the same in 1988. On the other hand, we see what such activity obscures, namely, the proper recasting of modern socialism in the presidential context, for under both Hollande *and* Aubry, the real issues facing the modern left were not addressed; doctrinal, ideological, even policy renewal never undertaken. Old and inadequate ideas were carried forward through to the presidential elections and, perhaps even worse, although this in great part because of presidentialism itself, the candidate Hollande put forward a flimsy programme presented hurriedly to the country as a legislative and governmental programme (ironically, the dissident left would subsequently regard this programme and his abandoned lyricism as the promise betrayed; e.g. he had said at the Le Bourget meeting during the campaign 'I love people' while others are fascinated by money' (*J'aime les gens quand d'autres sont fascinés par l'argent'*)). The party was now bound into five years of government, having won the legislative elections of June 2012. Was it a party now entering government without a real programme? Yes it was. Or did the President have a programme of his own? No he did not. As the left's presidential candidate, although he projected a very downplayed image, during the campaign he did the usual leftist, near-populist, near-revolutionary rhetoric for the party faithful; but in debate he was quiet, unassuming, straightforward and, in fact, rather dull. Was dull normal? In his last campaign speech in Toulouse, he spoke of the left's ten years of preparing for this victory: they had waited, struggled, and reconstructed themselves. In fact, as we have seen, they had done nothing of the kind. We should stress here in parenthesis the party unity and well-run campaign in 2012, were almost like an atonement for the disunity and lack of proper support for Royal's 2007 campaign (which had itself been extremely badly run by the candidate and her team (Gaffney 2012, pp. 199–205)).

François Hollande, with the image of an unassuming, straightforward, rather jovial party man had, nevertheless, taken on during the campaign for the party faithful the language and gestures of the master Machiavellian, François Mitterrand. He made a symbolic visit to Mitterrand's grave in Jarnac at the beginning of the campaign (*Le Point.fr* 9/1/12), as if gathering inspiration. The left loved it, but did not register how much this contrasted with Hollande's overall image; Mitterrand himself having not been 'normal' one iota. Perhaps normal was not, is not, after all, enough. In the election, as we have mentioned, for a while, his far left adversary, Jean-Luc Mélenchon, with his own high rhetoric of 1789 had been in part responsible for the radicalisation of Hollande's rhetoric. The longer-term consequences of this rhetorical contradiction were two, and very serious; one was party political, the other related to character. Politically – it began from around December 2012 – the left of the party in the Assembly began to organise as a '*fronde*' against the betrayal of campaign promises. As regards Hollande's character, the right depicted this duality as a sign of hypocrisy. Ironically, both critiques exploited the highly rhetorical register of *inter alia* the Le Bourget speech. Hollande's general self-depiction as 'normal' was, arguably, necessary to throw into relief Sarkozy's not-normal, exaggerated image, and to legitimate the persona that Hollande was displaying. It, nevertheless, was a highly ambivalent and, paradoxically, volatile notion, in that it meant many things, which we shall address below. And it would be tested against two fundamental challenges – both of which would undermine it severely: first, normal (however defined) as measured against the exigencies of the presidency; and second, normal, as measured against the deployment of normal as a mode of daily comportment. It met its first anecdotal challenge (in terms of its appearing hypocritical) through its association with moral exhortation e.g. against the arrogance of the ruling elite carelessly speeding, when the new President's car was clocked driving at 170 km per hour (*Le Huffington Post* 7/6/12). This trivial incident was a microcosm of the difficulties Hollande had folded into the character of his presidency at the outset. The challenge would become a defining crisis with the 'Valériegate' 'Tweet Affair', which we shall analyse in Chapter 4.

Presidential character

This raises the question of what the French presidency is for, and what kind of President the French expect (if they know) and, ultimately, how presidential function and public expectation interact. And it is here that things become as complicated as they are consequential. In a word, can the French – can the *system* of the Fifth Republic – really cope with 'normal' in the context of the inordinate focus upon the persona of the President? Sarkozy certainly was not normal, but he was accused of not being presidential either (in fact, paradoxically, both in polls and by the commentariat, part of his being not presidential was ascribed to him being too 'ordinary' in the sense of being 'unpresidential' and on occasions vulgar (*'casse-toi, pauv' con'* (Gaffney 2012, pp. xvi–xvii)). This raises the question of what exactly is normal, and what normal means? For it came deliberately to dominate Hollande's first crucial month in office, before being overturned by Trierweiler's 'tweet' and a series of other mishaps, as we shall see, and each of which set in train a negative dynamic of unpopularity which would very rapidly make Hollande the most unpopular of Presidents. This in turn raises the question not only of what normal actually meant, but what its consequences would be. 'Normal' was emphasised again and again, as we shall see. Such a stance would have major political consequences, few positive, most negative. Did 'normal' simply mean the opposite of Sarkozy, which was what was meant in the campaign? None of the French Presidents had been normal. So this was arguably a significant new departure with a lot of ramifications for the political process. 'Not normal' is why the Fifth Republic (1958–) is not the Fourth (1946–58) in that the latter had screened out enhanced leadership status, and the Fifth Republic's central feature was its re-imposition (Tenzer 1998). But this is not what Hollande meant by 'normal'. Perhaps Hollande also meant not like Sarkozy, but not like the other Presidents either – including Mitterrand. This is one of the implications of such a claim. Opposing normal to unpresidential 'bling' may have been Hollande's campaign intention, but the assertion also strongly implied honest and straightforward, as a new kind of presidency. Ironically, Sarkozy, in spite of everything, could claim the same, although a more aggressive kind of honest and straightforward, and a more striking style. Perhaps more problematic in the longer term, was that Sarkozy's real 'fault', the essence of his in part 'unpresidential' image, was his lack of what we might call a national cosmology and cultural narrative. Following in the footsteps of de Gaulle, Pompidou, and Mitterrand, such an absence was startling (and Carla Bruni took it upon herself to rectify some of the historical, literary, and cultural lacunae). The point we wish to make here, however, is that Hollande's persona did not really offer any antidote to this defect in Sarkozy's presidential character. We shall examine this in detail in the next chapter.

Change brought in by Hollande's presidential conduct would contrast most, in fact, not with Sarkozy, but with the dark arts (and high culture) of the mysterious and equivocal François Mitterrand, the hero of the left and the character the candidate Hollande had so copied when addressing the troops in his rallies. The highly rhetorical (uncharacteristic) Le Bourget speech (*Libération* 22/1/12) which launched his campaign was a mix of classic Mitterrand and Sarkozy's 2007 campaign launch '*J'ai changé*' speech. The 10,000 activists loved it, but it contrasted strongly with his 'normal' style (and it was not just for the activists, there were 350 journalists present too). This early use of high rhetoric was quickly toned down, but implicit in its use was the idea that very soon 'normal' would become a rhetorical trap. After election, any move from normal, simple, and honest, would also raise the issue of a style that had been deliberately deceptive. Even more consequentially, consequent in the sense of reducing dramatically Hollande's symbolic comportmental room for manoeuvre, 'normal' has as its true antithesis not Sarkozy nor even Mitterrand nor even the regal Giscard, but de Gaulle himself. We shall come on to this and its consequences below. However, we can say here that this being the case, the Fifth Republic's symbolism was entering unknown territory. And the Fifth Republic is utterly dependent upon its own symbolism. The helicopters and paraphernalia reminiscent of an American President in the little town of Tulle waiting to fly the new President back to Paris on Sunday night of 6 May 2012, suggested that the machinery of the very grandiose Fifth Republic presidency remained, throwing into relief the emerging dichotomy.

In this, Sarkozy was far closer to what *has become* the spirit of the Fifth Republic's constitution than Hollande said he would be. And did the French really want what was normal? This of course raises the question of the 'monarchical': what it is and what is its place in the symbolism of the Fifth Republic. It is clear that for most of Nicolas Sarkozy's presidency, *his* kind of presidentialism was disapproved of. The monarchical nature of the Fifth Republic presidency, however, remains. There is not only deep symbolism in the French presidency, the President is also the central political player, and this interacts with the symbolism of the presidency. Moreover, it soon became clear that all the acquired prerogatives of the President (e.g. nominating ministers, representing government at home and abroad etc.) would remain. Hollande, like all his predecessors, remained the central political (in spite of his denials during the election campaign) *and* symbolic leader; so that all his decisions and style would be compared relentlessly to these.

Practically, over and above the challenges the new President and government had to face in the European and wider global arena immediately after his election, the fact that at least six million voters had voted for Marine Le Pen, the inexorable rise in the unemployment figures, and the awfulness of the problems in the deprived suburbs, where even the police would not go anymore, would determine the 'character' of the presidency, and the image of the President, and this very rapidly. The nature of the Fifth Republic is such that these developments would almost automatically trigger a call for a less normal type of leadership style, and if it did not come from the President, he would be seen as *inadequate*, and it would emerge elsewhere. To a certain degree, just as Sarkozy had stamped his presidency with a certain character within a week of his victory, so too had Hollande.

The office itself, therefore, as well as circumstances, had the potential to force 'abnormal' onto the agenda and challenge the President's persona. As regards being normal, Hollande also had a kind of leftist 'echo' in the strident and (relatively successful at this time) persona of Mélenchon, but also the potentially undermining images of 'strength' emanating from figures like Marine Le Pen (and Sarkozy, if his star were to rise again ...), each a threat to 'normal' as 'a method'. Once 'normal' is adopted, it is difficult to manoeuvre it. Because of the requirements of office in the Fifth Republic, 'normal' might well slide into 'mediocre' or 'inactive'. And the reason 'normal' is difficult to manoeuvre is because it echoes its antithesis, that is to say that Hollande projected normal as not normal: 'normal' would rally a divided nation around itself/himself. Once this failed to happen, normal became an extremely negative trait. A further danger of a 'normal' image (reminiscent of an earlier UK equivalent in the *Spitting Image*'s withering depiction of the monotone John Major when UK Prime Minister) was, particularly in Canal+'s *Les Guignols de l'info* (a satirical puppet show similar to the UK's *Spitting Image*), the question of the satirical depiction of Hollande. We shall come back to this issue of satire, but can make two points here. First, satire is of great significance in French political culture and has, arguably, been politically very consequent, at least since the French Revolution. Second, for reasons we shall see below in connection to the 'Valériegate' scandal, satire and cynicism demonstrated how vulnerable such a persona as Hollande had constructed and deployed would become. In satire, and soon – very shortly after his election because of 'Valériegate' – lampoon, his 'normalcy' would be translated into hilarious mediocrity, and his persona transformed into a mediocre *and* indecisive figure (Trierweiler would stress this latter trait, '*indécis*', in her 2014 book). 'Normal' became synonymous in satire with mediocre, even stupid with, for example, the Hollande 'puppet' wildly exaggerating the real tendency of Hollande to say 'uhhh' between words and phrases. This raises the intriguing issue of whether certain 'personae' are mutually exclusive or, more than others, vulnerable in a highly personalised regime, and whether types of persona are generic to the presidency, and if so which, or whether all types can, in fact, be adapted to the office. This discussion constitutes the main part of our analysis in Chapter 3.

Hollande had demonstrated a 'Mitterrandian' style and discourse in some of his party rally speeches (the less regal, more combative style of Mitterrand in the 1970s). This impersonation always received wildly enthusiastic reception among the hall and stadium audiences, and it was this enthusiasm that was partly transmitted to the wider public: Hollande as leader of socialism and heir to Mitterrand. But there are limits to such blends (I'm normal but I'm not normal). Discourses can be mixed – the move from high rhetoric to a fireside chat style is compatible (although problematic). Blending contrasting *personae* images, however, is more problematic; one can relatively easily step from the grandiose to the 'normal'. De Gaulle was able to do it very successfully on several occasions (Jullian 2000) (although we should remind ourselves that to say that de Gaulle's image from 1958 via the ORTF was state controlled is not an exaggeration (Chalaby 2002)). Stepping in the other direction, from the normal to the grandiose, is infinitely more problematic. We shall come back to this.

Hollande impressed again when he formed his government. There were almost no hiccups, just enough (e.g. the appointment of Christiane Taubira to Justice) eyebrow raising for some commentators, for others admiration for such bold symbolism balanced with social-democratic sobriety (the Prime Minister, Ayrault) and experience (Fabius at Foreign Affairs), an equal number of women, and an opening out to the Greens (with one ominous hiccup over Cécile Duflot's remarks about decriminalising cannabis). There was also a sense of resolve in the *non*-appointment of Aubry. The country had chosen by default this most bland of all its seven Presidents, yet it seemed positive about him, and he, competent, unassuming (and the antithesis of Sarkozy) seemed to be invoking a new kind of presidency.

Such a question raises several more, and the *raison d'être* of this book. For there is something inhibiting of understanding in the way observers approach French presidential politics. First, all observers seem to assume they and everyone else know what presidential means, and what 'charisma' is. Most media observers assume to know why

Sarkozy fell; then why Hollande was elected, and all this without criticism of what these issues really meant or what was really involved. What we hope to demonstrate is the role of the persona of the President and, here, the consequences of Hollande's choice of persona during his campaign and in the early weeks and months of his presidency. The 'Hollande phenomenon' is a rich opportunity to study the French presidency, and understand what it is. And we cannot understand Hollande without understanding Sarkozy's presidency, or either of these without understanding truly what the French presidency itself is about, what it is *for*, why it is the way it is and, indeed, the character it has taken on as an 'embodied' political institution since 1958. For whether it is Mr Bling Sarkozy or Mr Normal Hollande, the French presidency, the leadership office in one of the world's most powerful nations, is a very complex and ill-understood institution, and the regime and culture it is embedded within are equally complex and ill-understood. In order to grasp the real significance of the Hollande presidency let us analyse how the Hollande presidency took on its 'character', as it unfolded. What we contend is that Hollande's claim to be *'un Président normal'* defined his presidency for better and worse, and shifted if not the paradigm of the Fifth Republic Settlement (see Chapter 3), then several of the conventions hitherto enacted within it, which brought with it, almost immediately, a series of problems.

Sarkozy certainly was not normal, but he was accused of not being presidential either. So what exactly was normal? The opposite of Sarkozy? None of the French Presidents was normal in that sense. That is, as we have said, precisely why the Fifth Republic (1958–) was not the Fourth (1946–58). Perhaps Hollande was not like Sarkozy, which is what he intended, indeed fixated upon, but was not 'presidential' either. If that was the case, the Fifth Republic would enter upon a period of unanticipated difficulties. So we come back to what 'normal' meant, and what it meant for Hollande. He seemed to suggest during the campaign that it meant respecting the Fifth Republic's Constitution. But this too would have utterly transformed the Republic – the Prime Minister not the President would name the government ministers, the President could not just call referendums at will (that was just the start of what a truly constitutional Fifth Republic presidency would mean). The Fifth Republic's Constitution had been made for de Gaulle, by de Gaulle, but he then simply ignored it or, rather, exploited all its ambivalence, as did his successors who adopted and added to a kind of acquired behaviour a range of possibilities as we shall see in Chapter 3 (Debré 1974). A President who followed the letter of the Constitution would transform the Fifth Republic utterly. But de Gaulle had bequeathed gravitas and a style that 'befitted' the office of President. In this, Sarkozy was actually closer to what became the spirit of the Constitution than Hollande suggested it was. The French had seemed since 1958 to not really want what was normal, but what was monarchical. Playing the part of the 'Good King' might compensate, in that here 'normal' implied understanding the lives of 'normal' people while remaining distinctive, emphasising, nevertheless, a kind of omniscience; but there is a symbolism in the French presidency that the 'Good King' mythology (i.e. more normal) disguises and, besides, it too is a very complex mythological idea; in fact, Mitterrand had used it in the 1986–88 period to great effect, but his style was the antithesis of Hollande's style. We shall come back to this in Chapter 6.

Hollande's claim to being normal had implications beyond the understanding of his advisors, one of the main being that by stressing that he would be normal (unlike Sarkozy) the emphasis upon persona remained as acute. In a word, France moved from a preoccupation with one character to an equal preoccupation with another. Let us examine some of the wider implications of the discursive/symbolic claim to the President as 'normal', and the manner in which this extends to an attempt at a kind of 'domestication' of the presidency itself.

What is the nature of the office itself, and how did Hollande 'envision' it? He saw it as the antithesis of Sarkozy's treatment of it. He would have it 'normal', 'simple', respectful, and so on (all these, his expressions). Everything that 'Sarko' was not. He would not be involved in every detail or be present at every moment, like Sarkozy, and there would be decorum and poise in his presidency (Sarko was everywhere all of the time, and was called the 'Hyperpresident'). At the heart of this idea, is the traditional distinction (echoing of the King's Two Bodies, an originally medieval idea distinguishing between the king as both sacred and profane (Manow 2010)), between public life and private life (with an added implication, nay assertion, that each would be exemplary) (Saussez 2013). The idea of his candidacy as moral as well as normal was stressed repeatedly by Hollande; and implicit in his 'normal' critique of Sarkozy was the moral issue of Sarkozy's having mixed the public and the private. This 'moral' disapproval was given a powerful symbolism by Hollande's disparaging, cursory treatment of the outgoing President (and his wife) on inauguration day: keeping the exchange between the presidential incoming and outgoing couples too brief, not accompanying them to their car, turning quickly on his heels, etc.; all this symbolised a kind of moral, exemplary President ejecting the unexemplary President from the sacred office. This symbolic gesture of 'dismissing' Sarkozy on inauguration day implied disapproval of his predecessor *because* Sarkozy was incapable of stopping the private self from crashing into the public President. This is why Valérie's tweet had such effects, and threw Hollande's own depiction of the presidency and himself into (comic) relief and – and this is lethal in France – into ridicule. There is a deep cultural context here regarding 'face' and the royal court of, in particular, Louis XIV (king of France 1643–1715). Similar ritual ostentation – and lampoon – still inform the presidency today. Once the 'tweet' affair broke, all of the satire on TV, in cartoons, or online, focused on the idea of a weak man or a fearful king in his palace utterly overwhelmed by the feud between two caricaturally dominatrix women.

The question of normal, therefore, raises several other questions, especially that of the mythological exigency of the Gaullist presidency. Even in the played down mythology of Hollande's campaign, there was constant reference (by all the participants and in particular their spokespeople) to the election as 'the meeting of a man with the people' (*une rencontre entre un homme et un peuple*), a near direct quote from de Gaulle. Whether or not this jarred with Hollande's down-to-earth persona (can one talk of a mythological 'normal'?), it nevertheless raises the question of whether these strange notions of destiny (the antithesis of social democratic thinking) were reflected upon in Hollande's campaign, for they would come into play later and severely damage his presidential status in the first year of his presidency.

Hollande gave the impression many times and the assurance often, that as President he would be presidential; a strange juxtaposition with normal. We mean by this that he made it clear that he would not interfere in governmental, let alone party matters. In reality this was not true, for it would have thrown into relief (if not into crisis) the whole notion of the presidency in the Fifth Republic. And it did not happen. Hollande, not Ayrault, chose his ministers. His first FR2TV interview (see Chapter 4) was *also* a call for a parliamentary majority for the left. Calling to order Cécile Duflot (over remarks about cannabis), and a host of other things – demonstrated that the President would continue, even in domestic policy and politics, as the main political actor, so the political fundamentals of the President's rule remained the same; and in reality, Hollande became as 'activist' as Sarkozy as he tried almost continuously to reverse his growing unpopularity. The appointment of his government was a case in point here.

Although it was met with public curiosity and interest, it was a government formed in the spirit of Hollande as party leader. This was not remarked upon very much at the time, but was an indication of how things would develop. One of the reasons it was so large a government was because Hollande was ensuring that all the party faction leaders and allies of the PS were represented. It was like the signatories to a *motion de synthèse* at a party conference. What it was not was a government ready for rapid and decisive action, as would become clear when, as soon as the government was formed and the legislative elections over, everybody went on holiday (Visot and Lachèvre 2014).

Normal is highly problematic, in that the office lends itself to grandeur; in fact, it demands it. And the comportment of the President has repercussions upon the image and behaviour of every other actor in the system. If he is to be like a nice Prime Minister, what should the actual Prime Minister be like, and all the ministers, and so on? What should be his conduct towards 'rivals' on both the right and left, and within his government? And what should happen if for any reason his authority stumbled (e.g. international (sense of) affront to France by, say, the US, or Germany, or a required comportment and decisiveness after say a terrorist attack, or riots or strikes)? The 'call' for strong leadership would be highly consequent in the circumstances of a President having established normal as normative. This makes his appointment of the workaday and equally 'normal' Jean-Marc Ayrault a further indication of the difficulties surrounding executive image. Moreover, Ayrault had no more governmental experience than Hollande; they were allies and old friends; but symbolically, the executive now had two 'normals'. This, in fact, had never happened (Pompidou and Messmer is an arguable comparison). But this division of symbolic labour meant that Hollande would have to try to lose his normal image at the first crisis. The first crisis, Valériegate, however, was more a farce than a crisis, as we shall see in Chapter 4.

We need, therefore, to widen our study to an appraisal of what the French presidency is; not simply constitutionally and politically, but culturally and mythically; and what the 'scope' for the President is, rhetorically and performatively. What are the deeper structures within the institution, and in the French '*imaginaire*' that have created, maintained, and influenced the presidency. Only with an appraisal of this nature will we be able, not only to see past the trivial, day-to-day chronicle of the Hollande presidency, but to see the dramatic role this latter played against the backdrop of a very complex political institution, and why the comportment of the President was so dysfunctional in the regime. In the next chapter, by drawing upon the founding and development of the Fifth Republic (Gaffney 2012) and the character, style, and rhetoric of each of the Presidents, we can establish the ideational and evolving structure of the Fifth Republic's presidency, and the elements of character, style, and rhetoric that constitute it and inform its 'performance'.

3
From the Gaullist Settlement to Celebrity Politics

What then might be the 'elements' constitutive of presidential character and performance in the Fifth Republic? It would be helpful to elaborate a theoretical framework for the study of character and performance in the presidency in the Fifth Republic, and its role in the political process. It will take into account phenomena relevant to how, and the effects of how, political actors acted in 1958 (Denquin 1988; Ferniot 1965; Hoffman *et al.* 1963; Mitterrand 1964; Mollet 1962; Rémond 1983; Sirius 1958; Touchard *et al.* 1960), the particular conditions of performance, and the wider stage (institutions and culture) of 1958; and the longer-term consequences of these three aspects upon the subsequent development of the Fifth Republic as it moved forward through different Presidents into the media age and later into the culture of celebrity politics (Bell and Gaffney 2013). We have to start by distilling de Gaulle's view of the world and of action within it and how these created the Fifth Republic as an imagined entity.

The settlement

Because of the way the Fifth Republic was established, and because of who established it, and the republican, national, and personalist traditions it reflected, and the particular way that de Gaulle romanticised France, France in the Fifth Republic was originally 'envisioned' and then 'performed' in the following way (De Gaulle 1954, 1956, 1959, 1970, 1971; De Gaulle 1970a; Dreyfus 1982; Institut Charles de Gaulle 1981, 1990; Cotteret and Moreau 1969; Maitrot and Sicault 1969;

Touchard 1978; and see Bibliography):

- France is an entity
- France is a divided entity
- France is a beloved and fragile entity
- A sense of history is akin to religious sentiment
- France is exemplary
- The weight of history implies duty
- The motor of politics is the search for unity
- Persons/individuals can act upon history
- Persons/individuals can intervene dramatically
- Persons/individuals have a special role (they are special and can 'envisage' solutions). Their comportment is chivalric; France, therefore, the object of their chivalry, is 'feminine', and part of a 'quest' for a near-ineffable entity: 'All of my life, I have had in my mind a very particular idea of France. It is shaped as much by feeling as by rational thought. The emotional part of me imagines France quite simply like a fairy tale princess or the madonna in a painting, and fated to have an unusual and glorious destiny. Instinctively, I feel that providence created France in order that she achieve great triumphs or else undergo great misfortunes' (My translation). '*Toute ma vie, je me suis fait une certaine idée de la France. Le sentiment me l'inspire aussi bien que la raison. Ce qu'il y a, en moi, d'affectif imagine naturellement la France, telle la princesse des contes ou la madone aux fresques des murs, comme vouée à une destinée éminente et exceptionnelle. J'ai d'instinct, l'impression que la Providence l'a créée pour des succès achevés ou des malheurs exemplaires*' (De Gaulle 1954).
- Politics as drama involves individuals acting in order to re-establish the state/the health of the republic
- The French are capable of heroism and of foolishness
- Political institutions and constitutions are necessary but insufficient
- Individuals intervene in their arrangement, for better or worse, through action and discourse
- Institutions, constitutions and individuals are influenced by wider ideological, cultural and mythological factors proceeding from French history
- Political ideologies and doctrines appear to be coherent discourses
- Ideologies or doctrines are informed by ambivalence and ambiguity (mystery), mutability, and a range of discursive, rhetorical qualities; they can also 'discursively interweave' with one another (e.g. de Gaulle's blending republicanism and Gaullism being an exemplary but not isolated illustration).

The character of de Gaulle became central, and therefore France accepted 'romantic leadership' which involved accepting such a character, and folding into the paradigm of the republic the rhetorical consequences of recognition i.e. de Gaulle's 'life' (legend) as a saga: Desert crossings, Lonely certainty, Visions/envisioning, Cassandra-status of the leader, *Moi* or *Le chaos*, the legend of an exemplary life, the marginality of the hero, Recognition/non-recognition of the hero, Acclamation/rejection/ultimate 'pantheonisation' of the hero, France as cherished *patrimoine* (e.g. can be 'taken' to London, 1940), *Fatalité*, and Voluntarism (Drake and Gaffney 1996; Hazareesingh 2012; Institut Charles de Gaulle 1983; Tenzer 1998; Gaïti 1998).

At the level of political activity, the above factors heighten the role of relationships between leaders and everything and everyone. Individuals become echoes of a wider collective desire, or are imagined as being so. Leaders also have a special relationship to their opponents, to doctrine, and an imagined intimacy with history itself, with 'France', as well as with – interchangeably – 'the French', the public, the electorate, and 'opinion'. Relationships – e.g. the leader's relation with the party, but also to democracy and institutions, to wisdom and insight, to life as a quest, have a grammar that is independent of how political relationships are normally perceived in contemporary democracy (Garrigues 2012). This notion of a privileged relationship with both France and the French was clearly de Gaulle's own conviction, but we need to stress that it was an imagined relationship (with very real consequences) and was in great part maintained throughout his presidency by his own soviet-style control of the national TV and radio media (Chalaby 2002). His 'unmediated' relationship was not only mediated, it was this to the exclusion of other mediations. This was, in part, why the 1965 presidential election was such a national event; for the first time, or the first time in years, the national electorate saw not only political figures other than de Gaulle, they were also seeing candidates who dared to stand against him (Fondation nationale des sciences politiques 1970; Roche 1971). The presidency became instantly the most popular and influential office in the republic, and the presidential elections of 1965, 1969, 1974, 1981, 1988, 1995, 2002, 2007, and 2012 became and remain by far the most popular moments of the electoral cycle and the central political and symbolic act in the Fifth Republic (Baniafouna 2012; Bertolus and Bredin 2011; Bréchon 2013; Goguel 1965; Labbé and Monière 2013; Lewis-Beck *et al.* 2012; Pascal and Potier 2012; Perrineau and Ysmal 1995, 2003; Tiberj 2013; Touchard *et al.* 1960; Winock 2007; and see Bibliography).

The Fifth Republic, therefore, acts as a portal through which enter political resources normally excluded from the dominant republican paradigm, i.e. a whole range of interpretations of and mythologies about France, about political action, the role of individuals, and the various political relationships within the republic e.g. the relationship of the leader to 'France' and the 'French'. Interactions within this framework create a dynamic within political relationships, in particular, the constant appeal of, and appeals to, imagined alternative forms of political allegiance, relationships, and action/activity. Contrary to the near-universal characterisation of Gaullism as a form of Bonapartism or semi-bonapartism (Rémond 1982), these forms may sometimes be anti-Bonapartist, and pro-democratic (or anti-democratic, or even anti-personalist) but are pulled decisively into the formal political arena by the Gaullist settlement itself. The real interest to the scholar is not just that de Gaulle took power, but that he could do so in a French tradition, that he was 'possible', that his being perceived as 'necessary' was possible within French cultural paradigms (Gaïti 1998), and that 1958–62 established or re-established this quality of French political culture as a path-dependent constituent part of French political life, and a major influence on the development of the institutions. The Gaullist emphasis upon the special or providential character of the leader also created an inordinate focus upon the individual's qualities and character traits, a kind of path-dependent narcissism that has informed the Fifth Republic from 1958 until today.

The essential characteristic of the Fifth Republic, therefore, is the dramatic intervention of persona into institutional arrangements. And the persona brings with him/her inordinate reference to the historical/social/mythological basis for action on behalf of the people and their personal role within/relationship to all this. Once accepted, this triggers reactions throughout the polity and becomes the basis for political action. One of the main consequences of this is that the discourse of the persona comes centre stage, changing – in discourse – throughout the polity what the persona has changed at the level of political organisation. This in part is possible because, as we have argued elsewhere (Gaffney 1989), the 'isms' of earlier discourses are themselves more ambivalent and polyvalent than they seem. This means that republicanism is not just a set of core and associated values or beliefs, or the elaboration of doctrine (Nicolet 1982; Freeden 1996; Laborde 2008), but a discourse which would have itself these, but also contains myths and legends and 'exposure' to other discourses, and is in perpetual 'ideological maintenance' (Flood and Bell 1997; Berenson *et al.* 2011; Bréchon 1994; Hazareesingh 1994) or 'progression' at best (Fieschi 2004), in decline at worst (Andolfatto 2005; Benoist 1979), depending upon 1) its ability to interact with institutions and processes (cf. the decline of left Gaullism and the UDT in the 1960s (Capitant 1971, 1972; Debû-Bridel 1970; Hamon 1958; Mallet 1965; Vallon 1969)), 2) its ability to interact with persons, i.e. to be 'voiced' by a range of types of leaders and parties (perceived as rallies, *rassemblements* around the inspired leader).

A political identity or culture and action within it at any one moment is the consequence of the actions and interactions of individuals and groups within institutional, cultural, and discursive contexts; action such as de Gaulle's was a performance within a context. Politics is in that sense 'performative' (Gaffney 2014a). The 'coming of the Fifth Republic' has traditionally been seen through one of the discrete disciplines (political history, political science, constitutional law), and therefore as essentially a question of: 1) its own legitimacy vis-à-vis a 'real' republic; 2) the weakness and the institutional misarrangements of the Fourth Republic; 3) the virulence of the Bonapartist tradition (or at least heroic leadership tradition); or 4) a crisis of (state) authority; or else a combination of these (the list here is long; for these four essential approaches see, *inter alia* Andrews 1982; Berstein 2001; Berstein and Milza 1991; Bell 2000; Chagnollaud and Quermonne 1996; Chevallier *et al.* 2002; Debré 1972; Denquin 1988; Donegani and Sadoun 1998; Duverger 1961, 1974; Duhamel 1993; Goguel 1965; Hayward 1983; Hoffman 1967; Mendès France 1962; Pickles 1962; Rioux 1983; Thody 1998; Williams and Harrison 1960; Zarka 2009). Let us recast these four analytical perspectives in new terms, the terms of our alternative reading of the republic, because a proper understanding of the Fifth Republic in both 1958 and today means the realisation that it is more than any of these explanations, more than all four of them put together. Before elaborating on this, let us recast the four questions along the lines of our own more semiotic approach.

1) Is a Fifth Republican form of regime leadership and political action *conceivable* from a 'leadership restrictive' Fourth (or Third) Republic perspective? The answer is yes, because the overall constitutional difference between the republics is quite small. And all observers dwelt upon, and eventually accepted as republican, the Fifth Republic's constitutional version of personal power. In fact, the Fifth Republic is less about personal power than performed personal 'presence' and 'embodiment'; and constitutionalists of all types have ignored this and this near-same question: is a Fifth Republican form of regime, with its

emphasis on leadership and political action, conceivable from a Fifth Republic perspective which does not destroy a Fourth Republic world view (republican forms, democratic process and representation, economic growth, modernisation, both cultural and socio-economic, leadership, stability, etc.)? The answer again is yes (Williams 1972).

2) Second question: The weakness of the Fourth Republic has itself traditionally had a range of interpretations e.g. failure to renew elites properly, paralysis of, and yet shifting (because of Cold War) centre of gravity leading to instability and '*immobilisme*', virulence of extremes (Communism and Gaullism), and so on. Recasting this we would ask, in what way did the Fifth Republic appear to offer an antidote to the weakness of the Fourth (for example, how was the discourse of the state and the image of personal leadership and its relation to other forces deployed and perceived in 1958? (Gaïti 1998; Rimbaud 1997)). Were the perceived mis-arrangements of the Fourth Republic's institutions born of fear of personal leadership and a strong executive? Some have argued that there is very little evidence that the Fourth Republic was collapsing/weak (e.g. attitudes of people; booming economy, etc. (Williams 1972)). If this is true, the role of the symbolic politics of the type we have described – and especially the politics of a surreptitious *coup* – takes on even more salience (Tenzer 1998; Nick 1998), that is to say that de Gaulle's coming back to power in 1958 needs to be fully grasped as a 'performance' upon a stage or within a cluster of symbolic imperatives, e.g. sense of crisis, vulnerability, role of providential leader, sense of state impotence, fear of a coup, drama, acclamation, desire for protection and deliverance (Parker and Kosofsky 1995).

3) Regarding the virulence of the beast that the Fourth (and Second and Third) Republic was trying to suppress, essentially Bonapartism, we can say that perhaps it was virulent but it was not the beast the Fourth Republic's politicians thought it was, and in a sense they created it (Gaïti 1998); in a word, de Gaulle, particularly because of the 1944–46 period and his Bayeux and Strasbourg speeches of 1946 and 1947 (De Gaulle 1970a), and the brief success of his RPF party (Charlot 1983; Audigier and Bavarez 1998), 'existed' within the Fourth Republic as a refused alternative. Perhaps the Fourth Republic is really to be understood as the exclusion of a discourse and mythology, namely, Gaullism, through institutional arrangement and political comportment (in the name of modern and rational democracy), but an exclusion which established the conditions for its return.

4) Re: the crisis of (state) authority. In a sense, this begs all the questions. It is partly tautological: in 1958, the state was in crisis because

the state was not working. If we change our perspective slightly, we can say that instances of the lack of respect for republican state authority were there in parts of French tradition (certainly into the twentieth century in parts of the army and the Church, for example) and, conversely, become effectively countered when there is a very practical fear of the army, which in turn offers the state a way forward: in this case, to recall de Gaulle to office in June 1958 – and the recall itself hauls together for a period of time the competing traditions and ideas (republicanism, fear of/allegiance to personal authority, fear of the army, and so on). The focus then becomes how the elements within the culture and within the institutional configuration and discursive range were assembled and deployed by a range of actors and comportments of actors to promote or enhance or allow for an incorporation into the polity of what we have called romantic leadership or romanticised presidentialism, that is, acceptance of de Gaulle's 'legend' as an appropriate and necessary form of national leadership.

The point we need to make most strongly here concerning the way 1958 has always been interpreted, is that the break/continuity approaches miss what is of fundamental interest (we find both approaches in Lachaise *et al.* 2011; Le Brazidec 2000; Pickles 1962; Williams 1970). What is important to an understanding of 'what happened' is how the transition was 'enacted', how the series of events relating to political leadership and its realignment within and of the polity (institutions, culture, discourse, and of course, here, person or persona) were played out or played themselves out to give us the Fifth Republic (Gaffney 2012). The essential point here is that there is a kind of separation yet intertwining of 'real' and 'symbolic' politics in both the Fourth and the Fifth Republics. In politics generally these are conflated, yet in varying degrees of influence. The Fourth Republic had attempted – as regards many things but especially leadership – to stress the practical and procedural, and to minimise the role of 'symbolic politics'. The events of 1958 gave dramatic 'play' to it, while almost separating it out from 'real' politics to the point where it almost replaces it, real politics having become essentially loss of state authority (especially in Algeria), '*immobilisme*', and tumbling governments, followed by trying to organise in the face of military insubordination; symbolic politics being the timed interventions and rhetoric of de Gaulle, and the growing allegiance to him by the political elites and the public.

With the conferring of office and power upon de Gaulle to address the issue of the loss of state authority, the events of May–June 1958 see the real and the symbolic enter into a different relationship until they have re-fused differently around de Gaulle's authority. The battle then between 1958–62 was, for the Gaullists, to keep them so. From then, there is a configuration of institutions with the political actors attempting to orientate them to a particular purpose. Their efforts are informed by ideas about politics (past, actual, and desired) and particularly about the role of individuals and about how particular actors interpret the actions and intentions of other actors (imagined allies and protagonists). At the institutional level, there is tension between those institutions which have a parliamentary purpose (the National Assembly, political parties, the government) and those with a presidential one (the presidency, but also, because of the new circumstances, political parties and the government). Over and above this, however, we can say that political action strategies and their accompanying discourses of leadership are not exclusive to any of the institutions even though they are privileged by presidentialism. They are, moreover, related both to institutions and to 'wider' or 'other' political phenomena such as constituencies, mediations, and discursive resources, and these constantly affect developments. And one of the main discursive resources in a highly personalised polity is a dramatic view of political action. It may be the case, for example, that '*ruptures*' (breaks), following crises, happen, but what is important for our understanding is which levers within the political system are thrown in order that, among the political elites and/or wider public/s, the impression or conviction exists that 'crisis' is upon us, and 'ruptures' can exist or are about to take place, are taking place, or have taken place. All of this means that the essential quality of the Fifth Republic is the 'performance' of leadership as both an 'act' and a pedagogy.

Let us at this point be clear about how we understand de Gaulle and Gaullism, because our view differs from the received view and certainly from those of his apologists. It is clear from our analysis that although we subscribe to the notion of de Gaulle's fundamental importance to the nature and development of the Fifth Republic – we probably subscribe to the idea of his influence upon the subsequent development of presidentialism more than most – we also take issue with the received view of what it was he did bring. It is the case that de Gaulle's admirers and followers (his mythmakers in some ways – not least himself in his Memoirs) have built a notion of de Gaulle and his importance that today is almost unassailable (De Gaulle 1954, 1956, 1959, 1970, 1971; and *inter alia* Malraux 1971; Peyrefitte 1994, 1996, 2000). The central thrust of this approach is that he was, indeed, a providential leader and that he brought 'Gaullism' and a *gaullienne* quality to French history and politics from the mid- to the late twentieth century. In spite of our analysis, we do not subscribe to this view. Ours is that through his performance in a particular set of circumstances, which themselves offered opportunities because of France's specific and specifically rich history and culture, he was able to take power, embed it, and pass on a style of presidency and its associated relationships to his successors. We stress the performative (and thereby de Gaulle's art and artifice) because, in spite of the idea of *volonté* in Gaullism, providentialism is teleological and therefore self-contradictory, except if what is meant is 'providential' in its literal sense of being sent by Providence. It is therefore a fantasy.

As regards the richness of Gaullism as a philosophy and as a set of prescriptions, we have outlined its implicit world view at the beginning of this chapter; as a doctrine (Institut Charles de Gaulle 1983; Sabatier and Ragueneau 1994), however, it is in our view minimal and can be reduced to a set of three perhaps four political truisms: national independence, a strong currency, a strong state, and a loose belief in social cohesion, welfare and well-being (*participation*); the undergirding of these and all other aspects of Gaullism being a profound emotional, and arguably clichéd (both in its imagery and affect) and infantile (in the psychoanalytic sense) love for and devotion to an equally emotional, although ineffable, idea of France. By seeing the Gaullist imagination in this way, by correcting our angle of vision, the centrality of the (myth of the providential) leader becomes clear. To paraphrase the poet Mallarmé – *'chargé de vue et non de visions'* – it is not the vision that is central to Gaullism, it is the envisioning. In fact, the vision (*une certaine idée*) is also ineffable. It is the 'seer' and our acquiescence in the idea that the seer has seen/can see that is the core of Gaullism.

Path-dependence and the evolution of the Fifth Republic

As regards the advent and the development of the Fifth Republic, let us now turn to ideational institutionalism and to path-dependence theory. Essentially, what we need to do is to gather our theoretical perspectives, and inscribe these into a more dynamic framework for understanding the Fifth Republic. We need to demonstrate how the symbolic, discursive, rhetorical, and mythological elements brought to mainstream politics by de Gaulle survived him, perpetually modifying the institutional thrust of the regime right up until the present day. This theoretical undertaking is particularly important because the literature in this area is – as regards France – particularly poor. It falls into two camps, each unhelpful: either an under-theorised Weberian idea of charismatic leadership as regards de Gaulle, and (therefore) 'disenchantment' (normal politics) in the post-de Gaulle period (this view is near-universal, e.g. Berstein 1989, pp. 267 and ff.; Weber 1964, 2004) or else an over-emphasis upon the presidential regime, but now that of the new media age in which attention to 'spectacle', political marketing, and *'la com''*, by both actors and scholars, is considered explanatory (Maarek 2014; Schwartzenberg 2011). We need to maintain our emphasis upon the institutions and upon culture while showing how these have moved forward through a range of levels, of interactions, of informing ideas, and of discursive and rhetorical registers, and how they accumulated and developed in the post-de Gaulle period to form the basis of contemporary politics.

Because of the nature of and relationships between the new institutions of government, and in particular the comportment, rhetoric, and style (Gaffney 2012a) of de Gaulle, the discourse of the regime became very responsive to dualisms, both in discourse and then in understanding and attitude. In a sense, this is inevitable: myths and mythological thought are designed to imply reality and give it or actions within it ethical significance. Leadership will become more and more a question of 'seeing' what is right as opposed to what is wrong, and perceiving what is true, and what not true. And particular styles of leadership, particularly if pronounced, will imply their opposites (strong leadership will imply weak leadership or absence of leadership in others; action will imply the *immobilisme* of adversaries, and so on). As a result of these developments, a series of opposites is fed into the normative paradigm of the republic, and is often mediated by or linked to individuals or personae, de Gaulle being a classic case, Mitterrand too; these dualisms or opposites will become almost the language of the republic; for example, mythical register/straightforwardness, providential leadership/procedural leadership, *compagnons/féodalités*, constitutional respect/constitutional abuse, lyricism/quietism, individual effort/collective effort, protocol/humour, conspiracy/transparency, presidential exercise of power and authority/abuse of same (*lèse majesté*), serenity/*'agitation'*, 'hyperpresidentialism'/*'apaisement'* and many more. These dualities imply states of mind and emotion. What they also do is make certain emotions and comportments inappropriate, because the 'President' is not 'real' in the sense of being an ordinary citizen, or even an ordinary human being. Claims to ethical superiority, certain types of humour, or claims to citizen-status – e.g. taking action as the person rather than the President, claiming the right to a private life, and so on – these traits and dispositions will be precluded for reasons of the special status of the President – and of course all of these dispositions apply to François Hollande. We shall come back to this at the end of this chapter and in our Conclusion.

Origins matter, but evolution matters too. Historical institutionalism is strong on the former but weak on the latter. Hay, in a 1998 article, theorising the political role of temporality, asserts: 'The order in which things happen affects how they happen; the trajectory of change up to a certain point itself constrains the trajectory after that point, and the strategic choices made at a particular moment eliminate whole ranges of possibilities from later choices while serving as the very conditions of existence of others' (Hay 1998). Not only does this help us begin to 'plot' the developmental evolution of the Fifth Republic, it further confers upon actors within contexts, the opportunity to affect development. One thinks of the French mystical philosopher, Simone Weil (1909–43) and her view that not anything was possible but that the future was not determined (Weil 1962). Specific patterns of timing and sequence matter; a wide range of social outcomes may be possible; large consequences may result from relatively small or contingent events; particular courses of action, once introduced, can be almost impossible to reverse; and consequently, political development is punctuated by critical moments of action or junctures of activity that shape the basic contours of social life (Pierson 2000). This leads Pierson on to the development of an analogy with economics and its idea of increasing or decreasing returns, that is to say that the path-dependent branches of development will be reinforced by time and sequence (e.g. it becomes harder and harder, with time, to go back on decisions taken because more and more opposite decisions would need to be made, and this in the context of other decisions taken on other subsequent branchings).

Presidential comportment in the Fifth Republic creates a path-dependent presidency; presidential decisions within constraints and opportunities fashion the presidency in a particular way. We might add that a further, almost opposite, element will also be incorporated into political exchange, that is to say the diminishing returns of romantic leadership. This means that appellative rhetoric, envisioning discourse, and the discourse of crisis, have constraining conditions to their success. One of them is the avoidance of overuse, another, rhetorical inventiveness or lack of it, another the danger, quite simply, of lassitude. They are political resources that need to be handled extremely carefully. Misuse can lead rapidly to indifference on the part of the listener, and ridicule on that of the speaker. 'Ordinary conditions' (for example, procedural leadership) may effectively counter such a register. A consequence of this is that political competition will often involve the strategic use of one or both of these by political protagonists. Having said this, abandoning romantic leadership in favour of procedural leadership, particularly when other factors pertain – e.g. the 'proximity' of the President – can have unpredictable if not negative results. Because of the singular nature of the presidency, all the Presidents have had to negotiate their relationship to the appellative and the procedural.

The Gaullist settlement introduced into mainstream political life a kind of mythological imagination. This is only one element of the polity. We should not fetishise our approach. By introducing this 'other' register into political exchange, and in the context of a representative, democratic system, Gaullism paradoxically brings in with it all its opposites which also inform political exchange. In practical terms, the successes of Gaullism's opponents (e.g. as early as the Municipal elections of March 1959) and the exigencies of 'normal' party life upon de Gaulle's political support, actually help this domestication and contextualising of romantic leadership's higher register, assuming it survives such opposition, which it did, enabling 'high' presidentialism to survive in a modern democracy. We shall come back to the question of leadership and the political party at the end of this chapter and in our Conclusion.

Let us just end this part of our discussion by speculating that the development of our framework will enable scholarship to revisit in a more thoroughgoing way many of the main events and developments within the Fifth Republic, and offer a sensitive reading of these: for example, the nature of de Gaulle's loss of authority following the social upheaval of 1968 and his failed referendum of 1969, and the conditions of and effects upon Georges Pompidou's simultaneous transition – as Prime Minister he 'solved' the 1968 crisis – from procedural to presidential leader (and the effect of this upon the institutions); the manner in which the left adapted to the Gaullist republic; Mitterrand's shifts through 'federator' of the centre-left, Damascene conversion to socialism (Mitterrand 1969), and appropriation of socialist discourse (Gaffney in Raymond 1994), and the repercussions of these upon government; the nature of Michel Rocard's personalised challenge to Mitterrand as an example of the institutional and cultural effects of the Fifth Republic upon the political parties (*idem,* the National Front and its personalised development in the Fifth Republic over and above the cult of the leader in right-wing populism); the various stages of the valorisation of the National Assembly in spite of the constitution: the role of Chaban-Delmas, Giscard d'Estaing, the political parties, alternation of majorities, and cohabitation/s; the role and nature of Jacques Chirac's 'renewal' of Gaullism in 1977; the fortunes of the non-Socialist left in the context of the institutions; the 1988–95 period of system dysfunction/near collapse of the PS; the exemplary nature of Jospin's leadership (1995–2002) and his stunning failure in 2002; the role of 'character' in Chirac's fortunes, 1995–2007; the endemic rivalries within movements or governments (one of the most spectacular, that between de Villepin and Sarkozy 2002–06); the shifting of presidentialism in Sarkozy's presidency towards the politically consequential incorporation of the 'private' into the public life thus extending and complicating, and enhancing further the role of 'character'; the interaction in Sarkozy's presidency of the 'private' and the 'ordinary', and the effects of these; the entry of women into the presidential paradigm; the understandable but unpredictable claim by Hollande in the 2012 campaign to be a 'normal' President in a normal presidency; and the dramatic consequences upon Hollande's fortunes and the nature of the presidency once 'normal' proved inadequate as a presidential norm. These few examples give an indication of how a new approach to the Fifth Republic might be developed.

Personal leadership and the Republic

In France, leadership as a political resource has always enjoyed a romantic form; strong, exalted, inspired, and exemplary. There are four reasons for this. The first is related to the process of state centralisation and nation-building and leadership's relation to these over the last 200 years or so. The fractured nature of French political elites (and their relation to one another and to social groups) has meant, certainly since the 1789 revolution, that political elites – monarchists, republicans, Bonapartists, for example – have invariably been a) in a relative minority and therefore b) have had a champion. Second, this means that there has been leadership – or rather competing leaderships – each championing itself, its 'vision' and its constituency, while trying to reach beyond itself and unite a range of groups (in order to change a relative majority into an absolute one, or at least one large enough to exercise power). Third, because of this situation, leaders have invariably either enjoyed a lot of power (often for only a brief period) or else have been institutionally kept from it. With the halting but ultimately successful establishing of the republican tradition over the last two centuries, this has meant a structure and process of republican institutions which have kept pretenders to power at bay, particularly 'Bonapartists' of one kind or another, so that 'strong' leadership was screened out from power, and regarded with hostility and suspicion, therefore becoming even more virulent in the wings of politics, creating surges, threats, and so on to republican institutions and increasing the latters' sense of vulnerability. Having said this, the republican tradition has itself had many heroes and leaders, but they have enjoyed smaller 'cadre' constituencies, or else have emerged only in crisis, and have themselves often been marginalised by the structures of the regime (e.g. Clemenceau after WWI, Mendès France in the Fourth Republic) (Garrigues 2012). The fourth and final factor informing this issue has been the images and language associated with this leadership phenomenon. Because the tradition is long and tortuous, the range is wide: strident, reconciling, historically sensitive, conquering, mythical, the guardian of memory or the patrimony, envisioning of the future. These are some of its powerful traits, and it is accompanied by a whole series of legends, and almost fairytale dispositions: exile and desert crossings, lonely certitude, tumultuous acclaim, sacrifice, rejection, and so on. We shall come back to this, as these aspects were the basis, as we have seen, of de Gaulle's claim to exemplary status. The point here is that whatever the range and depth of language and image, e.g. imagining and contemplating being illustrative of a personal or national *vécu* or lived experience, and containing implications and shared understandings (*présupposés* or *sous-entendus*) which refer to the wider culture, both language and image are quintessentially personalised and, generally, suggest isolated leadership (until the 'call' is made) on the one hand and, paradoxically, point to a rich and *shared* national heritage on the other.

Leadership, institutions, and culture

We can now make one further point. In fact, we have already made it, but it is worth restating: that in the case of the French Fifth Republic, it is the relationship of the leadership tradition to institutions and culture that is crucial to our understanding. The essence of the Fifth Republic, particularly when contrasted with its predecessor or even when contrasted with the formal, constitutional Fifth Republic, is that it is characterised by the institutional supremacy of leadership as performance. The Fifth Republic's advent, its institutional configuration, and its structures of political opportunity mean that acts of leadership would take on great salience: the 1962 reform (which meant the President henceforth would be elected by universal suffrage), the 31 January 1964 Press conference (whereby the President's pre-eminence was reasserted), the President/Prime Minister relationship, foreign policy, the comportment of the first and subsequent Presidents, the constructed relationship between leader and electorate (or other real or imagined constituencies (Anderson 2006; Gaffney 2001)), the use of rhetoric (Charteris-Black 2005; Herman 2008; Martin 2013), the exploitation of performance's relationship to both institutions and culture; all these will matter consequentially in a range of important ways.

The question of leadership's relation to culture is possibly even more important to an understanding of French politics than its relationship to institutions. And from our earlier discussion, however alluring the notion of Bonapartism might be superficially, it is an empty term signifying little of value. The notion of Bonapartism now has common currency in French political and academic exchange, and we have used it until this point because it is understood as having a particular meaning and we did not wish to confuse the argument further. It was given heightened intellectual and academic status after the publication of René Rémond's *La droite en France* (first published in 1954. New editions – and title change – in 1963, 1968 and 1988. Last edition, *Les Droites en France* 1992). Rémond's book has since become normative (revised versions are still in print and it is on every French Politics and French History reading list); its findings are assumed to be self-evident. Essentially, he identifies three types or families on the political right: Legitimists, Orleanists, and Bonapartists. These are seen as being in spirit, respectively, conservative, progressive, and insurrectionary. In contemporary France, these categories are used to 'read' a particular political movement, style, or persuasion. Giscard d'Estaing, for example, is seen as Orleanist; Chirac, Bonapartist, Sarkozy (early) Bonapartist (Duhamel 2009; Thody 1989). Such traditions clearly exist in French political history, but for us it is, in the first place the way they are expressed by persons, and in the second the way they interact (and this often within the same movement and even more tellingly, within the same person or persona) that is of real interest to understanding political action and its mutability and, by extension, the mutability (discursive nature) of political doctrine. Moreover, dividing the right off from the left in interpretation, as is the norm and is Rémond's own method, may have merit in separating out two distinctive approaches to the polity, society, and the state; but even here the ways in which elements cross over from right to left, or else what elements each side share, or which elements can cross – and so change in their import or even in their nature – are far more interesting than the notion that discrete political families exist through time; political 'families' are simply one of the conditions of performative political action. One could even argue that political families as Rémond describes them only exist through time because of such mutability, that is, they exist through time because they do not. They exist through time because they performatively transform themselves through time. They survive because they are not as they are represented in Rémond's classic distinctions.

The way in which leadership styles are not rigidly bound by doctrine (Mitterrand's 'legitimism', certainly between 1981 and the early 1990s, is one of the best illustrations) is one of the keys to understanding contemporary France, and means that we really need to look again at what we mean in the French case by leadership and its relation to doctrine. Regarding Bonapartism itself, perhaps the most relevant of Rémond's terms to our thesis, it is helpful to approach this phenomenon as being a form of leadership claim to followership which transcends doctrine (i.e. the 'isms'), but which is in a particular relationship to doctrines in that it presents itself as transcending them, and therefore becomes a particular political resource which purports to be synthetic and dependent upon the envisioning by a particular leader. In his/her rhetoric, the leader will establish a regime or government or particular order, an order in part imagined, given voice, by means of doctrines (and by traditional/ordinary French people), yet whose true realisation and understanding are dependent upon the leader and his or her exemplary understanding (we say 'or her', although it is clear that the structures underlying this kind of leadership are chivalric and, therefore, characteristically male) of the state, the nation, and France. This is much more helpful than seeing Bonapartism as a political family within the political right. The whole collective or individual gesture of allegiance to such a leader constitutes the (Bonapartist) adventure, lending it romance and commitment (and possible foolishness – hence the multiple negative connotations of the French expression '*l'aventure*'). To see Bonapartism in this way, as a style and a mythology (and a set of discursive political resources, particularly the creation of romantic 'promise'), rather than as constituting a political doctrine or family, is more helpful to understanding France, especially when trying to grasp the opportunity-dependent structure and mutability of political practice, and indeed doctrine, within the Fifth Republic. Once this is admitted, the biggest 'ism' of them all, republicanism itself, becomes subject to revision and becomes crucial to an understanding of the Fifth Republic. We shall come back to this.

One of the ways of grasping the relationship of the Fifth Republic form of leadership to culture is to grasp what a President or a pretender to the presidency lays claim to (i.e. why they are followed, or at least why they are 'recognised'). We have argued that it involves vision, envisioning, but also an awareness of a mystical patrimony. The 'promise' of leadership is like a treasured secret akin to notions such as how and why the Grail was smuggled out of Montségur (irrespective, indeed, of what the Grail actually contained); how and why this patrimony is to be passed on, and the fact that it must at all costs be passed on. These issues, therefore, raise the question of the leader's relationship to France and to the French, and in the contemporary period of course, the electorate and 'opinion'. These latter, however, should not be seen as the mundane expression of desacralised myth, i.e. that today's French electorate is the pale reflection of yesterday's Nation; that today's demystified consumers are the remnants of a mythical France. In discourse, the former is *perpetually* being transformed into the latter and, on a bad day, cf. de Gaulle, Giscard, Jospin, and Sarkozy's 'rejections' in 1969, 1981, 2002, and 2012, vice-versa: the fickle people/electorate oust the great man because they forget their debt, or have forgotten 'the vision'. Even when Culture Ministers talk about policy for the arts, let alone bolder claims about maintaining the memory of Valmy and Mont Valérien, or absences thereof – colonial atrocities, for example, they imply a shared and emotionally-informed patrimony. Depending on a range of factors: the conjuncture, the speaker, the performance, such transformations may or may not have political effects, and if they do they have such because of the particular institutional configuration of the republic and/or configuration of circumstances; but they are there all the time interacting in and with the culture which is itself pervasive. We could and perhaps should here caricature our own argument and say that, as regards myth, for the leader to know or imply that they know where the Grail they seek is hidden might be helpful. As regards the institutions, having a parliamentary majority is even more so. Our argument is not that France is a chivalric polity, but that there are elements of this within the culture, and that because of the institutional configuration of the Fifth Republic and the manner of its inception, such traits inform French notions of leadership and influence practical politics.

As regards the cultural qualities of leadership and their relation to institutions, we need only remind ourselves of the transformation in Mitterrand's image between 1986 and 1988, carried from great unpopularity back to re-election (Cole in Gaffney 1989a). We can catch here a glimpse of the role of culture in politics. He was President in 1986 but lost the legislative elections to the right and so, humiliatingly, was forced to appoint his adversary as his new Prime Minister. Once such a cultural phenomenon as, for example, exalted leadership status is given such institutional significance, the 'character' and actions of the leader/President then become significant, and will in turn inform the significance of subsequent character traits (as well as the significance of other discourses such as political ideologies; we shall return to this point).

Mitterrand's character between 1986 and 1988: wounded yet patient, tenacious, dignified, republican, parental, eloquent, regal, versus Prime Minister Chirac's contrasting (the existence of opposites/rivals here is also of significance for the continued influence of cultural elements in the polity): unintellectual, brash, disrespectful, impetuous, impatient. All of these traits – whether or not they actually existed in the two men is not the point here – inform the 'showdown' between the two in 1988; the presidential election campaign of 1988 being almost exclusively a (performative) personality contest between the two men, one in which Mitterrand humiliated his unworthy rival (a humiliation which laid the foundations of Chirac's winning the presidency seven years later). Subsequently, these events influence perceptions of leadership itself, particularly in characters such as Chirac (much of his effort over the following years was to overcome this image – and 'overcoming' it being part of the chivalric process (Madjar 1995; Desjardins 1995)), but also possible contenders for leadership such as Jacques Delors, Michel Rocard, Edouard Balladur, Lionel Jospin, Edith Cresson, Dominique Strauss-Kahn, Ségolène Royal, Nicolas Sarkozy, Alain Juppé François Hollande, and others, between the late 1980s and the 2010s. All contenders for leadership, of necessity, develop a 'persona' (only in part controlled by themselves and their team) which contains character traits that are culturally recognisable and in a complex set of relationships to leadership image. It is not without significance that of all the above, the least developed public persona was that of François Hollande.

Identifying these perceived and ascribed character traits leads us to look at the relationship of leadership to culture from another perspective, one we alluded to in our mention of the electorate/nation, namely, that of audience: in what way or ways is the institutionally privileged leader related to his/her audience? For if the institutions allow the leader to behave and 'be' in a certain way, such also has to be 'recognised' and 'allowed' by an audience or audiences, who may perceive themselves – or acquiesce in the leader's perception of them – as more than 'just' an audience, and as individually and/or collectively in a privileged relationship to the leader. This is a further aspect of how the person is attached to the culture through a publicly approved relationship to ideas, for example, ideas such as vision and grandeur. This is not, of course, always the case. Perception and ascription (by the audience), as well as intention and performance (by the performer), all operate at a range of levels (conscious, unconscious, implicit, explicit, implied, emphasised, and so on). The secrets of Montségur might be considered by the person on the metro on their way to work as of limited interest. They may simply be sensed, if at all. The follower is no more ever-attentive than the leader is ever-transcendent. Most leaders most of the time are rarely further forward in their thoughts than the problems at hand. The corridor conversations, the earthy asides attributed to de Gaulle and to others, stand in relief to the kinds of leadership we have been describing. But the more exalted types of leadership are 'there' in the institutions and culture. And, mythically, leaders are there even when the people are not. Much of the time, leaders are performing only to a restricted or even to a future audience (hence the 'desert crossing', for example, so strong in French political culture). De Gaulle gained his national audience in part because he had known no audience. This is even more the case for political actors who came after him. Lionel Jospin, for example, had, by 1995, many credentials of the left's version of the providential leader. But in spite of his national profile since at least 1981 (as party leader, Mitterrand's lieutenant, and later government minister), most French people in 1995 were barely aware of who he was. It matters how the political class responds, and this in turn is located within a particular relationship, in de Gaulle's case, to the Fourth Republic's institutions, to de Gaulle's own claims, and to others' – the people, the army, political adversaries, foreign governments – perceived responses to him. It should be emphasised, therefore, that there is a structure to this type of leadership of which one of the essential elements is having been unknown, or at least ignored in a phase preceding acceptance (and such applies to Jospin in one sense as it does to de Gaulle in another).

François Hollande in 2011–12 was an even more acute case than Jospin, and contrasted utterly his 'normal' undemonstrative style with the flamboyant Sarkozy, even more than Jospin's did with Chirac. Hollande won in 2012 in part because no one knew who he was. We can see how unlike 'ordinary' democracy this is. 1958 put the phenomenon of 'heroic', romantic, personalised, and strong leadership, and all its attributes: vision, sacrifice, loneliness, rejection, return, acclamation, etc., into the mainstream, irrespective of what else it put there, constitutionally, institutionally, practically. It is part of the Gaullist myth that approval post-dates possession of providentiality, so that a period of exile/wilderness must also be experienced (or else manufactured). This latter issue, as well as carrying the burden of being 'heroic', becomes difficult for 'non-heroic' professional politicians (e.g. Chirac, Sarkozy, and Hollande) but no less a requisite imposed by the type of leadership introduced at the beginning of the Fifth Republic; de Gaulle's authority was based upon his having been denied such. Hence the *recours* is the person who, Cassandra-like, is unheeded or unknown in an initial phase; established politicians, e.g. Jospin in 2002 (as opposed to Jospin in 1995), are perpetually vulnerable to a resurgent Cassandra-like figure, or rival leader, or else to a range of responses within the electorate to Cassandras. Sarkozy's relatively comfortable election to the presidency in 2007 was in part based upon last-minute revision of doubts about his character (doubts that would come back to haunt him after his election in 2007); *idem* doubts pre- and post-2012 about Hollande's competence. But from the mythological point of view being unknown must be followed by action.

Since this has been inscribed into the leadership myth in France, it has become a prerequisite of it. De Gaulle's own 'desert crossing' (1946–58, between his resignation as Prime Minister to his return) was exemplary (in myth, perhaps more than in practice. His great advantage here was that he was able to rely on the original desert crossing of 1940–44). Figures such as Mitterrand had to create their own versions (in his case, essentially transform himself from mainstream Fourth Republic politician to exemplary hero through a performance of rejection and redemption). As we have said before, this poses problems in an ordinary contemporary democracy such as France would have itself as being most of the time. This is why we see mini-desert crossings (arguably, a contradiction in terms) (e.g. Pompidou, 1968–69) or even discursive desert crossings – invented periods of contemplation, rejection – such as Chirac's (e.g. 1988–94, even though, in fact, he remained Mayor of Paris and not a very exemplary one). Whatever the reality of the notion, this phenomenon remains within the political culture, even to the extent that it may be caricatured. On this question of lonely reflection also rests the question of the leader's origin and intellect, and therefore wisdom; and there is a whole range of expressions of this. Both de Gaulle and Mitterrand were classic French intellectuals: well-read, imbued with French history and philosophy, writers in their own right, and so on. Others have had to substitute for these qualities high technocratic reputations, such as Giscard, or lay claim to all these things like Chirac (or his entourage for him), or try to mobilise other aspects of intelligence outside 'intellectualism', like Sarkozy, or a kind of 'efficient normality' which downgrades the importance of such constant preoccupation with such qualities, like Hollande.

These traits and others (courage, fortitude in adversity, a Machiavellian understanding of power relations in spite of virtue, and Machiavellian *virtù* in spite of power, a small band of eternally loyal followers, occasional betrayals, etc.), are seen as enhancing a leader's image. All of these elements accompany the leader's relationship to the people. De Gaulle's use of the referendum and other appeals for support should be seen in this light, e.g. the National Assembly dissolution in 1962, or through his – sometimes decisive – TV and radio broadcasts and press conferences; the happy irony, of course, being that de Gaulle's most dramatic 'unmediated' radio and television appeals were in the defence of the republic, against elements of the army who would overthrow it, the classic case being his TV broadcast of 23 April 1961 in defence of the republic against a threatened army coup, his '*Françaises, Français, aidez-moi!*' broadcast (de Gaulle 1970a). 'Republicans' quite rightly referred to de Gaulle's use of these appeals as plebiscitary. That, however, is the nature of a form of leadership which transforms both leader and audience/follower into a *symbolically* constructed romantic version of themselves, rather than being simply a form of political comportment antithetical to accepted republican forms. Hence too, de Gaulle's highly personalised response in his own appeals for support (1969 being the negative enactment of this; he was not, constitutionally, obliged to resign). His use of the referendum in this plebiscitary yet democratic way was arguably not anti-republican. In the republican, moreover, as we have suggested, lies the plebiscitary, and de Gaulle's *modus operandi* was constantly to remind people of such, e.g. threatening to resign if disavowed by democratic vote, having to remind his audience of their exalted symbolic national status, dramatically calling for republican support, mostly appearing legitimate in republican terms, although sometimes tilting over into 'just' rabid anti-communism (in the name of democracy), or simply appearing to be not playing fair, by abusing his arbiter status by keeping the 'state of emergency' Article 16 in place longer than necessary in 1961, by, in fact, pretty much ignoring his own constitution, and so on. He was nearly always just this side of the line (arguably just over it sometimes), but all of this in a particularly personalised way, that is to say, that what is significant for our understanding of contemporary France, is not the line (stressed by constitutionalists), but *him* just this side of it. This overall special, privileged relationship was symbolically backed up by the nature of his press conferences, radio and TV broadcasts, *bains de foules*, overseas trips, and state occasions. These latter were good examples of another aspect of de Gaulle's mythical relationship to 'France', in that state occasions such as the 1961 visit to France of US President Kennedy and especially his wife Jackie, or de Gaulle and Adenaueur's 14 visits between 1958 and 1963, meant that through pomp and de Gaulle's own style, France (henceforth) could behave and be treated differently from before. Because of de Gaulle's comportment, the Fifth Republic was seen as being different from the Fourth. What was by then considered 'traditional' republicanism as opposed to de Gaulle's regime (the Third and Fourth as opposed to the Fifth) was seen as lackluster. It would take this 'other' republic i.e. the non-Gaullist republic within the Gaullist republic, almost 30 years to regain a sense of its own exalted pedigree; in part thanks to the collapse of Marxism and socialism as alternative doctrines to republicanism, and the willful embracing of versions of republicanism by Mitterrand, Chirac, Sarkozy, and Hollande. We shall return to this.

Both institutionally and culturally, therefore, what the Fifth Republic did more than anything else was to redefine the relationships between President/the French, leader/follower, and in the immediate term negatively and later more positively, party/electorate (as the parties began to respond to the Fifth Republic), within the polity. The relationships de Gaulle established between himself and 'France' constituted a set of (imagined) relationships which contrasted with the 'other', the parliamentary representative set, and eventually influenced them (and in fact was also influenced by them through the partial domestication of high politics). The overall relationship between de Gaulle and the French was partly dependent upon the conferring of 'character' upon the leader as a kind of substitute for doctrine (even at times, policy). The republic existed of course in the doctrine/s of republicanism. Henceforth, it (and more) could also be 'apprehended' through the vision or understanding of an individual. This was fine in the case of de Gaulle. He was seen as having a vision; in fact, he became President because of this perception. In order to be properly deployed, this set of (imagined) relationships means that not only the leader must have a set of character traits (envisioner, keeper of the ineffable patrimony etc.) but the audience also must adopt a set of characteristics: a nation sensitive to the needs of France, a people trusting of their exalted leader, and exalting of him, and 'recognising' of him as in communion with *la France profonde* in a pre-intellectual or non-rational way. One of the people's, the nation's, new characteristics is that the leader is so wise that they can be perceived by him as susceptible to straying from the true path, even to the point where he may be rejected by them while remaining right, and they wrong, until they see the error of their ways. Given this feature in Fifth republicanism, the leader who seems 'mediocre' (and this can be defined in a range of ways) is in real danger of symbolic status collapse. Being 'wrong' is not in itself a disadvantage necessarily but there are right ways to be wrong. It is this crucial and complex set of relationships that significant actors of the 'old' system of the Fourth Republic and early Fifth Republic could not grasp, and were swept away by (between 1958 and 1962 and again between 1962 and 1965). Although he opposed de Gaulle and the establishment of the Fifth Republic, François Mitterrand was one of the first to understand this, recognising that the presidential election and the notion of the personalised 'rally' were fundamental to the republic. This relationship leader/people is privileged, but not immutable. What goes up, comes down; and all the Presidents (including de Gaulle) have known real reversals of popularity (less so, Pompidou). What is characteristic of the Fifth Republic is not the benign nature of the relationship but arguably its opposite, its intensity. Earlier in this chapter we identified some of the fundamental elements and attitudes to the Fifth Republic within the wider context of republicanism and French political culture generally. Let us now sum up our points in order to establish the conditions upon which Fifth Republic leadership 'performs' in the age of celebrity politics.

The conditions and characteristics of Fifth Republic leadership

- The relation of leadership not only to the institutions but more importantly to culture is central to understanding French political history over the last 50 years.
- Because of the heightened role of the performing persona within the republic, the institutions of the Fifth Republic (e.g. the pres-

idency, its government, the bureaucracy, the media, the political parties, the electorate) carry within them an ambiguity about legitimacy and democracy, thereby maintaining ambiguity about the nature of the regime. The ambivalence is enhanced by the plasticity and mutability of discourse and ideology themselves.

- A new leadership form and style (and, developmentally, forms and styles) are seen as necessary for maintaining the integrity of the state, the nation, the patrimony, and last but not least, though last, the republic.
- The acceptance of this romantic view of leadership legitimates both 'personality' and 'character' as significant elements within the polity, as well as a heightened style of dramatised politics.
- French culture, history, and political experience have confronted and negotiated a dynamic/critical tension between republicanism and strong leaders. In Vichy and with de Gaulle in 1944, France had had recent experience of this tension, a tension that was carried into the Fourth and later Fifth Republic.
- The Fifth Republic has seen a perpetual and dramatic relationship between leadership and institutions, audience/s, and culture/s, a relationship that has dynamised and altered its trajectory through institutional cycles.
- The two crucial relationships of the Fifth Republic have been those of a) the leader/President whose relationships are to his audience/s and to 'France', and to republicanism/s, and; b) the political parties' relationship to their audience/s. Unlike in previous regimes of any kind, these two sets of relationship co-exist and even compete with one another, even though the audience/s competed for are identical or near identical. The concomitant of this is the complexity of the relationship between leadership and the political parties themselves (Bréchon 2001; Delwit 2014). We shall return to a discussion of this in the Conclusion.
- A consequence of this latter has been the division of executive power between the President and Prime Minister, and this relationship, whether conflictual or not, has been a significant influence upon, and in many cases has actually 'driven' much of the politics of the Fifth Republic. Since the introduction in 2000 of the presidential five-year term, however, this relationship – and it is not the only one – has become dysfunctional, particularly in the Hollande presidency, as we shall see.
- 1958 (and 1962, 1965, and thereafter) are best understood not as witnessing the institutionalisation of charisma, or its routinisation

(Weber 1964, 2004) but as the bringing of *persona* into the institutions, and making these sensitive to it, drawing it forward in time and throughout the polity.

- The task of political analysis is to establish the conditions of leadership as a framework for performance, and to analyse this latter. The misunderstanding in the literature, e.g. that without the political parties the leader is nothing; or without a majority the President is nothing, is to miss the point (although both of these are in themselves by and large true).

- The political party in France is not simply an organised aggregate of interests, or an organisation that sees itself as designed for power and office, but an organisation which needs to survive within a culturally-charged institutional configuration in which its own 'party drive' is no longer its organising principle, but has become, along with a competing leader-oriented 'rally drive', one of the conditions of its performance (and survival and prosperity) (Graham 1993).

- The practical consequence of these conditions is that political parties are in a novel relationship to political processes, and to organisational, discursive, doctrinal, but also symbolic, cultural, and mythical factors. The way in which this difficult combination of influences is maintained and carried through time is, in great part, through leadership. The party leader or other claimant therefore needs a particular team that is not simply an emanation of the party but is in a critical relation to it, and in a particular relation to his/her and the party's audience/s, that is to say, in a personalised relationship reminiscent of the king's knights or musketeers, and independent or as if independent from party. This is an extremely tall order and often malfunctions (e.g. the UMP post-2012, a 'rally' party which had lost its leader and descended into personalised faction-fighting); and has a nefarious impact upon policy and doctrinal elaboration (e.g. the PS 2002–12); and upon political loyalty (e.g. Hollande's difficulties increasing dramatically from 2012 because he was not the undisputed leader of the party, and because he had brought into government rivals who neither feared him nor had any allegiance to him).

- All of these factors, true for the leader, are equally true for rivals to leadership, rivals from other party leaderships or from within parties. The doctrines and ideologies emanating from political parties, as well as from other institutions and organisations – e.g. the education system, popular culture, television – and from individuals (e.g. de Gaulle, or Jacques Delors, or Coluche, or political philosophers, and other 'voices'), are best understood as discourses which because of interventions may adapt over time. The 'isms' of the Fifth Republic: Gaullism, Socialism, Communism, Republicanism, etc., can be fruitfully analysed in this way, i.e. in terms of their capacity to adapt and the modality of their adaptation, and in terms of their relationship to discourse on the one hand and leadership on the other (Bréchon *et al.* 2000; Gaffney and Kolinsky 1991; Nora 1984; Thody 1989).

- The outcome of all this is the creation (and the sustaining over time) of a leader's persona as an 'actor' within the configuration. There is a person, but also a persona who is an 'imagined person'. This persona has a range of qualities and character traits and, to be successful, possesses traits which correspond to, reflect, and inform the nature of the Fifth Republic: fortitude, vision, constancy, superiority (and ordinariness where necessary), and so on. We should say in parenthesis that success itself is an extremely complex issue, and may have as its own prerequisite, as we have seen, failure. The configuration will of course favour some parties and leaders, and encourage some personae over others (the significant entry of women into the paradigm is perhaps the most startling and interesting illustration – or counter-illustration – of this, in the recent period, given the male-centric nature of the chivalric mythologies informing leadership). There will, moreover, be a very wide range of types and traits competing at a range of levels. The 'characters' will be identified through a range of phenomena such as cultural recognition, repetition of idiosyncrasy to create 'style' (Gaffney 2012a), appeals to dispositions and emotions within the public (and/or as perceived by and mediated by the media), and so on (Ballet 2014). Through character and persona, style will involve the display of discourse and image, that is, the perceived and received discourse and image of the leader (and changes to and within these). There will also be generic character traits linked to former Presidents and to protocol-sensitive France itself; but the genre is mutable.

- One of the major conditions today (from circa 2000) is the new celebrity culture and its related new media, and the effects of these upon political life (Drake and Higgins 2012; Corner 2000; Corner and Pels 2003; Finlayson 2002; Street 2012; Wheeler 2012). The new celebrity culture, *la presse people*, and so on, have had major impact upon Fifth Republic politics, as leaders are drawn into the exigencies of celebrity politics – and France is drawn as no other polity is because of all we have discussed. These new conditions – over the last 15 years – are not the cause of heightened leadership politics in France, as they are in most other polities, but are, in part a consequence of French leadership politics; one of its consequences as well as one of its formative conditions.

All of these factors: electorate, institutions, parties, personae, and the relations between them, move forward through time, normally accompanied, in the French case, certainly until 2002, by an unpredictable, or potentially unpredictable, electoral cycle. All of this can be seen as a dynamic structure of path-dependent opportunity.

Institutions and performance, therefore, interact through time and space. Institutions (the presidency, political parties, the media etc.) are themselves culturally informed and respond in particular ways and offer particular advantages to (equally culturally specific) performances. Performances take place in this context through time and at particular 'moments' (elections, 'crises', 'events', conjunctures within the configuration – an interesting 'clash' of performances for Hollande in 2013 was the 'Syria' and 'Leonarda' crises happening at the same time (see Chapter 5)), and have a particular resonance and, given a particular institutional or circumstantial configuration at a particular moment, allow for a range of performances which create political advantage/disadvantage. The Fifth Republic is particularly interesting in this respect in that it offers to individuals inordinate opportunities, far greater than in comparable polities. What we see (in reality or in appearance) is a consequential choreography of political performance. Alternative performances are also taking place, and the aim of adversaries is to transcend, outshine, stop, deform, or discredit the other's performance. In practical terms, this involves the continuous work of a core team of supporters (in part, paradoxically, in order to enable the performer to appear alone), and counter moves against adversaries, and in the Sarkozy presidency, for example, a veritable industry of press leaks, collusion with sympathetic media, countering unsympathetic media, perpetual media intervention, constant core team calculation of the standing and prospects of their candidate (with the widespread use of private focus groups and opinion polls). In the case of Hollande, partly in reaction to Sarkozy, there was a significant failure to pay attention to this notion of image.

The persona must be accompanied by a discourse and an image that have themselves certain qualities, and help create the 'character'. The character, moreover, must be seen to appear to overcome difficulties, right wrongs, transcend and domesticate 'crises', blockages, and so on.

And the character must also have a range of qualities, not least competence in all areas of political life, be able to effect a 'gathering' of forces, have vision, be in some respects an outsider or appear to be so, be 'original' in some way, and show qualities such as fortitude, understanding, resolve, compassion, concern, single-mindedness, and courage. More recently, moreover, as regards character and image, gender and sexual dimensions have played a significant part (Alter and Cherchève 2007; Clerc 2006; Deloire and Dubois 2006; Girard 1999). Over and above all this, or rather beneath all this, lie the very slowly shifting tectonic plates of political, social, and economic choices: decline of ideologies, relative depoliticisation, changing attitudes, fundamental evolution of lifestyles, changes in the media etc. (Berger and Luckmann 1991 [1959]; Bourdieu 1984; Mendras and Cole 1991).

Character traits

The characters of leaders therefore perform within these contexts. Let us address the question of the character traits of leadership in the Fifth Republic. One can identify five types.

Firstly, there is what we can call *characterial capital traits* (I adapt John Kane's idea of 'moral capital' (2001)), that is to say, a range of expected, anticipated, assumed, traits that a leader possesses or appears to possess when they become a leader (of a faction or party, a government, a republic, or even none of these, when for example one makes a claim to leadership with no constituency at all). Most leaders have or pretend to a Cassandra quality and/or a (self)-ordained leadership status – Charles de Gaulle being the most illustrious example ('*L'homme du 18 juin*'). Characterial capital is the accumulated recognised character traits of this type of leadership.

The second type and related to these are more consciously ascribed, even demanded traits. We can call these *generic traits* – i.e. traits generic to an office or a kind of leadership (Kohrs Campbell and Hall Jamieson 2010). They are conferred and required traits; for example, there are *presidential* character traits, which – especially in the 'dyarchic' Fifth Republic – distinguish the style and comportment of a President from a Prime Minister (this latter, however, will also have a cluster of generic traits). These traits are often unremarked (that is how a President or Prime Minister behaves), and are thrown into relief when behaviour seems to veer away from the generic. As regards prime ministerial character, this is what happened when Edith Cresson (Prime Minister 1991–92) plummeted in the opinion polls for, in the view of opinion makers, the media, and public opinion, transgressing prime ministerial protocol with a particular style and language that contested the generic comportmental traits of leadership (Schemla 1993; Wilcox 1996). In his first two years as a President, Hollande suffered particularly from this.

The third are *cultural character traits* and are linked to myths of leadership. The valence of these will be very dependent upon institutional configuration. For example 'strong' leadership in the Fourth Republic (and in republicanism generally) could be contained, even screened off from political effect, or overcome by other forces. But these myths are deep and widespread in French culture, and are doubtless related to the myths of French history itself: chivalric traditions, religious traditions (particularly Christian, both Protestant and Catholic), and provide an array of traits – visions, envisioning, solitude, devotion, certainty, endurance, goodness, sacrifice, and so on; and all imply in the lexicon of character itself the opposites of these.

Fourthly, there are what we shall call *real traits*, that is both the actual traits, and the ascribed traits directly linked to the individuals themselves. We say 'ascribed' as these traits may not always be actually possessed by the individuals (are not 'real' in that sense) but are taken as belonging to them, taken as real. For example, JFK a happily married practising Catholic, Margaret Thatcher and the trait suggestive of an 'Iron Lady'; the assumption of the trait *seemed to* correspond to the person, and was held as being true. We should stress here that these traits and character traits in general will have inordinate influence within French politics because of the long cultural tradition of personalisation, and in the case of the Fifth Republic because of the institutional configuration.

The fifth set is what we might call *new traits*, i.e. ones which come into the system, are unexpected, or else have little valency in some circumstances but then have new valency in others. These, once introduced or embedded, may then become part of the 'received traits' (the other four types), or else fall away from valency. For example, the *'hauteur'* of de Gaulle could not be immediately followed without ridicule (in fact it is a dangerous trait to use at all), so the (cigarette-in-the-mouth) Pompidou style becomes part of the presidential canon (while some of the *gaullien* style is also his because he becomes President and he *replaces* de Gaulle). Another might be a modernising tendency that contrasts with a very protocolary style (Giscard d'Estaing in fact deployed both simultaneously). Mitterrand's style was very (but not only) *gaullien*, and so on. Sarkozy moved backwards and forwards between ordinariness and a kind of nervous regality. Hollande, in his first two years, was of course 'normal' (and this was underpinned by his barely repressed sense of humour), but it was very soon inadequate; and his ability to reach for *hauteur* was cursed by his claiming a non-presidential 'normal' status during his election campaign.

The range is very wide, and all traits, e.g. *hauteur*, may exist in all the categories. It is not that each has its own (though this is arguably true to a certain extent) but that traits which may have effects will come from one of these sources so that we need to see character traits as being political resources. A range of phenomena: looks, habits, style, image, tone of voice, objects even, and so on are related to these traits, or may imply traits (cf. Thatcher's handbag, JFK's aversion to hats, Giscard's wearing a lounge suit for his official photograph). 'New' traits, or real/ascribed, mythic cultural, or institutional traits may also emerge or merge 'into' the character, as in the case of, say, Mitterrand who in the winter of 1986, *becomes* a wise, understanding, and listening counsel to France's discontented; and it is at this time that we also see the beginning of a true 'character' onslaught upon his Prime Minister, Jacques Chirac. Alternatively, a leader may 'seek' a character trait – e.g. be seen as tougher, or try to be seen as less tough, more human and so on, cf. François Hollande reaching for gravitas over Syria in August–September 2013, only to end up 'scrapping' with Leonarda, a 14-year old Roma girl from Kosovo (we shall return to this). Finally, one may *lose* a character trait, and this can have major consequences. The classic example is de Gaulle's huge loss of prestige in 1968 when he was perceived as having lost his grip (simply by not returning quickly enough from a state trip to Romania), i.e. not by allowing May '68 to happen, but by not 'recognising' its political significance (this was arguably what *transferred* presidential character from de Gaulle to Pompidou, who did respond correctly to the 'events' (Frerejean 2007)).

Presidential use of humiliation also does not simply occur, but is built into the system. It is therefore, or its desire is, a political sentiment constitutive of the Fifth Republic. It is interesting that de Gaulle's sacking of Pompidou, Pompidou of Chaban, Mitterrand of Rocard, for example, involved a demonstration of presidential ascendancy *and* a concomitant humiliation of the Prime Minister (Gaffney in Helms 2012). Not all sackings involve this, and not all humiliations will be of Prime Ministers or by Presidents. Moreover, some of these will be institutionally strategic – one can argue that part of de Gaulle's reasoning in this domain, and arguably all of Pompidou's, had a political logic. Some, however, were in great part simply vindictive, such as

Mitterrand's of Rocard in 1991. Irrespective, however, of which is which, they happen because the system allows for and encourages them – such sentiment is part of the system. The halting of Chaban's *Nouvelle société*, and the disregard for/attack upon his parliamentary support had major political effects. Similarly, the cavalier 'disposal' of Prime Minister Rocard by President Mitterrand had severe short- and long-term political consequences. Conversely, President Sarkozy's perpetual assaults upon the authority of his Prime Minister, François Fillon, diminished Sarkozy's own status – humiliating is an art. Conversely again, Hollande's failure to rein in the outspokenness of some of his government ministers, Arnaud Montebourg in particular (while cavalierly sacking the luckless Environment Minister, Delphine Batho), seemed like personal weakness. These traits have major effects and are part of the system. One of the effects of this overall feature in the system is to make it more volatile. We have just mentioned Mitterrand's (we would argue mistaken) inverted *lèse majesté* in humiliating Rocard, but we can also say that it altered the political process quite unnecessarily. The nature of the Fifth Republic encourages leadership capriciousness. Just as humiliation can be used capriciously by the President, it can also – because it is so active within the political culture of the Fifth Republic – in certain circumstances be something the President himself suffers. It is ultimately linked to atavistic notions of fear of the leader, and of rebellion against omnipotence, but to disregard it (as, for example, Hollande did regarding Arnaud Montebourg) is to sacrifice an essential character trait of leadership.

Another feature of this volatility of personality traits is that it does not just involve Presidents or Prime Ministers. The system is *'disponible'* to personality. As we shall see, 'personality' implies personality as a *narrated tale*, so that it can be used by leadership contenders against incumbents or *'héritiers'* (Angeli *et al.* 1969). Slaying of opponents therefore becomes – like JFK jumping a generation when he took the presidential nomination in 1960 – part of the system. The political careers of figures such as Jacques Chirac and Nicolas Sarkozy are based upon this notion of incorrigible, irrepressible (testosterone-fuelled?) personality drives in which barons (e.g. Guichard, Pasqua) are toppled by young Davids. Such slayings or near-slayings can therefore reach right to the top, whereby Presidents themselves can face humiliation. It is arguable that Giscard's defeat in 1981 was lived as a humiliation, a sense of indignation that would adversely inform the succession politics of the non-Gaullist right for 20 years. Similarly, the left's losing the 1986 elections was lived by the right as a (short-lived) exquisite humiliation of Mitterrand. One of the consequences of Chirac's huge mistake in dissolving the National Assembly in 1997 was not just the return of the left to power for five years but the humiliation of the sitting President for having misread the topography of presidential authority. The perceived friendly 'local bank manager' style and image of Hollande created for him an unpopularity linked to a perceived 'inappropriateness'. The failed policies of his government – rising unemployment, flatlining economy – were perceived as being directly linked not just to the policies themselves but to his personality. And it is a commonplace of French politics that the personalities of the major players are almost clinically pathological in their obsessions and depressions: fear of humiliation and failure having haunted almost every major political figure in the Fifth Republic from (and including) de Gaulle onwards (Clerc 2014; De Sutter 2007; Maier 2001).

The Fifth Republic presidency, therefore, has from its inception displayed a series of emotions, sentiments, states of mind/being, and character traits of more or less (but infinitely more than is generally assumed) political consequence. Through the behaviour and style of the Presidents, through Memoirs, biographies, the media, and public memory, each of the Presidents has a series of character traits seen as contributing to the character of the presidency itself. We can capture these best if we take them in some kind of chronology, but many are shared (so the de Gaulle list will in fact be the longest) and bequeathed to the evolving office. Some have major effects in particular circumstances. All, we should add, were given heightened currency by the fact that the *first* President was such a *character*.

De Gaulle: A sense of personal destiny/mission/vision, Arrogance, Personal courage, Political acumen, Paternalism, Personal austerity, A desire for protocol (Déloye *et al.* 1996; Fleurdorge 2001), Great intelligence (and culture), A tendency to depression/despair, Capriciousness, Pessimism/optimism, An emotional relationship to France, Great wit (and earthiness) 'off', An assumed magical relationship to the people/France/the nation, A conviction of having been misunderstood/rejected. **Pompidou** (carries several of the above and introduces): Managerialism, Dignity (of a more sober kind, plus in the face of grave illness), Economic competence, Sense of duty, Sense of what is required, Naturalness, Political realism, Culture (art). **Giscard** (carries several of the above and introduces): Modernity/desire to modernise (almost as a fetish), Aristocratic sense of self and of France, Technocratic problem-solving approach, Fiscal mastery, Strong sexual appetite (rumours of) (this also true of Mitterrand and Chirac),

Humiliation/Resentment in defeat. **Mitterrand** (carries several of the above and introduces): Bringing of the left to power as part of personal mission/destiny, High culture, Political brilliance, Economic incompetence, Machiavellianism, Vindictiveness, Mysterious health problems (Pompidou also), Wit, Patience, Humanity (Mazarine), Reliance upon privileged inner circle (applies to all but most associated with Mitterrand), Secretive (of dark secrets: again applies to all, but most associated with Mitterrand), (Stoic) Decrepitude. **Chirac** (possesses some – though shares fewer – of the above, and introduces): Brashness, Impetuousness, Unpretentiousness, Public awkwardness/private warmth, Need for counsellors/dependence upon, Ideological relativism, Deficiency in culture/ethics/intelligence, Energy/enthusiasm/ lack of rancour, Whiffs of financial corruption. **Sarkozy** (carries several of the immediate above but like Chirac far fewer of the previous Presidents, and introduces): Driven (adolescent?) virility; Tirelessness (an almost Gaullist *volontarisme*), Emotionalism, Amorousness, Vanity, Friendliness, Unfriendliness, Temper, Frankness, Inappropriateness ('*casse-toi* ...', and 'bling'). **Hollande** (fewer still of all of the above, and introduces): Initially a normal/simple anti-Sarkozy character (and, unsaid, anti-DSK character), Accessibility/friendliness, A claim to moral exemplarity, An initial 'ethic' of slowing the tempo of the presidency, '*Bisounours*'/*Président Bisou* (cuddly), Quiet (misplaced?) confidence, Involvement with two, nay three, attractive, dominant women – incapacity to control them, Lack of *grandeur*, Mediocrity, Lack of decisiveness ('*Flamby*'), Lack of leadership, Developing sense of inadequacy, (After 'Closergate'), foolishness, coldness (towards Trierweiler), Dishonesty, cruelty, obsessiveness, indecision (After Trierweiler's book).

We have, therefore, a range of 'qualities' related to the presidency: the way that France, history, individuals, politics, and ideas are perceived by the leader and by the French; the President is central to political life; and the President is a persona with consequential character traits derived from a range of sources; and each of the Presidents has added to the developing range of available traits. Let us now examine the first two-and-a-half years of François Hollande's five-year term (Chapters 4 and 5), and then appraise his presidency (Chapter 6) in the light of the events and the theoretical arguments we have elaborated here.

4
The First Year. The Normal President and Time

This chapter and the next will evaluate and analyse the first two-and-a-half years of François Hollande's five-year presidency and explain not simply 'what happened' but also the way the new President and government contributed to the way politics and the republic itself developed, how they perceived what was happening, how what happened happened, and how François Hollande and his government and the opposition responded to the challenges and 'events' of the period. 'Year I' (May 2012–August 2013) was a process whereby Hollande put into practice (often by not taking action) his conception of the presidency. It became increasingly clear, however, that the new President and his image, style, and actions were evidence of a mis-reading of the practical politics demanded by the prevailing situation, and an equal mis-reading of the symbolism of the presidency and its 'performative demands'. Year II, from August 2013 to the September *rentrée* 2014 saw a series of initiatives to counter and remedy the deteriorating situation, all to little avail as an accumulating series of setbacks, gaffes (*couacs*), and inadequate initiatives and responses (invariably reactive rather than proactive) saw the popularity of the President fall to a level (by September 2014 in some polls he was at 13% and falling) that raised the question of whether he would even be forced to resign.

In these two chapters, we shall evoke the events of the first two-and-a-half years, concentrating in each on moments which illustrate the problems facing the presidency, such as Valériegate, the Cahuzac affair, Syria, the European elections, the return of Nicolas Sarkozy to frontline politics, and the near-eclipse of President Hollande from a frontline role. In Chapter 6, we revisit the issues discussed here and in Chapter 5 in terms of the theoretical appraisal of Fifth Republic presidentialism that we made in Chapter 3, and identify what the 2012–14 period tells us about the nature of the Fifth Republic. Let us bear in mind, therefore, from our earlier theoretical analysis that our concerns are essentially: the nature of the relationship of (the persona of) François Hollande to the office and to 'France' and 'the French'; the cultivation of those two relationships; the way in which the new President carried with him into the presidency his qualities and character traits that we identified in Chapter 2: President 'normal', 'France simple', anti-Sarkozyism; moral rectitude; the ambivalence of his 'left' character (Le Bourget v. *'culture de gouvernement')* (Evin 2012); Hollande as a solution/response to the economic and social 'crisis' France faced on the one hand, and the rejection (in 2012 by, in fact, a small majority), after five years of public exasperation, of Sarkozy's personal and presidential style on the other; and finally how, through action and inaction, these traits 'played out' after Hollande took office and created the near political crisis the regime found itself in barely two years into the Hollande presidency.

A first point to note, and which was an ominous first miscalculation by the President, was that there was not one hour of honeymoon period in 2012. The relaxed attitude of the new President; the pictures that followed the soaking he received at his inaugural, and then his several overseas trips, were of him on holiday in August in polo and chinos with his partner, Valérie Trierweiler, as if there were indeed such a honeymoon period. Such 'normalcy' and the slow pace of presidential action were Hollande's first demonstrative steps in rejecting Sarkozy's flamboyance; but the need to react immediately stemmed from a quite different source. Sarkozy's 'hyperactivity' from 2007 had masked the fact that 'action' had become an exigency upon rather than a choice of the presidency. The illusion was that perceptions of Sarkozy's character made him appear *over*-reactive, but swift responses and initiatives had, in fact, become normative.

The changing nature of public expectation had characterised all three of the last presidencies, Chirac, Sarkozy, and Hollande's, and should have been seen as evidence of the changed nature of the presidency and of political life. The same dramatic need to act – to mend what his campaign called the broken society (*la fracture sociale*) – had been expected of Jacques Chirac in 1995 (less so in 2002 as (re)election itself over Le Pen was itself the dramatic act, although it would reappear quite quickly after his re-election) – hence the almost immediate social strife – following radical budget cuts and the *'plan Juppé'* – leading to the catastrophic dissolution of 1997 where the President lost his parliamentary majority. The same was true of Sarkozy; and of

Hollande. The President as in part a crisis manager – that there was a crisis to manage was an essential part of the claim to legitimacy – had been created by each of the three last incumbents, Chirac, Sarkozy and Hollande ('I shall be the last King', Mitterrand had said), in part by the changing nature of society and the new media, and in great part by the new five-year presidential term (passed in 2000, in force in 2002) which profoundly altered (Duhamel 2008) the nature and rhythm of the republic. We shall come back to this in Chapter 6.

François Hollande celebrated his victory in his adopted county town, Tulle, as well as in the Place de la Bastille in Paris. As we have seen, Hollande claimed to want to be a 'normal' President. And in Tulle, footage of *'Président Bisou'* showed him as nice, witty, friendly, and unpretentious, a truly almost 'accidental' President. He was, of course, a 'party man': a politician of consensus, backroom deals, compromise, and muddling through. As a leftist presidential candidate, he deployed a highly rhetorical leftist rhetoric (at Le Bourget, in particular – a rhetorical concession that would become a reference point for party dissidence, as we shall see in Chapters 5 and 6); in debate, on the other hand, he was quiet, unassuming, straightforward, and rather dull, apart from his one foray into high rhetoric, his *'Moi, Président'* of his TV debate with Sarkozy; ironically, a rare rhetorical foray that would come back to haunt him.

International President normal: The first clues

Let us look at what the new President did do and did not do in his first month, and the nature of the relationship between 'action' and 'inaction'. Foreign policy was illustrative of the issues at stake when Hollande first took office. Given France's importance as a world power, a member of the UN Security Council, the world's fifth largest economy, a nuclear power, and historically the most active political player in the European Union, and having the second largest diplomatic network in the world after the US, the orientations, challenges, opportunities and possible outcomes of French foreign policy under President Hollande in 2012 and over the next five years were of fundamental importance, especially to his presidential image. The irony was that no one had mentioned foreign policy in six months of campaigning for the presidential elections (if we count the Socialist Party primaries, not for a year). Ignoring foreign policy has become the stuff of domestic campaigns everywhere. In France, the electorate was less interested in France's overseas *grandeur* and *rayonnement* than in – as de Gaulle once said – the price of artichokes. The French presidency, however, was almost made for foreign policy initiatives; and not only made to *take* foreign policy initiatives but to be *à la hauteur* of them; to step up onto that stage and take up arms against the sea of troubles in defence of that beautiful creature, France. This was de Gaulle's intention and his attitude to international action as protection of France. We shall return to this issue below when examining the French intervention in Mali in January 2013 (Beau 2013), and later France's response to the idea of military action in Syria in September 2013 (Gaffney 2014), and Iraq in 2014, but can say here that individual initiatives at the international level define the French presidency.

To be the French President was to be ready, willing, and eager to take on, even initiate, the *grandes querelles* of this world, as de Gaulle used to call French foreign policy. Without those quarrels – and the leadership style that goes with them – the French presidency actually looks somewhat bizarre: other Europeans go about their business with a more down-to-earth Prime Minister or Chancellor (sometimes not quite down-to-earth, like Berlusconi). France, on the other hand, displays all the pomp and circumstance of history's eyes upon its men of destiny (to date, only men) to meet the heady challenges of France's leading role in the world. De Gaulle dared to contest the hegemony of the superpowers; and each French President since: Pompidou, Giscard, Mitterrand, Chirac, and Sarkozy has played a leading world role, e.g. Chirac remonstrating with the Americans for going unprepared into Iraq (echoing de Gaulle telling them not to escalate in Vietnam), and Sarkozy brokering peace with the Russians in Georgia, and leading the way in the war in Libya.

It is surprising to the observer that during the election campaign, Nicolas Sarkozy did not make more of his foreign policy achievements to try and throw Hollande's lack of experience into relief, and push to the fore their different styles in relation to the office (Boniface 2012). Even in the interminable three hour debate between the two men in the last week of the election campaign, for only a desultory ten minutes at the end (when, according to viewing figures, most people had given up and gone to bed) did the candidates talk of their foreign policy proposals. However, if we count European and EU politics as part of foreign policy, there was some discussion of France and its neighbours during the campaign. Not that the discussions were particularly positive. For Sarkozy, a lot of the European policy proposals in his campaign for re-election consisted of saying – flirting with xenophobia – that he might abandon the Schengen border agreements and pull up the drawbridge. Hollande, flirting with anti-German feeling, said he would re-negotiate the European fiscal treaty, painstakingly drawn up by Angela Merkel and Nicolas Sarkozy. Virtually every candidate was anti-European, and the pro-European centrist, François Bayrou, hardly made reference to Europe. Ironically, both Sarkozy and Hollande, like Bayrou, were actually committed pro-Europeans. In the 2012 campaign, as we have seen, Hollande pretended to be the spiritual son of the Florentine François Mitterrand. He actually was more the spiritual son of the eminently European, Jacques Delors, and used to say so on every possible occasion (much to the lasting irritation of Delors' actual daughter, and Hollande's rival for the party's presidential nomination in 2011, Martine Aubry). Hollande assumed office in May 2012, however, without a European or a foreign policy narrative at all; and was immediately thrown into a series of top-level international meetings, the relentless intensity of which no incoming President had ever seen, and which would orientate French foreign policy, and fashion in part Hollande's presidency, his status, his allies, his future, and his image for the presidential term.

On the day of his inauguration, Hollande flew to Berlin to talk to Angela Merkel about the Fiscal Treaty. And it is worth pointing out that down the years, all French attempts to make the Germans agree to something Germany thought was, in particular, fiscally or economically unsound, ended in the French going home empty handed. It had always been a given of European politics that France lead in Europe politically and Germany economically (Krotz and Schildt 2013; Marcowitz and Miard-Delacroix 2012). To contest this meant France leading in neither, which came to be the case. After Berlin, it was to the US for a first meeting with Barack Obama (to tell him he was pulling French troops out of Afghanistan), then to a G8 summit (which he used to say were a waste of time), then to a NATO summit (he opposed France's reintegration into NATO's military command structure), then the G20 summit (in part a Sarkozy invention) then, immediately, a European summit in Brussels. This was a series of challenges of great complexity for a man whose overseas experience was nonexistent, and which had, for the most part, been organised with Sarkozy in mind.

Two weeks in and he was doing rather well. This is an unusual phenomenon in French politics: Presidents, through a difficult to analyse combination of *virtù* and *fortuna*, have often been lucky in foreign policy, using their presidential status and France's '*rang*' to advantage. We can make two remarks here. One is that Hollande's success was partly due to the relatively symbolic, albeit relaxed, nature of these five occasions, Obama, for example, very laid back in an open-necked shirt without a jacket (at their first meeting he teased Hollande for being too formally dressed). Little bargaining is done, and much of these occasions is for photo-opportunities and symbolic assertions of cooperation and solidarity. Our second remark is linked to the question of persona. It is arguable that it was indeed the 'normal' aspect of Hollande's persona which lent him the success, that is to say, that circumstances such as these summits lend themselves, paradoxically, given the grand occasions they are, to a normal presidential persona being successful, by mixing with more 'normal' heads of government rather than heads of state. And the first two weeks of Hollande's mixture of ease and friendliness (in a context of the public knowing that he had no foreign policy experience) seem to have been well received *because of* the normal persona. The question still remains, however, as to whether such a persona in a President (rather than a Prime Minister) is ultimately constraining if circumstances change – which they always do, and did – calling forth the need for a more dramatic type of persona. A further point is that, successful or not, *everything* was focused upon the persona of the French President, and therefore became a crucial element in political developments.

When, at the start of his presidential campaign, François Hollande said he wanted to renegotiate the Eurozone Fiscal Treaty (essentially, make the Germans go back on their elaborated treaty, and pump more money into the European economy), it was not taken seriously. It sounded as if Hollande was just making it up, and that he would pay the price with stockmarket chaos, as well as Mrs Merkel's ire if he did not measure his words more. In the event, *fortuna* was good to him. It soon became clear that he was not alone in wanting more emphasis on growth and less on austerity. Many, including such sound voices as *The Economist*, were coming to the same conclusion. Italy supported France, as did Greece, even the German SPD – who earlier had winced at Hollande's assertions – started to look more sympathetically at the idea. Hollande drew attention to the fact that the Treaty had not yet been ratified by the participating governments (ironically, Greece being one of the few that had). The German CDU faced setbacks in the May 2012 North-Rhine Westphalia elections, and Mrs Merkel, herself facing further elections in 2013, began to change her emphasis. The grip of fiscal austerity seemed both politically as well as economically questionable. So, as the Eurozone went for some (limited) growth, it looked as if one person had been right all along. François Hollande! He knew he had to fly off, two days later, to the US to tell Obama he was pulling French troops out of Afghanistan early. When he arrived, Obama told him the US wanted stimulus growth in Europe too. It is true that the US, Germany, and France, all meant very different things when they talked of a growth strategy for Europe and the Eurozone; and in a very short time the Germans reasserted their insistence upon fiscal austerity, insisting upon structural reforms as a prerequisite. Nevertheless, the devil was in the detail, so for that moment, Hollande looked not just competent in Washington, Camp David and Chicago; but even possessing of forethought, and confounding of his critics. This is an illustration of a series of examples of a kind of 'normal' approach by a 'normal' persona that actually worked. For a while at least.

On his return from these five summits, Hollande held a very 'normal' TV interview with the – somewhat obsequious (he would become less so in later interviews) – TV journalist David Pujadas (Tuesday 29 May 2012). Here, Hollande stressed again his 'normal' nature, and developed it by stressing that he wanted to *'Faire simple'*, i.e. not just *be* normal, but *do* things in a simple, straightforward manner; so he referred to the fact that he had himself come to the FR2 TV studio, rather than summoning journalists to the Elyseé (as had been Sarkozy's practice, and would become Hollande's once again). He did, however, confer *grandeur* on France itself, suggesting that whatever he was like, 'France' itself was *'a grand pays'*, a powerful country, thus conferring upon the entity France, and therefore himself as its self-conscious representative, a certain grandeur. Here was perhaps a way out of some of the constraints of being normal, a more than normal use of the 'object' France, and an emphasis upon doing rather than being, even though the doing involved 'the simple' in this instance. This is a good illustration of the 'play' of the person and the office. It was a demonstration – given that Hollande had returned from his immediate meeting in Camp David, Chicago, etc. with his prestige intact, if not enhanced – of 'normal' as a successful personal performance. An indication of the pressure, as it were, upon the persona to enhance his status was Hollande's reference to how he would talk to Vladimir Putin about the growing Syria crisis when he came to Paris later that week, as if his *personal* intervention (with his tough personal counterpart) could alter Russia's position (in fact, the meeting was a failure and their joint press conference 'glacial'). The rhetorical aim, however, was to depict himself as equal to the mighty 'virile' leadership of the intransigent Putin, as an early indication of Hollande's recourse to 'self'.

The downside of international 'success' was that Hollande's profile, normal or other, created expectations of normal but effective leadership, particularly in domestic politics. We shall come on to this below. There has been, certainly since de Gaulle, arguably since the end of World War II, a certain logic driving French foreign policy which means that divergences on domestic policy have not been reflected in huge differences in foreign policy. Even the Communists when in government with the Socialists in the early 1980s and again in the late 1990s, did not counter mainstream foreign policy (and in certain areas – regarding national sovereignty, for example – were very 'Gaullist' in their approach). There is a tension between the more Gaullist approaches and the more 'Atlanticist' ones (a more open Europe, more pro-American), but even here changes are usually evolutions of policy, not breaks of policy. And the Atlanticist and Gaullist strains within French thought do not really oppose individuals, rather they exist within the fabric of French thought, and even within the individuals themselves, like Giscard and Mitterrand, in fact all of them, even de Gaulle, Gaullist on some issues, more Atlanticist on others. For Hollande, this meant that no stark party or ideological reorientations of foreign policy would oblige him to use his persona forcefully. In contrast, he would grow to use foreign policy and the international stage in direct attempts to enhance his persona. No French President since de Gaulle (and even he promoted more continuity than change) had dramatically altered French foreign policy; foreign policy rarely lent itself to such changes. Nevertheless, the 'high', assertive Gaullism informing French foreign policy (this applies just as much to 'Atlanticist' Presidents), and its bearing down upon the 'character' of the presidency, would be an issue as soon as a crisis, international disagreement, or opportunity arose. Very soon into his presidency, Hollande stressed his Gaullist heritage by visiting *Le Terrible*, one of France's nuclear submarines, with all the symbolism such a visit entails. This is, of course, part of the job description, but underscored the role of the new solitary President acknowledging the nuclear might he oversaw. Very rapidly, Hollande would start to use foreign policy as a political resource to enhance his presidential character, although, paradoxically, in an 'Atlanticist' rather than Gaullist manner (see Chapter 5).

Hollande did not take France out of NATO's military command structure, although he had opposed it when Sarkozy reintegrated in 2009. And Hollande and the French Socialist Party's overall foreign policy was not markedly dissimilar from the mainstream right's. The

French left had had ten years (2002–12), as we have seen, to revisit, redefine, and recast everything from ideology (and presidential style) to policy, including developing foreign policy orientations which would better adapt France to a globalising world (and its former colonies). Because of the leadership dilemma in the PS, as we have argued, the 'discourse of the leader' could not be used, nor even the persona of the leader constructed. In part, this was because the 'leader' did not exist until the primaries, arguably until *after* the primaries (there is an interesting comparative analysis to be made here with the US primaries where the reverse is arguably the case). This contrasts strongly with the long-term development of Mitterrand's persona as PS leader from 1971 to 1981, and with Jospin's from 1995/6 until 2002, albeit in very different circumstances. For Hollande, it was 2011 – from nowhere – into the Elyseé in 2012. What this meant was that Hollande's 'Gaullism' (i.e. a non-normal generic character trait of the presidency) would be deployed, necessarily, through a series of gestures that would confer upon him assertive – and more masculine – connotations, even though the decisions taken were arguably too pro-American to be 'Gaullist' as regards policy itself. We shall return to this when we look at Mali and Syria. The effects of a French President's foreign policy image upon his domestic image is a complex one. Sarkozy, for example, seemed to gain no great advantage from his bold action on Libya. Nevertheless, this does not mean that it does not have effects; and at this point in 2012, for Hollande, his overseas image was initially quite positive.

With Merkel, there was a somewhat arrogant France v. Germany style (Hollande the man v. Merkel the woman?); with Obama, Hollande looked rather clumsy next to the naturally elegant Obama; in the general conviviality of the (almost exclusively) heads of government NATO and G20 meetings, Hollande seemed to fit in, in a 'normal' manner like the others, more, in fact, like a head of government (Cameron, Merkel) than like a head of state (Obama, Putin). All of these issues or traits – a slight arrogance, inappropriateness, clumsiness, and ordinariness – would eventually have negative effects. The meeting with Merkel was frosty, and relations with Germany went on to deteriorate further; but for our purposes, what is crucial is that – contrary to 'normal' – Hollande was already using his presidential 'self' as the embodiment of France not giving in to austere and exacting Germany. His public 'friendly tension' with Merkel, as he called it, saw the personalised use of hostility to prevailing European policy, tinged with the slight virility issue mentioned above. This was an early example of a kind of 'misdirected personalisation'. It was a strategic/discursive misuse of his office because, by the end of the year, it had escalated into wild and acutely personalised attacks by Hollande's own party upon Germany as the cause of Europe's ills, and upon the 'selfish intransigence' of Merkel herself (this expression, used in one official draft party document but later dropped, evidenced the anti-German atmosphere that was being allowed to develop). And his Industry Minister (*Ministre pour le redressement productif*), Arnaud Montebourg, referred to Mrs Merkel's 'blind ideological thinking' (*aveuglement idéologique*) (Cotta 2012). In the end, Hollande ratified the agreement he had said he would change, without a comma having been altered, but the longer-term effect was the further development of France's hostile, or at least contradictory attitude to the Franco-German relationship and, as a consequence, the further ceding to Germany of leadership in Europe.

Nevertheless, Hollande's early foreign policy experience was positive given, in particular, that it was more concerned with 'display' than with negotiations or intergovernmental conflict. Hollande learnt very early on that initiatives and gestures were (in spite of their seriousness) relatively easy in foreign policy. This ease encouraged Hollande in his subsequent foreign policy decisions, some of them politically and sym-bolically beneficial – Mali – some not so – Syria. It also demonstrated to the Americans that the French President was alone in being able to undertake major foreign policy initiatives without consultation, hence their fêting of Hollande on his February 2014 state visit to the US. All this because of French presidential privilege, a not very 'normal' feature of the executive in a Western democracy, that Hollande would come to rely on.

'Normalism' and presidentialism

This international aspect of the presidency raises the question of what the French presidency is for, and what kind of President the French expect. And here complexity arises. In a word, could the French really cope with 'normal' either in domestic or in foreign policy? But, against Sarkozy, this was what Hollande had built his presidential character upon. And over the first two years, foreign policy stances depicting a 'strong' François Hollande came to be used to shore up his collapsing domestic persona. This raises the question, taking foreign and domestic policy together, of the structure of presidential persona, and whether different character traits deployed in each are compatible. We are anticipating our narrative here regarding domestic political initiatives but can make the following point. The relative success of Hollande's intensive international tour in May 2012 contributed to his sudden decline in domestic popularity because it was not accompanied by domestic initiatives, and the two are crucially related in the French presidency, whether or not it is the President who takes the domestic initiatives. Previous presidencies had begun with major initiatives at both the international *and* domestic levels. Although the political rhythm and the relationship between 'political time' and 'mediatic time' (Pingaud 2013) were very different, and the domestic initiatives were 'fronted' by the Prime Minister and government; the Debré (1958), Pompidou (1962), Chaban-Delmas (1969), Barre (1976), Mauroy (1981), Rocard (1988), Juppé (1995), and Raffarin (2002) governments all took vigorous domestic initiatives in tandem with international presidential performance. Some of these led to severe economic (Mauroy) or political (Juppé) crises, but that is not the point here: presidencies begin with major domestic initiatives and programmes which take place *alongside* international presidential performance. The exceptions here are first Giscard who waited two years (before appointing Barre) while 'interfering' overtly in domestic politics, alienating his first Prime Minister, Chirac; second Sarkozy whose domestic initiatives did not reflect his campaign promise; and third Hollande whose storm of international activity was not reflected or echoed in any substantial immediate domestic initiative by him or his new government. The history of the Fifth Republic indicates that presidential status is not only linked to both the international and the domestic, but that these are linked to one another; and what is more, as regards presidential status, international initiatives 'serve' or are a function of domestic performance, not the other way round.

On 6 May 2012, Hollande was elected President of the French Republic, beating his 'Bling' predecessor, Nicolas Sarkozy, in part, because Hollande was not 'Bling'. On 17 June, Hollande was plebiscited again by gaining an absolute majority for his Socialist Party and PRG allies in the parliamentary elections that followed his victory. The left now controlled the National Assembly, the Senate, the Regional Councils, and most of the large Town Halls. With the presidency in its hands as well, this meant the left controlled virtually everything. Neither François Mitterrand as President (1981–95), nor Lionel Jospin as Prime Minister (1997–2002), had dreamed of such 'full powers' (the headline in *Le Monde* on 18 June – *pleins pouvoirs*, a historically problematic term in French, suggesting dictatorship!). François Hollande and his Socialist

Party dominated all the national elected institutions. The 'normal', once eminently forgettable, Mr Hollande was arguably France's most powerful President ever.

After his election, he appointed his government. As a gesture, everyone including the President took a 30% salary cut. There were a lot of them to do so, 35, later 39 ministers in all (only five of whom had had any ministerial experience). There was also gender parity, a first in French politics, and several new ministers of 'diversity' (Taubira, Pellerin, Vallaud-Belkacem). It was as if the new, exemplary President would now transform the unjust regime into an exemplary republic. This had been both his implicit and explicit campaign promise. The Socialist left had never been so strong politically. Hollande and his new Prime Minister, Jean-Marc Ayrault, had also meticulously blended all the party factions into the government including the 'left' Arnaud Montebourg, Benoît Hamon, and 'Aubryists' Pascal Lamy and Marylise Lebranchu, and several of Hollande's own close associates, for example, Michel Sapin and Stéphane Le Foll. This meticulousness was understandable but strengthened the impression of the political tempo slowing down more and more when public expectation demanded the opposite. Apart from a few very small measures (e.g. fractionally raising the minimum wage, raising the 'back-to-school' allowance by 25% for those eligible) the impression rapidly developed that there was no interim plan other than time-consuming consultations with 'the social partners' before any action would be taken. There also had to be legislative elections which we shall come back to.

In the country, the sense of growing crisis, however, was marked. Peugeot-Citroën announced 8,000 redundancies; unemployment was rising alarmingly. Air France announced 5,000 job losses, and there was an estimation of 60,000 redundancies from firms nationally, and a report that the annual number of small firm's closing would be 50,000. Hollande's first response as the new captain of the ship now heading directly into the hurricane was, as we have seen, after a somewhat desultory interview on France's national 14 July holiday, to go on a three-week holiday. National disbelief soon turned to record levels of unpopularity. If Hollande had stayed in Paris working with a small team around him, while others – and the French themselves – took their holiday (with an 'I'll come down for a long weekend' to his partner, Valérie Trierweiler), Hollande's presidency might have started in a fundamentally different manner. Indeed, the symbolism of staying behind at the office-palace to sort out France's crisis problems could have made a profound statement about Hollande's desire to find new solutions for France's old problems.

The reasoning was, once again, that he wanted to demarcate himself from his hyperactive predecessor, so he took no demonstrable action at all, preferring to be seen swimming, and strolling around having selfies taken in Brégançon. The friendly holiday 'beach snaps' style of photos given to the press – i.e. the antithesis of Sarkozy on Bolloré's yacht – was nevertheless a hostage to fortune for an incumbent in a crisis, irrespective of the social context suggested by the photos themselves. This was clearly part of a strategy. Hollande wanted, according to one source in his 40-strong *cabinet* of aides and advisors, to 'return to the normal functions of the institutions' (*le retour à une pratique normale des institutions*) (Thomas Weider *Le Monde* online 1/6/12). When Hollande met his new *cabinet* he told them, as he had his government, that henceforward their own activity would be 'sober, modest, and simple'. 'Passion' would be taken out of the republic and, crucially, his role would be concerned with the longer term, the government's with the immediate and shorter term (*ibid.*; Bugat 2012; Chavelet and Grépinet 2011). This approach broke down very quickly, but it is an indication of how concerted and formative was the adoption of an approach that both practically and symbolically was a repudiation of Sarkozy's style. One unforeseen effect of the preoccupation with being and doing everything that Sarkozy was not, was to convey the impression that the political process was both being diverted from urgent purpose and that it was 'slowing down' rather than responding to the sense of crisis. President Hollande's defining himself in relation to his predecessor rather than to an 'imagined' France and an imaginable 'François Hollande, President of the Republic' stemmed from a more fundamental failure to respond to the subtle norms and exigencies of the office he held.

By September 2012, after he and Mme Trierweiler returned from holiday, the new President's popularity was already below 50%, and that was just the beginning. It then went into free-fall; by the spring of 2014 it was below 20% in most polls, by September 2014 down to 13%. France was facing a public spending crisis – in health, pensions, and welfare; and a government debt of 90%. It is arguable that, in spite of spending cuts and tax rises, no adequate measures were set in train, nor even proposed for the most part, in his first two years in office until the appointment of Manuel Valls as Prime Minister in April 2014, and even then little happened in the immediate term. The government in the first year was partly directed at simply undoing many of Sarkozy's measures (the most unpopular being the repeal of Sarkozy's law allowing people working more than the 35-hour week not to be taxed on the extra hours); and subsequently re-introducing some of them. For the larger problems, the government seemed to offer nothing except tax increases. It was estimated that these might overall need to be increased by a total of 20 billion euros. If France was to meet its budget deficit reduction target of 3% of GDP by the end of 2013, it would need to make savings of 33 billion euros. It did not reach its target; it was later estimated that by 2016 the deficit would still be at 4.7% and government debt at 100%, the highest in the EU.

During Hollande's inauguration as the seventh President of the French Fifth Republic, it poured with rain all day long. Inexplicably, no one offered him a raincoat or the protection of an umbrella. As we have mentioned, he spent the day's ceremony drenched to the bone, his sopping wet suit and shirt flattened against him. It was almost like a sign. It seemed, politically, to rain ever after. At the 8 May 2013 commemorations of the Allied victory of 1945, one year after his inauguration, Hollande was there, of course, as was his government, the military, and the veterans, but the Champs Elysées were deserted. The year before – to show how near to the people he was, and as he had throughout his election campaign – he went walkabout into the crowds, shaking hands and kissing babies. A year later, there was no one to shake hands with, no women to *faire le bisou* with, and no babies to kiss. There were not even any Japanese tourists. How did he get to this point of hostile indifference in just one year? Why was there such concerted inaction as it were, such mismanagement particularly of 'communications', and above all, certainly according to his critics (Fondation Copernic 2013; Parti de gauche 2012), such ineffective leadership? That is the lesson, the question raised by his first year. Hollande would have done well to have heeded Machiavelli's advice:

> A wise prince then...should never be idle in times of peace but should industriously lay up stores of which to avail himself in times of adversity so that when Fortune abandons him he may be prepared to resist her blows.

It is our view that beyond the political miscalculations and policy mistakes, an explanation of the deteriorating situation requires attention to the question of the performance of the presidential persona as part of a symbolic relationship with the President's audience.

A normal President's constituency

One issue which affects all those elected to office but takes on a personal dimension in such a highly personalised presidential system, was Hollande's 'constituency'. The French Socialist Party would have itself, like most leftist parties, as representing the poor, the unemployed, the ordinary working class, white-collar workers, pensioners, and the public sector (at least). In reality, it mainly represents this last – it had lost much of its working-class support by the 2000s, either to the UMP or the FN. By 2012, it was the party of teachers and social workers and an army of state employees who made up the inefficient quarter of France's divided workforce. There were, for example, twice as many public sector workers in France as in Germany, and there was a widespread view that a significant number of France's public sector workers were seriously not doing much most of the week (Shépard 2010), and were contractually and financially 'privileged' by the left (*Le Point* online 27/10/14). There was a generally-held view even by many on the left that this situation needed reform, yet the President's rapid unpopularity meant an initiative against his diminishing constituency would have made his situation dramatically worse. From 2012 Hollande and his government were perched on this tottering constituency – within the year, he had lost all the others who had come back to the left; the young, the workers, the elderly, the curious, the middle of the road, and those who could not bear Sarkozy. By 2013, however, even his public sector constituency was crumbling beneath him, mainly because of tax rises and the rising cost of living. 'Bashing' (a term used a lot in the French media) the rich was to have been the effortless solution, but such rarely brings in revenue unless it is part of a coordinated plan, and Hollande's unthought through 75% tax on the very rich (those earning over a million euros p.a.) was deemed unlawful by the Constitutional Council. Other declared intentions – eradicating *niches fiscales*, taxing income on capital, reducing the burden on small business – ran out of steam. The one solution the government applied was therefore to 'bash' everybody else instead by putting up taxes. (By the spring of 2014 it reversed tax increases for 1.8 million low-paid workers, but could only pay for this by taxing mid-range earners more). Moreover, the incremental nature and very badly 'communicated' announcements of tax rises – across France's myriad tax system – (with endlessly contradictory statements being made by both the President and government ministers) – created a mood of real uncertainty in both businesses and households, and saw a dramatic decline in inward investment.

Over and above this, Hollande's special constituency of public servants of one kind or another was one of the reasons for France's poor productivity and performance. But truly reforming the inefficient public sector would be electoral suicide. Indeed, Hollande, rather than cut the public sector, said he was going to increase the teaching population by 60,000 – a breathtaking decision given the overall budget deficit. Sarkozy's partial solution – abolished by Hollande – seemed, in retrospect, a good one: simply, for every two civil servants who retired, one was recruited. On top of this, in France, if one is out of work, there is often little incentive to find work; many of those out of work receive a large percentage of their salary (often over 60%) for one even two years after redundancy, partly paid for by the state and by individual contributions; employers paying the other part. Hollande therefore could only hope to sort France's economic difficulties if he took a strong line on structural reforms of the kind Schröder (also a social democrat) had taken when German Chancellor in 2002, in terms of both public sector employment and creating the conditions in the private sector, particularly small and medium-sized firms, for increasing recruitment of staff.

Rather than propose a series of immediate structural reforms, the President and government began in a very cautious way, as we have mentioned, setting up 'days' where discussions (*dialogue social*) would take place. There was a highly publicised 'social conference' in July 2012 where there was a great deal of debate by unions and business, but very little emerged from it. The overall consequence of this was that the executive would lose the initiative in all areas of activity. Even by mid-June (*Le Monde* 8/6/12; *Le Figaro* 10/6/12) the media were giving strong voice to a public sense that the government had no idea how it was going to reduce the public deficit and state spending, or reduce unemployment. The consequence of this, along with an accumulating series of 'gaffes' which by November 2012 had become commonplace, was that the government appeared to be utterly disorganised. We can make two related remarks here. The first is that this was, in part, a further response by Hollande to distinguish himself from Sarkozy, and avoid all 'spin' or '*la com*'' (Artufel and Duroux 2006); but the consequence would be the accumulating gaffes and insufficient coordination between government members; on one occasion the Prime Minister, the Finance Minister, and the Industry Minister said three different things about a topic on the same day. Another reason was Hollande's own capacity to make pronouncements without having consulted his own advisors or ministers first. The second remark we can make is that this avoidance of a coherent communications strategy betrayed a failure to grasp contemporary politics, because every failure to take the lead meant that the media and especially social media would fill the gap, pushing the government into a constant series of reactions rather than actions and, over time, altering the contours of the presidency. To counter the media saturation of the Sarkozy presidency, Hollande returned to the old-fashioned weekly talk to the press by the government spokesperson, then Najat Vallaud-Belkacem. Given the nature of the contemporary 24-hour media, particularly the lightning speed of gossip and hearsay, and the journalists' constant 'fact-checking' i.e. asking for government comment to a news story, and all compounded by the lack of coordination, the first year of government became a growing cacophony of mistakes and blunders. Both the President and Prime Minister changed their Director of Communications but the lack of real reflection on this meant that little difference was made. The longer-term result was the increase in the use of *'Le Off'* (off the record and unofficial briefings), but it is arguable that this made matters worse (*Libération* 15/11/14).

Related also to the new nature of the media, two separate 'movements', the *'Pigeons'* and, soon after, the *'Poussins'* caught the government off-balance from the summer of 2012. Together, they brought together on social media networks, start-ups, artisans and small businesses fearful of rumoured new tax rises. These flared into virtual protest movements garnering tens of thousands of signatures almost overnight, and threatened to turn their virtual protests into real ones. The government confusedly backed down (Pingaud 2013). Since the left had last been in power (1997–2002) the new media had grown in size and influence exponentially, and the newly-elected left was simply unprepared. The government's own attempts at 'spin' were also problematic. Deals between Airbus and Lion Air, then later hopes of selling *Rafale* fighter planes to India, for example, were trailed with the press, then modified as sales became less certain, making the government look as if it had failed (in late 2014 the Indian deal came back to the table). What all of these dilemmas point to is a conflation of 'mediatic' and political time, the former over-running the latter. We shall return to this in the Conclusion.

During his election campaign Hollande had told the workers at the Florange blast furnaces in Lorraine that if he was elected President he would keep the furnaces open. In November 2012, the government announced their closure. Exactly the same thing had happened to Sarkozy in 2009, going back on a highly-charged emotional promise about jobs to a specific cohort of workers. The notion of a 'betrayal of promises' entered Hollande's presidency (compounded in the Florange case by the publicly-voiced disagreements of Industry Minister, Arnaud Montebourg who drew great media attention to the issue by criticising his own Prime Minister (Astruc 2013)). The 650 were eventually found new jobs, although the local economy was seriously damaged. The political damage, however, was considerable because of the same ideas of deceit and betrayal that had been directed at Sarkozy now being transferred to Hollande. He tried to improve his image from November by beginning a series of visits to towns and villages (using the expression *à la rencontre des Français*), even involving overnight stays and meetings with the general public. His unpopularity, however, was by this time so marked these dwindled very quickly; even his physical security from crowds was in question. By March he tried to restart them. By April they had all been cancelled (*Le Point* 7/7/14). In November 2012, the Cahuzac scandal began to break (we shall look at this below). By December, there had been several by-elections. The PS lost each one of them badly. By then too the party in the National Assembly was beginning to demand changes, and the increasingly virulent left of the party, the part we might refer to narratively as 'leftist emotionalism', i.e. the 'old' left that still dominated the party's rhetoric and to which Hollande had appealed in his campaign, began calling for a reversal of the more 'social democratic' policies Hollande and Ayrault were trying to promote (e.g. tax relief for business in the CICE proposal (*crédit d'impôt pour la compétitivité et l'emploi*) put forward in November 2012). The dissidents started to call for a left radicalisation of policy (essentially a stimulus to growth), the moment, in fact, when Moody's downgraded France's TripleA status. In October 2012, the Ayrault government introduced the vaunted *emploi d'avenir* and *contrat de génération* programmes (essentially to promote young people's employment). These were designed (100,000 per year) to produce 500,000 contracts over five years. At the end of their first year, only 20,000 had been signed. In January 2013 unemployment was up for the 19th consecutive month, that is 250,000 since Hollande's election. The following month it climbed another 35,000 and passed through the 10% barrier (by autumn 2014 almost half-a-million had lost their jobs since 2012), and the figure rose unrelentingly throughout the period.

Normal as moral

Hollande had fought the election campaign claiming he would be a normal and simple President, like a Prime Minister, in fact. But even though the President may act *as* a Prime Minister, intervening directly in government business and domestic policy, the President does not act *like* a Prime Minister. As we saw in Chapter 3, the presidency is a major site of ambivalence, and is in a complex relationship to the French and their problems, anxieties, desires and reflections. There is a psychic dimension to the French presidency and its relationship to the French. And there is arguably an element of clinical narcissism in the French and their desire for a President (when everyone else gets on with having a P.M. or a Chancellor for political affairs) as both their political leader and their head of state. The President embodies metaphorically (in a near-literal sense of the term!) the French state itself. To stray from that or ignore it is highly problematic. It is not just, therefore, that unemployment and then taxation were going up. They were, and continued to do so, but it was also about what the relationship of the President was to the country in times like this. It was not just his policy intentions that mattered, but his emotional relationship to the people his policies affected. And Hollande seemed to only display a general *bonhomie* in his first year which became less appropriate as the situation worsened and the 'gaffes' accumulated. And the increases in taxation, as the only visible solution, created in the minds of all those who did not vote Socialist the notion that this was a very old and predictable left in power rather than a new and reformist one able to respond to the exigencies of economic management in the twenty-first century (the irony being that the left of the party thought the opposite).

Apart from 'normal' as a character trait, the other essential trait displayed by Hollande – we have seen this in relation to Sarkozy – was a strongly emphasised ethic. This can hook on to, as it were, issues such as a devotion to France, or republican integrity, or modernisation, or confronting injustice or righting wrongs. And the persona of the President can be used to mediate ideas and their ethical dimension. However, to state this overtly, to lay claim rhetorically and repeatedly to integrity and moral superiority, had ramifications. Hollande's constant stress upon his greater moral status to Nicolas Sarkozy (in January 2012, he had referred to Sarkozy as *'un sale mec'* (a low-life bad guy, *Marianne* 7/1/12)) and upon the idea that he would bring integrity through his own example and that of the team around him was to expose him to constant scrutiny – and soon lampoon – almost from the moment he took office. The searchlights would seek out not just the simple and normal persona and its variants, but every ethical implication of every action. 'Normal', 'simple', and 'ethical' were bound to descend very quickly into farce: Hollande's claims to virtue would, if undermined, turn farce into tragedy. Every personal characteristic, trait and failing, especially anything to do with personal morality and ethical standards – anything that suggested he was 'just like the others', or else hypocritical – would be exposed to scrutiny and take on inordinate significance. Each move he made would be subject to moral appraisal. He had said there would be no more corruption, no more bling, no more scandals, no more headlines in the *Hello Magazine*-style press. There was, however, a year of nothing else. Three 'scandals' in the first year alone stood out. The first happened almost immediately, during the legislative election campaign.

Valériegate and the presidency

Normal meant for Hollande showing, through this new presidential style, that the presidency was exemplary. This is why 'Valériegate' was so important. 'Valériegate' seems trivial yet turned out to be one of the most important and problematic events of François Hollande's presidency in terms of the way both his presidency and his image were perceived from then on. It had two other consequences. It robbed his presidency of exploiting Trierweiler's potential role which could have been of great significance in countering his 'greyness'; and it reasserted the focus upon the personal in a negative way, lending his presidency a soap opera edge involving the mutual enmity of the two women of his life, this being made much of in both political satire and mainstream political comment.

'Valériegate' was so trivial one would hardly believe it could be of any significance whatsoever, yet it altered the nature of his presidency from normal to trivial (Hollande's son Thomas was reported as saying that this incident ended his father's claim to a normal presidency (*Le Point* 12/7/12)). This brings us back to our earlier point about the trivial having great influence in France's symbolic politics. Between the two rounds of the parliamentary elections, on Tuesday 12 June, Hollande's partner, Valérie Trierweiler (the 'love of my life' as he told *Gala* magazine in 2011) tweeted (she had 80,000 followers, many of those fellow journalists so soon there were hundreds of thousands of tweets) her support for the dissident Socialist candidate, Olivier Falorni, in the La Rochelle constituency (who, it turned out, was a personal friend of Trierweiler). That was bad enough, supporting a candidate who did not have the backing of the President, but the tweet was a direct attack upon the official Socialist Party candidate, backed by the party and, personally, by the President. The official candidate was Ségolène Royal,

Hollande's former partner of 25 years, and the mother of his four children. The incident gripped the media in all its forms and threw the presidency, the government, and the party into disarray and the country into incredulity. For weeks the media talked of nothing else. Why had she done it? The new President's potential honeymoon with the French after his relative success in his international meetings shuddered to a halt in the tweet's wake. It now seemed that Valérie Trierweiler harboured a blind jealousy for and deep dislike of Ségolène Royal. The public was aware of a coldness between the two women, but there had been an assumption that Trierweiler was comfortable as the victor over Ségolène, 'yesterday's woman' – in both love and politics. Nothing was farther from the truth. The tweet incident publicly projected Trierweiler, the new President's partner, as highly emotional, wilful, and possibly unstable.

Royal was the Party's presidential candidate in 2007. In the aftermath of her defeat (by Sarkozy), she narrowly failed to take the leadership of the party in 2008 (André and Rissouli 2012; Courcol and Masure 2007; Lienemann and Cohen 2007); and in the primaries for the party's candidacy, she gained only 6.7% of the party vote. She did, however, support Hollande in his 2012 campaign, and was rewarded with the respect of the party barons, and an unofficial assurance that she would become the President of the National Assembly in the new 2012 Parliament. Throughout this period, her opponents in the party, like Laurent Fabius and Martine Aubry, came to terms with her, but her 'rival' had not, even though Trierweiler had been with Hollande since 2005, and Hollande's relationship with Royal had been over for years (Lévy 2006). According to some reports, the idea of seeing her at the summit of the Republic (President of the National Assembly is the fourth highest office of State in protocol terms) and therefore often alongside François was too much (Courage 2012).

After 'the Tweet' and the furore it created, it became clear to the public, and especially to those around the President, that not only did Trierweiler possess a barely controllable dislike of Royal, but it might erupt in some form at any time. This was politically dangerous for the President. Even the new Prime Minister, Jean-Marc Ayrault, called her to order. It then emerged that Trierweiler had lobbied successfully to have references to Royal's 2007 presidential candidacy removed from Hollande's campaign video; she had also lobbied at the Rennes campaign meeting of Royal and Hollande: they were not to touch, to speak together, to appear together (they did very briefly), nor kiss (they did not). On the night of his victory on 6 May, when Hollande did give

Ségolène a public, reconciliatory peck on the cheek (the public and the paparazzi had so been waiting for it!), Trierweiler walked across the stage to Hollande – in front of the celebrating crowds at the Place de la Bastille – and said 'Kiss me on the mouth' (she can be seen mouthing this on the YouTube clips), which he did, rather less enthusiastically than she, it must be said. This all makes brilliant copy, which as a journalist she would have known, for it is both funny and pathetic. But these funny, pathetic, soap opera incidents seriously affected Hollande's two-month presidency. Why? For a host of reasons.

The first is that Trierweiler herself was a puzzling figure for a new 'First Lady'. Somewhat aloof, professionally independent, protective of her own privacy (as she told the media in interviews on several occasions); she was seen by many as the quiet power behind the throne (which she now suddenly seemed in danger of knocking over). It was she, for example, so the official story went, who helped Hollande take the decision to run for the presidential candidacy. She also said she did not want to be a '*potiche*' (a trophy 'First Lady'). Perhaps she would be like the radical Danielle Mitterrand, she mused in one interview (but that was long before First Ladies found themselves quite so much in the spotlight). Her tweet certainly demonstrated her independence, but it was less like a gesture by Danielle Mitterrand (who had gone to meet with Fidel Castro); or the magnificent and independent Eleanor Roosevelt, who Trierweiler also claimed to admire. Her tweet was more like a gesture by the headstrong and politically disastrous Cécilia Albéniz, Sarkozy's second wife (and the great love of *his* life). She too had interfered at the beginning of his presidency, damaging his image (then almost immediately leaving him for another man). Albéniz and Sarkozy had carried downmarket celebrity culture right into the Elysée. Hollande had been elected in part because the French disapproved of this '*peopolisation*' of the presidency (although the relationship was a contradictory one: disapproving yet fascinated); and he spent most of his campaign distinguishing himself from Sarkozy on those grounds. He, as President, he intoned, particularly in his '*Moi, Président...*' intervention in the TV debate, would bring back decorum and gravitas to the office (ironically, at the time, this albeit ungrammatical series of *Moi, Président* completely overwhelmed Sarkozy, leaving him speechless).

As a working journalist (for *Paris Match*), as we have mentioned, Trierweiler said she did not want to be a *potiche* First Lady. But then she kind of did. She said publicly, immediately after the elections, that she did not want to be dependent either on a man or the state; later she said she wanted to be a link (*un relais*) between the President and the

French. This duality created very rapidly a sense of public distrust, and her uncertainty betrayed a self-centred caprice, in an ingenuous relationship with both the office and the media. And, contrary to her stated desire for privacy, she was in the media all of the time, for example, on the cover of magazines almost unendingly in early and mid-2012, and giving interviews. And her omnipresence wherever the President went (on one occasion she assaulted a journalist), suggested a sense of media attention-seeking; and she often made 'people' magazine-style remarks. In January 2013 on a visit with Hollande in Algeria she told a group of children, but it was as if to the surrounding journalists, that she had 'fallen in love with the man rather than the President'. Returning from Algeria where she had had a high profile series of engagements with children's charities, she was seen at both the Yves Saint Laurent and Dior fashion shows, and with the Princess of Monaco. Later in May after returning from a humanitarian visit to Mali (where, looking immaculate – perfect 'brushing', high heels – she was photographed and filmed playing African drums on a mud floor surrounded by poor women with no shoes at all ...), she attended with great publicity the Cannes Film Festival. This contradictory political persona continued; in March 2013 she took the authors of *La Frondeuse*, a biography about her, to court for invasion of privacy – which made the sales of the book soar (Bouilhaguet and Jakubyszyn 2012); all this until the Closergate scandal broke. By 2008, President Sarkozy's public/private drama with his ex-wife Cécilia and new wife Carla had seen his popularity drop to 36%. Hollande in his campaign was, as we have seen, going to put a stop to all this *'peopolisation'* of political life; and yet within weeks of his taking the presidency, Valérie had become the highest profile and least popular First Lady of the Fifth Republic. Very soon polls saw Trierweiler disowned by the French with a 67% disapproval rate. Hollande was caught on camera being told by a local woman not to marry her, and that the French did not like her. There was an equally hostile feeling against her assuming such a central role, given that she and Hollande were not married (and although reluctant to be a First Lady, nevertheless had five staff working for her at the Elysée. A PR consultant might have been a better idea).

We have mentioned the relative confusion by and about Valérie Trierweiler regarding her prospective role as 'First Lady' or, even worse, 'First Girl Friend', as the US press called her. What this marginally interesting issue actually raises, however, is the central issue of, not what the First Lady is but what the presidency is. And in this case, what a 'normal' presidency might be. This, in turn, raises the question of the largely unexplained relationship between the character of the presidency and the character of the President (and their relation to the public), a modern version, perhaps, of the King's Two Bodies, the temporal and the transcendental. And this incident, the tweet, coming so early in Hollande's presidency, significantly affected both bodies and, more importantly, what Hollande himself would have himself and his presidency to be. We shall return to this in Chapter 6.

The idea of Hollande as hypocritical was the immediate result. Other questions were immediately raised. He had personally contacted Royal and lent her support in her campaign, complimenting her personal election manifesto: hence Trierweiler's anger. Hollande's act could have been seen as understandable given their history, but with the tweet, questions immediately were raised as to whether a President should become involved in the legislative campaign in a partisan way, particularly as he had said he would not (unlike his predecessor...). Yet here he was encouraging a very particular parliamentary candidate (who happened to be his ex-partner). Hypocrite! Tartuffe! It is clear from this that 'normal' carries with it a series of associated traits: honesty, reserve, appropriateness, calm – each of these qualities was being revealed as questionable. Trierweiler immediately became (and this would remain for the duration of the presidency) a potentially loose cannon. In fact, she turned out to be an Exocet missile, as we shall see. For the rest of June 2012, she was nowhere to be seen, which in some ways was even more striking than her previous omnipresence throughout the campaign and in the first weeks of Hollande's presidency. She was not even there to meet Aung San Suu Kyi when she visited Paris at the end of June 2012. And the triviality of the tweet affair increased significantly the lampooning of the new President in the press and online media. The tweet affair conferred upon her a very negative publicly-perceived character, and raised several issues about his. Fifteen months later the revelations in her 2014 book were all designed to take Hollande's 'received' character and replace it with a 'kiss-and-tell' version of its opposite. This brings us to the question of 'character'. Let us turn to this.

The character, or rather the perceived character, of François Hollande as President was undermined by 'Valériegate' because it brought into relief doubts about his resolve, doubts that had existed about him (just as doubts about Sarkozy's volatile narcissism came back to haunt him once he was elected in 2007). The damage was all the greater because it is the constructed and imagined relationship between the President and the French which drives the Fifth Republic. To make matters worse, as a result, a series of caricatures came in to play (as they had for Royal when she was presidential candidate in 2007; in her case, caricatures running the gamut of female stereotypes from Madonna to Witch (Lambron 2006; Bacqué and Chemin 2007)). Hollande's damaging caricature was that of an indecisive man who had failed to respond to the whole issue making him seem more ostrich-head-in-the-sand than otherwise; and all this in the context of his being torn between two strong-minded women (throwing into even greater relief his very physical ordinariness, and lending a Feydeau farce quality to the affair), who now, in turn, took on caricatural female qualities, of the mother hurt and the vengeful mistress (currently locked in the wardrobe), and so on. Royal was reported to have said some years earlier that Hollande could never take any decisions. Another of his rivals, another woman, Martine Aubry, during the Socialist primaries for the candidacy, referred to Hollande as the 'Gauche molle', the latter word having sexual connotations of impotence. Was France being run by a man who could not control his women who, transformed into harpies, were fighting over *him* – slamming doors and making him want to hide – it was as if 'Mais n'te promène donc pas toute nue!' as well as 'Tartuffe' were being performed in the Elysée Palace, and this only four weeks after his election.

The French showed little interest in the parliamentary elections themselves; the only two 'stories' (out of 577), in fact, were the battle between Marine Le Pen and Jean-Luc Mélenchon in the Pas-de-Calais and, latterly, the fight between Hollande's 'Ex', Royal, and Trierweiler's friend, Falorni. Royal did not profit from Trierweiler's attack; she was crushed by Falorni; gaining only 37% to his score of 63%. Her hopes of becoming the President of the National Assembly were over (Claude Bartolone was elected). And there was more trouble ahead. Royal felt – as probably did Hollande – that she must regain, if not the upper hand, then her dignity. Her future role within the left was therefore fragile and problematic. Both women therefore became a 'problem' for the new President, given that one could only prosper if the other did not. Just as the idea that Trierweiler might become for the rest of his presidency potentially very embarrassing for the President, so too at the level of 'character' did Hollande seem now *permanently* vulnerable to indecision. If you are looking for the root cause of a problem, *Cherchez la Femme* – look for the woman. It is a sexist cliché, but it took hold of François Hollande's presidency in the first weeks and lasted until he and Trieweiler separated, and then came back with a vengeance in the form of Trieweiler's book in September 2014. It also meant that the soap-opera aspect of 'celebrity politics' was established at the very beginning of Hollande's presidency and would run throughout – the next 'episode' being Hollande and Royal's elaborate 'avoiding' of each other at the UN in October 2012, all of it monitored by the *'presse people'*.

Changing the tempo; scrambling the signifiers

The second 'moral' hostage to fortune was the myriad of little lifestyle changes Hollande and his entourage undertook in order to (ostentatiously) remove ostentation from the presidential function: he would take trains instead of taking jets. In reality, his taking trains – usually accompanied by Trierweiler – became media events (and the couple never seemed to have any luggage); and he might take the train there and the jet back (which had to fly there to get him), or else take the official limousine back, which once was clocked at 110 miles-an-hour on the A1 motorway. Hollande told his ministers off for taking private jets to get about, and then used them himself, even to go from Paris to Lille, a 59 minute train journey (*Le Point* 25/01/13). He would live simply, except that Trierweiler expensively renewed (with public money?) the furnishings for their summer holiday residence in 2012. It no longer mattered whether half these things were true; the damage was done because of the earlier claims to moral rectitude, and the new conditions of social media. It was estimated by the public accounts committee (*Cour des comptes*) (*Le Monde.fr* 3/9/14) that by July 2013 Hollande had taken 14 domestic plane trips, 21 car journeys, and one TGV; by the same time the following year, two TGVs out of almost 60 domestic trips.

Sarkozy had scrambled the 'signifiers' of what the President and presidency were. Hence Hollande's anti-Sarkozy campaign image. But Hollande's own image would further scramble the signifiers. Could 'scrambled' be blended? There were precedents. And in myth, there are transitions: Prince Hal becomes Henry V in a spiritual transition. Hollande's supporter, Stéphane Le Foll remarked that Hollande was taking on the identity of a head of state (*François Hollande s'installe dans les habits du chef de l'état*) in this semi-mythical way; but whether these two types – the ordinary and the kingly – can co-exist remains problematic. There are many precedents for the 'kingly' (both de Gaulle and Mitterrand are examples), and of their very presidential 'stepping down' as it were through an act of ordinariness (e.g. through humour); making the gesture in the opposite direction – from the ordinary to the presidential, is a much harder task. This is why the early images (e.g. *'Président Bisou'* during the legislative elections) were so important. Had François Hollande introduced a contradiction into the presidency? Let us try and understand what that entity is he may have introduced a contradiction into. Let us bring in here some of our discussion from Chapter 3. What are 'the signifiers', the elements constitutive of presidential performance? What was the French presidency, or what should it be? Do we need to go back to the origins of the republic to grasp its significance? In one sense yes, but not in terms of finding the original 'meaning' of the presidency, but in terms of discovering what de Gaulle and others brought to the functioning of a presidency in a republican framework (or a republic in a presidential framework). What we have argued is that the Fifth Republic is both very complex and particular as a political entity, in that the republic should not be understood as simply 'presidential' or that it would have itself so. Rather, it is the 'performance of the presidential' that is crucial; complex, in that the role of the 'self', the 'character', the 'persona' of the President (and other pretenders to leadership) should be the focus of our attention; by attempting to 'perform' normal and ethical, the exigencies of the presidency militated against the former, and a series of incidents and especially the tweet affair militated against the latter.

The fall in Hollande's popularity was vertiginous. In early 2013, the successful military operation in Mali and the freeing of a family held hostage in Nigeria barely made a blip on his popularity ratings (even though the military intervention was itself widely approved of). By this time, a qualitative decline in not just Hollande's popularity but his credibility had taken place. He had said he would, throughout his mandate, stay in touch with the people through provincial tours and visits, for example to his adopted département, Corrèze. Hostility or even worse, indifference, met him everywhere. By spring 2013, as we saw, the provincial visits had become a PR disaster and were stopped. And when it seemed things could not get any worse, the third scandal broke, the Cahuzac affair, which was of nuclear proportions.

The Cahuzac scandal

The Jérôme Cahuzac affair was the catalyst for a series of crises which engulfed the government in the early months of 2013. It started off as a relatively 'discrete' issue, involving only one man, albeit a government

minister: did Jérôme Cahuzac, the Budget Minister, have a secret overseas bank account? And if he did, he would have to resign (he said he
did not have one). But the shockwaves from his resignation on
19 March 2013 (yes he did have a secret Swiss bank account, and admitted as much) seemed never-ending. *Mediapart* had run the story on
Cahuzac's account on 4 December 2012, so the affair dragged on for
months. What was astonishing was that this was not foreseen – not the
Swiss bank account, which some insiders were clearly aware of – but the
fallout. The reason why the fallout was not foreseen was the same
reason why the President and his team got into such difficulty: they had
over-played and underestimated the consequences of the use of claims
to moral exemplarity, did not understand what the political consequences of overt and constant claims to morality were, nor the symbolism of leadership in relation to these. The Cahuzac affair was a personal
tragedy for Cahuzac and a sad comment about politics (he was a tax
fiddler whose job it was to – with due righteous indignation – chase tax
fiddlers). But politically, it was Hollande who was the real victim. The
new administration had created a climate of ethical exemplarity. The
campaign itself had been predicated upon the idea that post-Sarkozy
there simply would be no scandals; although it was not Hollande's own
integrity which was being pilloried at this point but his incompetence.
If he knew the truth about his Budget Minister he looked bad; if he did
not, he looked equally bad. The press compared Hollande unfavourably
to the authoritative Mitterrand: none of whose ministers would have
dared lie to him. Hollande's earlier campaign association with
Mitterrand, to the point of quite literally impersonating him – e.g. in
his Le Bourget speech – now made him look somewhat comical.

In the same spring of 2013, Carla Bruni-Sarkozy, having taken up her
pop career again, released an album containing a song that depicted
Hollande – allusively – as a rude and silly penguin (who would get his
come-uppance). He had – as part of his moral rectitude – acted with
dismissiveness towards the outgoing presidential couple on his inauguration day. Now President Hollande had, in turn, become a figure of
derision. As new Cahuzac revelations appeared by the day, the
President flew to Morocco on an official visit (3–4 April). As if suddenly
aware of the growing crisis before he left for Morocco he made a brief
statement, saying that Cahuzac's lies were 'unforgivable' and that he
was going to bring in measures to stop it happening again. A full press
conference would have been more appropriate. One newspaper
cartoon depicted him as an ostrich with his head in the (Moroccan)
sand. He held a short press conference before leaving Morocco to try

and retrieve the situation, but by now the derision had become deafening. By 8 April 2013, he was promising major changes including making all government ministers declare their fortunes and tax arrangements. Many of the results would turn out to be embarrassing; one result was to set a trap for future miscreants and further government or presidential humiliation, another was the sense that by the spring of 2013 events like these, along with a lot of 'empty' rhetoric and posturing, were actually replacing government policy elaboration; there developed the sense of a President and government finding things to do – '*sociétal*' issues such as Gay marriage (see below) – rather than making bold economic reforms.

On Wednesday 3 April 2013, Finance Minister Pierre Moscovici was questioned in the National Assembly and denied all previous knowledge of Cahuzac's misdoings (there was widespread suspicion that both Moscovici and Hollande were not telling the whole truth about what they knew). The right-opposition UMP called for a complete government overhaul, thus beginning the pressure for an unstrategic forced government reshuffle. The far-right National Front called for new elections. The Left Front, which could attract a lot of Hollande's former supporters – even his MPs – called for a new constitution, as did some in the Green Party, which was in coalition with the government. Hollande would have lost any elections badly, and perhaps be forced to resign. The sense of chaos grew by the day and lasted several weeks with a developing public conviction of the government's complete incompetence. And the sense of political crisis would recur at each moment of scandal or defeat, and there would be many.

The government ministers quickly had to declare their assets. The ones with little fortune declared immediately (although in most cases declaring the value of their homes when they bought them rather than their current value immediately lent the whole procedure an air of suspicion). No one seemed to have a car – all used ministerial cars, two of them declared their bicycles adding a sense of farce to the proceedings. No one had investments in the dynamic economy. Property (or properties) was the main source of wealth. And there were eight millionaires in the government. The combination of voyeurism and the perception of large fortunes made the situation even more farcical. One of the little-remarked upon features of this affair was that Hollande arguably made the situation worse through self-dramatisation. By being solemn and righteous-sounding in his pronouncements, upon something he had implied he would ensure did not happen in the first place and for which he had been elected to make not happen, made him seem particularly unpersuasive. It was then reported that Hollande's friend and the treasurer of his 2012 campaign Jean-Jacques Augier had a (tax avoiding) account in the Cayman Islands. Rumours emerged concerning Laurent Fabius' personal finances (*L'Express* 7/4/13). Social media was alive with speculation about the whole government, giving a sense of chaos to the transparency issue (*L'Express* 12/4/13). And, significantly, one poll showed that 70% thought politicians sounded off too much about morality, and 55% believed that all politicians were corrupt (*Le Point* 11/4/13).

The negative impact of these three issues made Hollande appear dishonest as well as aimless. By the end of the first year, in all polls, the French overwhelmingly did not know where the government was going, or where the President even wanted to go; but what was worse, no one believed what he said anymore. This was compounded by the constant discrepancy between all economic indicators put out by the EU and the IMF on the one hand and those of the government or President on the other, the former always being more accurate. The most important issue facing the President as he began the second year of his presidency was that of his credibility, and whether, only one year into his term, he could sustain the course. All this came at a time, spring 2013, when 7 in 10 of those polled already thought Hollande as President was a disaster. And this was now serious because the public was clearly angry, and worse, utterly disillusioned with politics. When a population – particularly one in the middle of a crisis that France was going through, with unemployment now over 10% and factories closing every day – believes that all politicians are corrupt (*pourris*), this helps the extremes, in particular the extreme-right who stood to gain significantly from this growing sense of economic, political, and now moral crisis. The fragility of French politics was exposed by the Cahuzac affair. Much of the sense of political stability in France is based upon the multi-faceted and interactive relationship between the French and their President. François Hollande seemed to have lost the French somewhere along the line. This was primarily because of four things – two things he did not do, and two he did. First, as we have mentioned, he did not make clear how difficult the economic and social trials were going to be; second, he did not make clear how deep the cuts in spending would be; third, what he did do was to tell the French that, ethically, his rule was going to be a new dawn; he was going to 're-invent the French dream' – *réinventer le rêve français* had been one of his campaign slogans in 2011–12 (Hollande 2011) – but he clearly had not; in fact, the situation was turning into something of a nightmare in terms of social costs; fourth, Hollande now presided an atmosphere of vaudeville in terms of political performance and the issues taking the executive's attention and, more than ever, the growing view that month after month the President and government were not properly addressing the economic situation. Beyond this, along with the several scandals, one issue in the first year of Hollande's term further undermined his and the government's authority, even though the issue itself had widespread public sympathy.

Gay marriage and *La France Profonde*

On 18 May 2013 'Gay marriage' became law in France. The movement against the law, however, was a stunning political success. Not in terms of outcomes; the law was passed, but in a country that measures its political significance in its demonstrations, rallies, and mobilisation, the *Manif pour tous* was the most successful right-wing phenomenon in decades.

Four major marches in Paris between November 2012 and May 2013, large demonstrations in a host of other cities and towns daily, and 'spontaneous' lightning demos throughout the period, and a media presence worthy of a Coca Cola or Nike advertising campaign, put millions of people on to the streets. For the final demonstration on 26 May, 500 buses and a dozen trains were hired to transport demonstrators from the provinces to Paris. Three massive processions from various points in the city each converged on and filled to overflowing the open space of the Place des Invalides. And this was after the bill had passed into law.

Who were they? Right wing, yes, for the most part. Quite a few small, extremist groups and violent far right groups such as *Génération Identitaire* and the *Gud*, for example, on the edges of the movement. There was also a racist element with for example the bill's sponsor, Christiane Taubrira, the black Justice Minister, being likened, even by children in demonstrations as well as the far right press, to a monkey. But to concentrate on these as explanatory of what had happened would be to miss the movement's significance. The movement also had its 'Neuilly' aspect, Barbour jackets and Burberry scarves aplenty; and the deep involvement of Roman Catholic Church organisations – of the official 37 organisations constituting the *Manif pour tous*, 15 did not really exist, outside the demonstrations themselves, and most of the rest were linked to the Church (and most of these to the creepy wing of the Church. One of the most prominent, *Civitas*, even the

Church shied away from). Along with the fundamentalist Catholics, some Muslims, Protestants, and Jewish organisations, even some Buddhists, supported the movement. But for the most part – and this is the essential point – it was families – and in fact children and young people by the thousands. Families, and many 18 and 20 somethings in numbers the right had rarely seen, and people from all the regions of France took part. And they were peaceful; they came, they demonstrated, they went home. Most of the arrests on 26 May (350 in all) were on the edges of the demo or in fights between the police and hard right groups afterwards.

The then Minster of the Interior, Manuel Valls, told families not to come for their own safety. They came in their thousands. For the 26 May demo there were 4,500 police on duty – to which should be added an equivalent number of the *Manif*'s own security and crowd control people, many of these keeping the hard right groups away throughout the day. That made 9,000 people just for security. It is true that the leadership of the movement radicalised, sweeping its main spokeswoman, the eccentric but media-friendly Frigide Barjot (that is not a typo) to one side, creating a highly-organised umbrella group called 'French Spring' (*Printemps Français*) which talked of civil war. Not since the 1930s had France seen its right materialise in this way, as a massive and peaceful and concerted social movement. For the last 50 years, the French right has always been behind on everything progressive: decriminalising homosexuality, abortion laws, divorce, contraception, equal rights, and civil partnerships. And it gained nothing from these rear-guard struggles against progressive policies (Giscard's reforms only passed because the left voted for them). The 1984 protests against cuts to private/church education are a rare example of success. That was not the case with this protest. The large demonstrations awoke or reawoke a Girondin France alongside the hard right. Revolutionary hats, calls for liberty, and even talk of the Vendée genocide of 1793 featured in these demos. '*Tout et n'importe quoi*' poured into this protest movement, whose dynamic was not only about gay marriage but about profoundly held cultural values. Why did this phenomenon occur? And what were its consequences? Overall, France is not anti-gay, is probably much less so than most countries. And there is a general tolerance on sexual and 'lifestyle' matters. The national majority in favour of gay marriage is significant. But the *Manif pour tous* was fuelled by four things beyond its extreme right connections, all of which were related to the presidency and the left generally.

First, the movement flourished in a national climate of utter exasperation with the government and the President. By 2013, François Hollande was the most unpopular President in Fifth Republic France. Public hostility to the *Manif* was muted because it was an anti-Hollande movement. Many were furious that the Gay Marriage Bill took up so many hundreds of parliamentary hours – although the real fault was the filibustering by the parliamentary opposition – to the detriment of finding solutions to the financial crisis the country was in (in the UK, at the same time, a similar bill was passed in half a day). The perception was that *'Questions de société'* were deliberately being substituted for more pressing economic concerns. Second, the French public generally had had little exposure to Gender Theory. Few, even in academia, had read Judith Butler (Butler 1990; Butler and Scott 1992). French attitudes to gender were quite traditional. And what we might call political homosexuality, Gay Pride, was seen, especially in provincial France, as an Anglo-Saxon import. Over and above this, the legislation was seen by many as a Trojan horse for IVF-for-all and surrogacy, and therefore in their view, the commodification of children (and because of proposed changes to the *Code Civil*, the wiping from their memory of their 'origins'), and dramatic social and cultural changes as a result. It would not have dramatic effects at all, not at the wider social level (although the social and psychic issues regarding the children involved is a different issue, but that debate was not addressed), but it was a highly emotional subject in a country that sees itself as holding children and childhood as sacred. Third, the left bore a large responsibility for letting all of these things coalesce into major social protest. All of the progressive legislation of the 1970s mentioned above (divorce, abortion, contraception etc.) came as a result of political activism and commitment but also of debate, often lasting years. On the gay marriage issue there had been no debate. Over the previous ten years the Socialists had debated little of interest, apart from who was going to be their presidential candidate. Hollande promised to heal the wounds of Sarkozy's divisive rule, yet within a year of taking office France had rarely been so divided. At one level, Hollande could not have hoped for a right-wing movement like the *Manif pour tous* that sent the mainstream right into turmoil, and saw far-right rioters appearing at the end of demonstrations. Surely, this could only profit the left? That was, however, a serious miscalculation. It is true the mainstream right was divided by the protest. It got involved, but was riven with internal division as a result, and it was effectively leaderless on the issue. Marine le Pen and the Front National, on the other hand, profited greatly – and would do so even more in the future. Le Pen herself was not a great supporter of the *Manif* movement. Officially, the FN did not associate with the protest. Individual members did – such as Le Pen's neice, Marion Maréchal-Le Pen, and many of the extremist groups had clear – or, rather, unclear – links to the FN. But significant parts of the political constituency that the *Manif* created would flock to the FN in the future. Over and above this, the movement also released into the political arena a million-strong new anti-Hollande movement, comprised mainly of ordinary families, mainly provincial, mainly Catholic, but demonstrably 'normal' in their vast majority. And their non-violence and discipline and latterly good-natured demonstrations, contrasting witheringly with the President and Interior Minister's forebodings of grave danger, lent dignity to the movement and ridicule to the left. Most importantly, this 'constituency' did not go away after the bill was passed, and continued into the five-year term as a potentially formidable force. Finally, the President and government's failure to respect this 'France' was a further setback to the left and the President's claims to represent all of France, and clearly rendered hollow the claims to heal the divisive wounds of the Sarkozy presidency, thus undermining the character of the President still further. In the space of a few weeks, the social protest of provincial France had (re)created *la France profonde* as a political entity.

The most important issue facing the President as he began the second year of his presidency was that of his credibility (Amar 2013). As the second year began, listening to both his Prime Minister and Finance Minister, Ayrault and Moscovici, one heard a now constant stress upon the idea that the President had fixed a course and knew where he was headed, as if vision and unpopularity were correlated. This actually is a deep tradition in French politics. By May 2013, almost everything seemed to revolve around the 'performance' of the President – his press conferences and interviews were moments where he could impress opinion – he never did, but these performances were always moments of opportunity and, until disillusion and indifference set in, expectation. In 2012, he had said that unemployment would start to drop at the end of 2013 (in fact, it did not, but continued to rise, but the President's credibility was undermined as soon as he said it). Most of all, the President, like all the political actors, needed somehow to find a sense of how to deal with the complexity of the culture and institutions he was operating within. No President of the Fifth Republic had become so unpopular, so fast. No other had shown how complex is the architecture of French political leadership. By the end of his first year in office in May 2013, political commentators were beginning to tire of saying that things could not get any worse for the French Socialist President and his government. And yet, catastrophe after catastrophe, things did just keep getting worse. Little of the government's legislation – apart from the tax rises – seemed to have any traction, whether it was in education, housing, pension reform, health, the civil service or justice. No bold decisions were taken on anything, so fearful were the Socialists of upsetting their disintegrating electoral base, and none of the structural reforms that other European countries were putting through had been replicated. Presidential and governmental activity largely took the form of increasingly iconoclastic presidential declarations of intent without substance. We have mentioned the CICE of November 2012 which was intended to offer tax credits, in particular to small- and medium-sized businesses and export firms, in the region of 33 billion euros over two years and reduce the salary costs of firms by 4% in 2013 and 6% in 2014 and, over five years, create 150,000 jobs. In the event, it was taken up by very few of these business (in part because its administration was so complex) and essentially by very large firms such as the postal service, *La Poste* and had no perceptible effect upon employment at all.

In March 2013 the President announced a 'Simplification Shock' (*Choc de simplification*) to help both businesses and households (France is notorious for its bewildering and constraining bureaucratic paperwork and rules pertaining to all aspects of personal, social, and economic life). The move was designed to identify, from 40,000 government directives, small taxes, ordonnances, and rules and regulations, and create a kind of 'bonfire' of these useless rules and conventions in order to make the life of small businesses and households easier. Some firms, in IT, for example, paid up to 90 different kinds of taxes (the tax code manual is almost 4,000 pages long – the Labour Code *Le code du travail* is only 3,000 ...). In early 2014 the French Finance Inspectorate identified 192 small taxes (e.g. on pinball machines) that could be cut. Of the 192, the National Assembly voted to abolish four of them. Of the 40,000 directives etc., 50 were abolished. Bakeries, for example, no longer needed to declare their summer holiday dates. Here was a further example of presidential initiatives creating a sense of their opposite (although we should note that a lot of changes did start to appear from the autumn of 2014 but with little fanfare).

At the beginning of Year II of Hollande's presidency, his attention turned to the Syria crisis (August 2013). Let us look at this in some detail as it was illustrative of the nature of the presidency. Then we shall examine the further developments in Year II.

5
The Second Year. Presidential Character under Siege

The first year of François Hollande's presidency saw his popularity slide almost relentlessly. In the first two-and-a-half years, there would be only one 'pause' (Mali January 2013) and two slight movements up (May 2013 when the *Mariage pour tous* bill was finally passed and May 2014 when he appointed Manuel Valls as Prime Minister). But more serious for him was the 'quality', as it were, of the unpopularity: the strong increase in the *'très mécontents'* – 'very unhappy' – and the rapid rise of polls indicating that he was considered a bad President, not up to the job, not presidential, and so on.

As regards perceptions of government activity, particularly on the economy, the sense was of policy measures seen as inadequate to the task and very slow in coming, out of fear of confronting certain constituencies or vested interests. The tempo of 'political time' and the legislative process seemed inadequate to the tasks facing the government. Grand announcements like the CICE tax allowances for businesses (mainly taken up by large firms rather than by small and medium-sized ones), or the *'choc de simplification'* announcement in spring 2013 – to address the bewildering complexity of French business' and French households' form filling and bureaucracy – were mainly presidential rather than ministerial announcements, although these, more than most, were also only ever the beginnings of long processes (especially all the *dialogues des partenaires sociaux*) which through their high-profile mediatisation drew attention to their tardiness. A further series of issues, e.g. the complex and confusing, and often publicly denied or contradicted, series of tax rises (e.g. in the autumn of 2012) – and the French tax system is complex; another major incident in September 2013 when the President and Prime Minister gave different dates (2014 and 2015, respectively) for the introduction of a barely-believed and ill-defined '*pause fiscale*' (on taxes); these issues began to heap ridicule on the President, so that by the end of that first year there was strong polling evidence that Hollande had become, not only extremely unpopular, but perhaps more importantly, considered as not fulfilling the presidential role. What exactly '*la fonction présidentielle*' meant remained somewhat an enigma.

Conversely, it is important to grasp how central the President was to everything, whether domestic or international, important, scandalous, or trivial. He and his advisers made every effort to start Year II on a sounder footing; in order to enable him to recapture what, on election, he had termed 'the normal function of the institutions'; and for his government to deal with the shorter term and he with the longer term as he had earlier stipulated to both his government and his *cabinet* (*Le Monde* on line 1/6/12). He told his ministers to stop arguing in public, and to clear press interviews with his office. To little avail. In March 2013, for example, three ministers – Muscovici, Batho, and Duflot, all made contradictory announcements on diesel fuel tax; and there remained the almost continuous outspokenness of Montebourg. Ministers (not all complied) were also to take only very short holidays and preferably in France. His Prime Minister, Jean-Marc Ayrault and he would take their short breaks in turn so the state did not close down for the summer (as France has a tendency to do). The government team was seen to be making every effort to put France back on its feet again. None of it worked. By 2014, polls suggested many French thought France was on the brink of dramatic social protest and upheaval right across French society. A widespread mood of national gloom and exasperation was in the air as evidenced by a myriad of polls. The problem was not just the economy, the rocketing taxes, the cuts, the unemployment, and the social divisions. There was a general sense that not only did the President not know what to do in terms of governmental policy, there was no sense of 'direction'. Presidential and governmental communications in this area were chaotic, given in part the deliberate idea conveyed that the presidential rendezvous was in a year's time when France would learn whether the President's unemployment forecast was accurate. Even more seriously there was deep confusion in terms of how a President was supposed to behave, what he was supposed to 'be'. And it was on this 'question of character' that he had been elected President in May 2012 (we shall return to this in the Conclusion). There seemed, moreover, to be a widespread sense that presidential discourse bore less and less relation to reality – the insistence on the predicted fall in unemployment by the end of 2013 being the classic example of this disconnect. In this sense, it was highly significant that the first major act of Year II was an aggressive act of foreign policy; one of de Gaulle's *'grandes querelles'*, and a highly personalised one at that. In terms of our analysis, the Syria crisis was an apposite beginning to Year II in that it saw a dramatic escalation of the presidential use of 'self' in François Hollande's presidency.

France and Syria: Hollande v. Assad

The first 'moment' of Year II was the crisis in Syria and France's decision to lead on the US initiative to attack Syria on the grounds of its use of chemical weapons against civilians in Ghouta, the eastern suburb of Damascus on 21 August 2013 (for a wider, theoretical analysis see Gaffney 2014). At the International Ambassadors Meeting in Paris on 27 August, Hollande launched what was a near-declaration of hostilities against Syria.

There is a slight irony in that during the Syria crisis in the autumn of 2013, America's oldest ally, France, became its newest ally; an irony in that it was not really true; rather, it was a diplomatic accident, born of UK premier David Cameron's hurried and unsuccessful attempt on 30 August 2013 in the UK Houses of Parliament to get backing for military action, and French President Hollande's decision to virtually declare war on Syria without consulting in Europe or even in the French political class. Presidential prerogative and presidential miscalculation were linked and nowhere better demonstrated than over the chemical weapons crisis of autumn 2013. After the shock of the UK's vote, American President Obama decided to consult his own Congress to maintain legitimacy and gain time. He referred to the UK's role, but made no reference to France at all. As a result of both Cameron and Obama asking for parliamentary approval, the French were left isolated internationally and in political chaos domestically. France's decision to wait until the G20 summit of 5–6 September before even beginning to build a coalition within and beyond Europe was also a sign of disarray.

There was another irony – the period of the early American Republic John Kerry was referring to (30 August 2013) when France and America were allies, was an early example of catastrophic French miscalculation. France did back America, overstretched itself, with the ensuing costs and government debt helping trigger the French Revolution of 1789. As Gustave Flaubert wrote, 'irony takes nothing away from pathos'. When de Gaulle told Kennedy, then Johnson, to stay out of Vietnam, his international standing skyrocketed. When Chirac told

Bush not to go into Iraq, the same thing happened. It is also worth speculating here that French support for the young American republic was arguably the high-point of Franco-American relations in the last 200 years. Misunderstanding has characterised relations ever since, and August–September 2013 was no exception. Our intention here is to examine how and why French policy over Syria was aberrant in the conduct of international politics and how the miscalculations were related to the presidential nature of the Fifth Republic itself. What the events of early September showed was that as a result of the French President's ability to act with greater impunity than his counterparts, he was in greater danger of making mistakes. He was weak because he was strong.

Let us look at the Syria affair against the backdrop of the events and their implications as 'performances' by President Hollande in August and September. François Hollande made three main rhetorical interventions on Syria (he had also said to *Le Parisien* newspaper on the 26th that airstrikes (*frappes aériennes*) were a possibility). All were highly personalised, as regards his depiction of both his adversary and himself. First was the speech at the Ambassadors Conference in Paris on 27 August where Hollande used the word 'punish'; second the interview in *Le Monde* on the 29th, and third a TV appearance on France's principal TV channel on 15 September. Taken together, these three interventions displayed moral outrage, personal commitment, the personalising of the self/the presidency and equally of the adversary, and the sense of imminent attack: 'I have consulted a great deal with the Americans and our European allies, and Arab League partners to gauge all sources of opinion, and tomorrow, I will hold a Defence Council and Parliament will be informed without delay' (Ambassadors meeting). This quotation demonstrates how centrally Hollande was placing himself in the unfolding events. Although there was no suggestion that the French would not be part of a coalition of forces alongside the Americans, we can see that the rhetoric was that of France itself on the threshold of an avenging attack in punishment for the massacre of civilians with chemical weapons.

The American and Russian Navies began sending reinforcements to the Mediterranean, and the French aircraft carrier, the *Charles de Gaulle* was put on stand-by in Toulon, as were French *Rafale* and *Mirage* fighter planes in the French base in Dubai. The following day, on 29 August, the UK Parliament voted down a call for armed intervention. On 30 August, John Kerry referred to France as America's oldest ally, comical in its implication; at no time had the French assumed they would find themselves alone alongside the US. Three days after Hollande's declarations and their tone of imminent action, on 31 August President Obama said he – as the UK had with its Parliament – would ask the US Congress for backing (given subsequent developments with the Russians this did not take place). The vote for this was to be taken over a week later, on 9 September (although the powerful Foreign Affairs Committee did give its backing on 6 September). But Obama's putting the vote to Congress (without a mention of France) brought the sequencing of Hollande's interventions, the Ambassadors Meeting and *Le Monde* interview, to a sudden halt. It also had two further implications, both of which undermined Hollande's status by asserting it. First, he was the only leader involved *not* asking his parliament for its backing (only the UK was constitutionally obliged), and second, paradoxically and comically, it made Hollande dependent, not upon his own parliament but upon the US Congress. It was as if Hollande had been freeze-framed. Adding insult to injury, on 2 September, Assad gave an interview to *Le Figaro* newspaper, as if mocking the French President. Hollande's continued silence was thrown into even higher relief by some of the left's spokespeople, because they sounded just as bellicose as Hollande had, using very undiplomatic language. David Assouline, Socialist Party spokesperson referred to the 'cowardice' (*une lacheté*) of the international community if it did nothing. The leader of the French Socialist Party, Harlem Désir, spoke of an 'appeasement spirit' (*esprit munichois*), implying a Munich 1938-type capitulation to Nazism (this is an even greater insult in France than the UK). Three days later, all the major players – Obama, Cameron, Hollande, Merkel, Putin – met at the G20 summit (5–6 September) in St Petersburg.

At the G20, Hollande became active in attempting to gather support (and he took Fabius (Foreign Affairs) and Le Drian (Defence) with him). This was, however, too late for a proper coalition of ideas to be gathered, especially as everything depended now upon the US Congress vote. 12 countries eventually signed a common declaration condemning Syria, but military intervention was not even considered. France was isolated. Perhaps significantly, Obama was friendlier to other leaders (Cameron, Merkel) than to Hollande, who in clips of the G20 meeting looked bemused and rather left out. The most significant 'event' of the summit however was Putin's (the host's) intransigent image and, paradoxically, his revelation during the summit, confirmed by Obama, that the two had had secret talks. It was clear; France was having no effect at all upon developments. On 6 September, Sarkozy (having shown 'leadership' on Libya) said to the French media that there was no leadership in this affair.

It was at this point that reports appeared in the press that German intelligence services were puzzled by the fact (their claim) that the overwhelming majority of the Ghouta gas victims appeared to be children and young adults/women, implying that the attack had been upon a single target like a school, the further implication being that this could have been done without rocket or aircraft intervention – i.e. might be the work of Jihadists. On 6, the Russian Foreign Minister, Sergei Lavrov, utterly refuted the US evidence implicating Assad. Assad (CBS 8 September), and Putin in *The New York Times* (10 September), also continued denying any government involvement. On 9 September, after all the leaders had left the G20 in indecision and with no sense of diplomatic direction, Putin dropped his diplomatic bombshell. He publicly offered to bring the crisis to an end by offering to broker a solution, the securing and handing over of all Syria's chemical weapons. Damascus agreed immediately.

A first point we can make here is the determined and 'crusading' nature of the French position up until Obama's decision to consult Congress, and the image of confusion and irrelevant isolation afterwards. The whole strategy, however, not just for France but for all the actors was problematic. It is clear that Obama was always reluctant to respond to his own self-imposed 'red line' (that Assad should not use chemical weapons) made one year earlier (and this makes the French approach even more puzzling, given that many knew this). But what were the aims of the French strategy? For France, it was to 'punish', but that does not explain anything. The term itself not only implied moral anger, but a very paradoxical mix of imprecision and finality. Would air strikes alone punish? How many? 2? 10? 100? 1,000? And would such strikes not have seriously endangered civilians? And would the strikes have dissuaded the use of chemical weapons? And surely this, rather than punishment, would be the only reason for the strikes.

A second point is that there clearly was no real coalition (the US had support from Turkey and Saudi Arabia for obvious reasons). Neither the French nor the US had undertaken the effort to build a coalition of the willing. Italy, Spain, and Brazil wanted the UN Security Council to find a solution. Germany was against any action. Russia, China, obviously, but also Japan was opposed. Egypt and Algeria were against, Canada very reluctant, the Arab League extremely equivocal. Domestically too, Hollande had virtually the whole political class against him outside the Socialist Party and the Greens. (The January 2013 Mali 'Operation

Serval' in contrast had been almost universally supported). Virtually all the other political parties across from the extreme-right to the far-left were opposed, so that figures such as Marine Le Pen, the UMP leaders François Fillon and Jean-François Copé (although he initially supported), Dominique de Villepin (who had opposed the 2003 Iraq War in the UN), and Centrists such as François Bayrou opposed the presidential initiative. Nathalie Kosciusko-Morizet remarked that Obama's virtual ignoring of Hollande was a humiliation. The radical leftist Jean-Luc Mélenchon was against, but even figures such as the veteran and former President Giscard d'Estaing opposed, saying that such decisions should go – in the spirit of the European Defence and Security Policy – via the European Council.

The largest question, however, and the one which raised the most concern, fuelling the idea of Hollande and France taking a frightening strategic decision in international terms, and whose non-discussion seemed to reinforce the sense of a lack of forethought, was the question of the possible dramatic consequences of Franco-US intervention upon the region. The reasons why the West had not intervened in Syria before were much more pertinent by August 2013. Intervening at a moment where the Syrian opposition was itself in disarray with the rise of the Jihadist Islamists in the opposition forces (that the Mali expedition had been fighting against) was highly questionable as an effective policy. Now the non-Islamist anti-Assad forces were often in conflict with them. By the autumn of 2013, in a country with both Sunni and Shia, as well as Alawite Muslims, Druze, Kurds, and Christians, large swathes of all of these groups arguably preferred Assad to Islamists. It is also the case that the West's bellicose position on Syria had created a large influx of European Islamists and others who joined the anti-Assad struggle, but this in order to set up an Islamist state ('objectively' helped, at this point, by France and the US). The autumn of 2013 was perhaps not the moment to develop the 'strategy' that the French were developing.

An equally serious consequence of intervention, or rather an equally necessary issue to take into consideration when contemplating intervention, were the regional consequences. International-led attacks upon Syria may well have ignited significant further strife in Lebanon (there were 900 French troops on the Lebanon-Israel border), perhaps see the conflict spread to Israel (Hezbollah had an estimated 60,000 rockets). Iran referred to Israel 'in flames' if the US and its allies attacked Syria. This is probably not what Iran would actually want (for fear of Israeli strikes upon its nuclear programme), but remained a possible scenario. A Hezbollah dominated Lebanon would mean, in the absence of toppling Assad – not, it is true, the declared intention of a France-US attack – a Shia dominated axis from Lebanon, through Syria, Iraq, and Iran. The potential changes to the security of the Hormuz straits would be increased and an all-out conflagration a possibility. At the end of November 2013, the radicalising Syrian opposition created an Islamic front with seven groups of the opposition joining in direct competition and conflict with the secular Syrian opposition. There is little evidence that any of these issues was discussed in depth before Hollande's 'punish' declaration was made, and arguably all the above issues would have been exacerbated by an attack.

From a sustained stance of imminent attack in August, President Hollande moved into one of near silence, as France became an irrelevance, and was treated as such by the Russians, Syrians and, in fact, the Americans. On 10 September, Obama made a TV broadcast (again with no mention of France) which was a clear indication, in spite of references to crimes against humanity, that the strikes were very unlikely – they were not in the US' interests. On 12–14 September, John Kerry met and discussed the crisis with his Russian counterpart, Sergei Lavrov, in Geneva. They held a joint press conference (with Lavrov referring disparagingly to 'a few European capitals' (*certaines capitales européennes*) i.e. Paris). Kerry indicated he would meet Fabius in Paris on the Monday, i.e. after the Kerry/Lavrov meeting, as if France were no longer central to negotiations.

This was the moment (15 September) Hollande broke his silence and appeared on TF1 TV on the primetime evening news in an interview with TV journalist, Claire Chazal. The interview was a perfect illustration of Hollande's dilemma and new approach: at the moment when, in Geneva, France's irrelevance was being thrown into relief, he persisted in his original rhetorical strategy of moral-personal righteousness, and now added to it an earlier and exceptional clairvoyance (and these to the extent that the impression was of someone in denial, if not slightly delusional). He began by repeating that the situation in Syria was the gravest tragedy (*La tragédie la plus grave*), and cited again in detail the overall loss of life and suffering. He then justified the French position in this way: 'As President of the Republic, the first question I had to deal with, not just in terms of my conscience, but in terms of the idea I have of what France is ...' (*La première question comme Président de la république que j'ai eue à régler, pas seulement autour de ma conscience mais de l'idée que je me suis fait de la France ...*). This was not only the gathering of the whole issue into a contemplative act followed by a personal decision with international consequences, the last phrase is a direct evocation of the opening lines of de Gaulle's Memoirs (*'Toute ma vie je me suis fait une certaine idée de la France'*, De Gaulle 1954). And he not only stressed his own solitary decision-making, but linked it to apparent success (the US is mentioned here but almost as the junior partner): 'The pressure France exerted – not just France, the US – pressure that was sufficiently strong, convinced Russia, Putin, to act'. And note: '*C'est la fermeté montrée par la France dans cette affaire*' which led to the diplomatic response by Putin. The word 'firmness' was used in the original Ambassadors speech. It is as if the same firmness shown to Assad was the decisive factor with Putin also. He then went on, once again, as if he were the architect of the current events: 'What am I doing tomorrow? I will receive Foreign Minister Kerry ... and the British Foreign Minister, and Laurent Fabius. And we shall draw up the next Security Council resolution'. The reality was that he was simply ratifying the deal elaborated over that very weekend between Lavrov and Kerry in Geneva. At three points in the interview, he restated the idea that his original intention had the intended result: that the threat of attack was *in order* (*pour faire ... évoluer*) to effect a change in Russian diplomacy. All of Hollande's behaviour suggests that France was taken by surprise by the Russian initiative, just as it had been by Obama's decision to consult the US Congress.

Hollande then accentuated his personal centrality in a cascade of first person pronouns – I think, I wanted, I refuse, me, I want, I have to say, I understand, I have, myself ... and many more (*Je pense, J'ai voulu, Je m'y refuse, Moi, je veux, Je dois dire, Je les comprends, J'ai d'ailleurs, moi-même*). He ended his discussion of Syria (Syria took up the first half of the interview) with a claim to unfettered freedom of action and to wisdom, and an affirmation of the pretensions of the French Fifth Republic presidency: 'Me, I do not rely upon any country, whatsoever. Not for Mali, not for Syria; I commit France or I don't commit France when I consider that our essential interests are at stake' (*Moi je ne dépends pas de quelque pays que ce soit. Pas pour le Mali, pas pour la Syrie, j'engage la France ou je ne l'engage pas quand je considère que ce sont nos intérêts essentiels qui sont en cause*). At one level, this is a meaningless statement, partly because it is not true, partly because it counters his argument throughout the period that it was personal, moral outrage in the name of humanity that prompted him; but it is also one of the baldest statements of what the institution of the French presidency would have itself: Gaullist, unfettered, and quintessentially personal, and how belatedly and almost indiscriminately Hollande now performed his office-as-personal-prerogative in the most overt manner of the French presidency. In terms of the efficacy of his approach, after every public intervention François Hollande had made since he became President, his ratings fell. This interview was no exception. Within one year of election, Hollande had moved from a self-effacing, *impersonal* interpretation of the presidential function to an authoritative and temperamental display of near-narcissistic imperium.

While both the UK and the US sought legitimation through democracy, the French President was able to go to war upon his own initiative. As a consequence, France did not appear particularly democratic by comparison. The left-wing Socialist Leader of the House, Claude Bartolone, argued on 4 September against a parliamentary vote on the very Gaullist grounds that it would undermine the President's constitutional (arbitrary) authority – the Americans' royal treatment of Hollande on a state visit in February 2014 was a recognition of the potential value of such an ally. Not very 'normal', it is true; in fact, incongruously, the normal President was, in a very un-normal set of circumstances, 'performing' a far more belligerent – although arrested – and far more personalised leadership than any of his allies, and a personalisation that mirrored the public and personalised behaviour of Putin and Assad.

In an attempt to assert French authority, the authority of the French presidency was significantly damaged and the Fifth Republic altered because, ultimately, Hollande could not do what he wanted. This was in part because the French President acted before he knew what the Americans were doing (and in spite of the noise, the French had no intention of acting alone), in part because public confidence in Hollande was so low, and disapproval of his stance so widespread, that his legitimacy to act was questionable. This brings us back decisively to the issue of the personalisation of French politics and its dependence upon a highly emotional language that stresses morality more than it does international law. When President Hollande implied immediate action against Syria, he said it was to punish Assad for using chemical weapons. We can see here that foreign policy was being conducted as an emotional function of personal leadership in an attempt to enhance it.

In one sense, Hollande, not for the first time, was saved by the right which was, since Sarkozy's defeat, in total disarray (we shall make an analysis of the French right in the period we are studying at the end of this chapter). For the previous ten days, since the Ambassadors meeting, the right had been saying everything and its opposite about

Syria, and about the President's prerogatives, the spirit of the Fifth Republic, about the rights of parliament, and the role of the United Nations. No one, right or left, offered reflection or clarity, let alone leadership.

The French government waited for the Americans, and then for the UN chemical weapons inspectors' report, while showing the French public heart-breaking videos of suffering children (but which were not proof of who had launched the attacks) in order to justify an action that the French military were not, as we have said, actually taking (on 13 May 2014, Foreign Minister Fabius further stated that Syria had used chemical weapons a further 14 times since the September crisis). There was very little discussion of whether punishing Assad (whatever that meant) ran the risk of making the civil war in Syria worse and, as we have said, dragging Lebanon, Iran, the emerging 'Islamic State', and Israel into the conflict, alienating the Russians for decades, and having no forward planning if Assad fell, or if Assad did not. (And by mid-August the following year, because of the Jihadist threat in both Syria and Iraq, the notion of overthrowing Assad had itself become highly questionable).

The uncoordinated and confused international reaction to the appalling events in Syria created a potential dynamic for a major non-military initiative supported by nearly everyone. If France had led on that, it would have profited internationally. But in order to do this it would have needed a sensitivity to the overall situation – for example, possible cooperation with Russia to elaborate a solution – that the government lacked. We shall come back to this in more detail in our concluding chapter, but can note here that, by 2013, the Hollande presidency had not only become characterised by the frequent, often simultaneous, contrasting of the domestic and the international, and the use of the latter to enhance his leadership image (the many world and EU summits, Mali, Syria, later operation Sangaris in the Central African Republic in December 2013, Iraq/Syria in September 2014), presidential involvement and public 'display' in all areas of policy also meant that, and again with increasing frequency, the Hollande presidency became characterised by the contrasting clashing of the serious and the trivial. This would develop with growing repercussions upon the character and status of the President up until the crowning humiliation of the publication of Valérie Trierweiler's book in September 2014. The Syria crisis, although of major international importance, was a good illustration of this issue of presidential display.

A first domestic incident immediately following the Syria debacle was the 'Leonarda affair'. Having been refused permission to remain, the Dibrani family, Kosovan Roma, were being deported from France. On 9 October, 15-year-old Leonarda Dibrani was detained by the police while on a school trip, and the family deported. The ensuing national outcry, particularly by school students, soon involved several ministers and politicians taking positions, in particular the Interior Minister, Manuel Valls. Public opinion remained staunchly in favour of the expulsion (70%). After ten days, the President himself made a long-awaited announcement to say Leonarda could return to France but only her. This strange intervention (she was a minor) was followed the next morning by a chaotic and very prolonged interview (by a BFMTV team who had travelled to Kosovo) with several members of the family including Leonarda and her parents remonstrating with the President via the reporters and demanding he allow the whole family to return. The spectacle brought Hollande's image to new depths. A BVA poll carried out for *Le Parisien* in December saw 70% of respondents state that the President had no place in such details of domestic policy. The contrast between the President's omnipotent style in his 15 September interview with Claire Chazal, and his being directly harangued on national television by a 15-year-old and her family illustrated the disarray in the President's image.

In the same month, October (and they continued until March 2014), the *Bonnets rouges* protests began in Brittany (the *'bonnets'*, hats imitated those of seventeenth-century Breton tax protesters) against, initially, an 'ecotax' which would adversely affect long-distance transportation. The movement coalesced, bringing in political parties (of the left, right, extreme left, and extreme right – an extremely unusual phenomenon), trade unions, and business and various other organisations – into a full scale 'regionalist' protest with a manifesto of demands. On 30 November 2013, at a protest at Carhaix there were an estimated 40,000 protesters. The civil disobedience, rioting, demonstrations, and damage (in particular to ecotax scanners above and by the side of motorways all given wide media coverage) soon saw the ecotax proposal withdrawn.

As the end of the year 2013 approached, the date of Hollande's strange gamble regarding unemployment approached too. His claim that unemployment (*'la courbe du chômage'*) would fall by the end of 2013 had never been believed. In February 2013, 84% said they did not believe it would happen (Pingaud 2013, pp. 134–135), and it did not, but continued to rise through the month of December – the rise did in fact slow slightly then – and then climb just as dramatically right through 2014. In the summer of 2013 at La Roche-sur-Yon, Hollande was filmed being appealed to at length by a woman who was long-term unemployed. His non-committal 'we're here to find solutions' was shown again and again on television.

Beyond issues of the economy, the international situation, and more trivial or incidental issues, the new year of 2014 would see the dysfunctioning of the presidency in the full glare of the cameras as Hollande's private life erupted into the public domain.

Closergate

In January 2014, François Hollande very publicly joined a long tradition of French Fifth Republic Presidents who have had affairs. Widespread attachment to France's privacy laws, and a press corps that generally agrees with them, combined with a generalised reverence for the office of the presidency have meant that rumours always remained largely rumours – until 2014. On Friday 10 January 2014, *Closer Magazine* revealed, with several photographs, that François Hollande was having an affair with the actress Julie Gayet. In the past, gossip did no harm because there always was, and still is, a generally more indulgent attitude to affairs of the heart and tolerance of 'liaisons' by both men and women (especially men). There was also the conviction throughout French history that power is the strongest aphrodisiac both for those who exercise it and those fascinated by it.

The nearest Charles de Gaulle got to sexual scandal was a vague rumour about a woman he knew in La Comédie Française. Stories of sexual intrigue – probably secret service smears – surrounded the Pompidous. But Valéry Giscard d'Estaing set the tone, and he encouraged it, seeing himself as a true Don Juan (Giscard d'Estaing 1988, 1991, 2006). Rumours still abound of many liaisons – did he and the softcore star Sylvia Kristel have an affair in the Elysée? Who was the woman he was with in the Ferrari when, driving though Paris in the early hours, he hit a milk van? He even happily encouraged rumours about himself, for example, that a President just like him had an affair with a princess just like Diana (Giscard d'Estaing 2009). Mitterrand was also linked to many women, including the editor of *Elle Magazine*, Françoise Giroud, the singer Dalida, and many more. Rumour became fact when he revealed he had raised a second secret family, and a secret daughter Mazarine, at the state's expense. News of another son emerged in 2014. The tone changed from the stylish and romanesque to the testosterone-fuelled with Jacques Chirac, referred to by his chauffeur (and then the world) as 'Mr 15 minutes, shower included'. His highly popular and respected wife, Bernadette Chirac, started a sea-change in attitudes when, in her best-selling *Conversation* (Chirac 2001), she wrote touchingly and honestly about how painful that aspect of her marriage had been. Hollande's predecessor, Nicolas Sarkozy, reportedly had affairs with journalists, including, allegedly Chirac's daughter Claude, but his dalliances and his very public life with his second wife Cécilia Sarkozy and later Carla Bruni were seen more as the passions of a man with not just uncontrollable ambition, but an uncontrollable desire for attention, affection, and their public display.

Even with that history behind him there were six factors which made Hollande's alleged affair with Gayet, sadly comical and politically dangerous. First, was the sea-change mentioned earlier. Attitudes had shifted, not so much about sexual mores and the weaknesses of the flesh – in fact, with the decline in religious observance, things are even more liberal. But cheating on your wife or partner, with intensity and frequency is seen – even in France – as sexist and the sign of a patriarchal society of inequality and disrespect. And sending his partner, Valérie Trierweiler, into hospital in a state of nervous collapse – which is what happened after the *Closer* revelations – was not seen as the act of a man of integrity (there were even rumours and a widespread public suspicion of a suicide attempt). Second, Hollande was elected in part because the French were tired of these celebrity scandals. He was 'Mr Normal' who was going to bring exemplary conduct to political life, and stop all the tabloid press gossip lowering the status of the presidency. He had said so himself. But his somewhat tortured relationships with former presidential candidate, Ségolène Royal, Valérie Trierweiler, and then Julie Gayet were never out of the headlines. Third, there was something comical and diminishing of the presidency in his slipping out not in a Ferrari but on the back of a scooter (driven by his chauffeur who also brought the croissants – you could not make this up), the easy victim of *Closer* paparazzo, Sébastien Valiela, waiting, camera at the ready, across the street. This too raises the question of the 'received grammar' of these affairs and the way they are depicted (e.g. Giscard, Kennedy, as opposed to Hollande) adding notions of ridicule. Fourth, there was the question of security. Why did he need bodyguards all around him in public when he took such risks in private? Fifth, even before this incident, he was the most unpopular President of the Fifth Republic to date. The sneaking out (this is how it appeared in Valiela's photos) was taking place at exactly the time that Hollande was taking the dangerous and unpopular decision to attack Syria. Sixth, the French had been subjected, perhaps the appropriate word given Valérie Trierweiler's widespread unpopularity (67% disapproval) – to a very high-profile First Lady; no presidential partner had had such a high profile, and whose relationship to the media had been so compulsive. Apart from the imposed silence after the tweet, she accompanied the President on virtually all of his engagements. After 18 months in office, the relationship publicly collapsed overnight. And her unpopularity remained at around 70% from then on. The sense of a continuing soap opera was the damaging consequence.

French commentators in the political class and the media, although obsessed with the scandal, caught up with the deeper political significance of all these things very slowly. There was real cognitive dissonance on their part regarding what was at stake here because the President does not have a private life like everyone else. He is the President. We shall come back to this point below and in the Conclusion. One might also say that when things are going well, the 'private life' of political figures is deliberately on display for all to see. That is how the French presidency thrives. Before his first press conference after the scandal broke which, for once, everybody watched, he had three choices regarding this very public affair: say something before, say something during, or say nothing. Each would be consequential in its effects. To the inevitable question, he chose the last, almost, saying (although bizarrely bowing his head while being asked) he would not answer questions on issues of his private life, but would respond in the coming days, before he and Valérie were scheduled for a state visit to the US, and the Obamas, in mid-February. All the commentators and the political class began to talk about redefining the status of the French First Lady who, constitutionally, has none at all. Politics would have been far better served if, rather than redefine the role and status of the First Lady, France had reflected upon the role and status of the presidency itself.

What does this titillating story in a gossip magazine tell us about the nature of presidential politics in France? One of the striking things about French reaction – probably unique among Western democracies – was that, at first, the political class, from Marine le Pen on the far-right, right across the political spectrum, with only one or two dissenting voices, claimed that this was about Hollande's private life and was not a political issue; and second, this was reflected in public opinion – the overwhelming majority of respondents on television, radio, and in public opinion polls (e.g. the *Journal du Dimanche*, 12 January) agreed that this was a private affair and Hollande had the same well-protected rights to privacy as any other French citizen. This was all framed, moreover, in a considerably more liberal-minded attitude to extra-marital affairs (although Hollande was not married to France's First Lady, Valérie Trierweiler – nor had he been to his long-time partner, Ségolène Royal). Hollande, however, was not 'any other' French citizen, and the affair undermined further the authority of the President, and even the legitimacy of the Republic, and this too for six reasons.

First, the indulgence accorded by the political class and public opinion to private life contrasted with the fact that France is the country where politicians and everybody else's private lives are the constant stuff of conversation, rumour, hearsay, and now, with the Web's relentless 24-hour scrutiny and discussion, minute, detailed attention. One only needs to mention the thousands of social media 'reactions' to the newspaper and blog reports on Trierweiler's admission to hospital on Friday 10 January 2014 to see how 'uninterested' the French were. In fact, a lot of people, particularly in showbiz and the media, already knew about Hollande and Gayet, hence, in fact, the *Closer* paparazzo's all-night diligence and patience over the road from Ms Gayet's flat – lent to her by a friend – just round the corner from the Elysée Palace. Second, another *Journal du Dimanche* poll of 12 January also claimed that 84% of the French had not changed their opinion of Hollande after the *Closer* revelations. This begs many questions, and probably tells us more about public attitudes to him than to dalliance. The President and his team took heart from these two polls. They were wrong to do so. Hollande was already so unpopular (down to a legitimacy-threatening 15% in some polls, 20% in most), an 84% no change response suggests a President who filled popular sentiment with utter indifference rather than approval or indulgence. Third, regarding the poll about his life being his private affair, it really depends upon what is meant by private life. The French presidency is already a very public, private life. The Hollande-Trierweiler couple, even more than the Sarkozy-Bruni couple, had been the highest profile presidential relationship the Fifth Republic had seen. Given the personalised nature of French politics, and especially of the French presidency, this incident would have a series of incremental, related, and over time, profound effects upon all those concerned, and even perhaps upon the French Republic itself. We shall come back to this crucial aspect of Closergate in the Conclusion. Fourth, there was the moral question of probity, for there was immediately a series of questions taken forward by journalists and politicians: was any public money involved in any of this? Whose flat exactly was it (and there were rumours there was a mafia connection)? And if he, as was suggested, was no longer in a relationship with Trierweiler, possibly for some time, this raised the question of her office in the Elysée and assistants, and her accompanying him on his official visits etc.. What was he doing getting the world to accept that although not married Valérie Trierweiler should have the status of a Michelle Obama; and what did Michelle Obama think of having to meet as an equal on the world stage just the latest of Hollande's girlfriends and, as it turned out, not even the latest (in the end, he went to Washington unaccompanied). What did the Catholic community in France and elsewhere think of Valérie and François being presented in February 2014 to the excessively admired other François, the Pope, who had agreed to make an exception to Vatican protocol in the French President's case (once again, President Hollande was eventually presented alone here too, and it is clear that the Pope did not seem inordinately pleased to see him). Fifth, there was the sense of vaudeville created by the whole affair. This was not Anna Karenin and Count Vronsky, not Leslie Howard and Celia Johnson. Hollande unfortunately looked more like one's friendly local family butcher – albeit surrounded by a plethora of frankly attractive women, which lent the whole issue the quality of a Feydeau farce. And the *Closer* pictures of Hollande arriving for his trysts on the back of a scooter disguised by his crash helmet lent an inspector Clouseau quality to the affair. And finally, there was the question of his real motivations. From a psychoanalytic point of view, this affair suggests the classic case of an unconscious desire to be found out, for reasons a psychoanalyst and his/her patient might know, but which the observer might wonder about. What might be the implications of such unconscious desire for Hollande's relationship to his own presidency? Behind the vaudeville depiction of a Feydeau character – bringing out all the clichés of over-excitable bourgeois French men – lay a more serious psychological issue regarding the President's motivations. Not his sexual motivations, but the psychic need to, as it were, be discovered – for such recklessness begs the question of the intention of discovery by a man who cannot 'face up to' his relationships not just with women, but perhaps even his presidency. An alternative or further problematic dimension is that the affair depicted a public man who thought –

against the office? – that he had a clear right to not one private life but several.

But the real issue, and the real interest here, was what 'Closergate' revealed about the French Fifth Republic and its dysfunctional mixing of the practical and the symbolic at the summit of power. Hollande was constitutionally the Head of State, but practically also the Head of Government. And one of the ways this strange office functions – unknown elsewhere in democracies, including the United States – is through the deployment of the 'character' of François Hollande, a character who came to power as we have seen as a straightforward, discreet, Mr Normal who would put an end to the look-at-me! attention-seeking, Nicolas Sarkozy. Hollande seemed, however, to have brought no more dignity to this highly-charged personalised and symbolic office than he accused Sarkozy of having squandered, and an equal or greater degree of media exposure of his relationship with Trierweiler. The French presidency became a malfunctioning version of the 'King's Two Bodies', one transcendent, one mortal (Manow 2010). The general evolution of the French presidency – since 1958, an institution popular with and revered by the French – had in the recent past, in part through developments in '*peopolisation*' since circa 2000, while heightening the role and frequency of 'performance' of the presidency, begun to drag the sacred towards the profane. Hollande, in fact, accelerated the trend. This would have major effects upon Hollande's already dwindling authority, and perhaps even the legitimacy of the republic, and draw him further and further away from his own intended aim of presidential distance from 'short-term' politics. And the publication of Trierweiler's book *Merci pour ce moment* in September 2014 (Trierweiler 2014) had a devastating effect upon Hollande's reputation, as (her version of) his private character was made very public, particularly this moment in January 2014, the Closergate issue and its aftermath. We shall return to this at the end of this chapter.

The Municipal elections and the Valls government

Rarely do local elections anywhere have such profound national resonance as in France. In the Municipal elections on 23 and 30 March 2014, France's governing Socialist Party (PS) lost more than 150 towns and cities. In terms of personnel this meant the loss of 35,000 local councillors and 5,000 advisors. The centre-right UMP made huge gains, much more than expected.

Members of President François Hollande's party had thought in the run-up to the elections that they might limit the damage, given that local politics is often very different from national politics, and France has a long and deep tradition of a 'Municipal Socialism' historically insulated from national concerns. Such hopes were misplaced. Town hall after town hall the left had held for decades went to the opposition, and a dozen of them to the far-right Front National. Out of 36,000 communes, this was not decisive in real terms, but its symbolic value was great. The local elections saw a Blue Wave (*Vague Bleue*) for the centre-right, but also a Navy Blue Wave, the '*Vague Bleue Marine*' – a pun on Marine le Pen of the Front National – whose party won 1,500 councillors in an advance, perhaps not as historic but more symbolic in its own way than the centre-right's. In Hénin-Beaumont, the FN even won outright on the first round. In some places, round two run-offs between rival lists saw no leftist lists on the ballot at all, just UMP, FN, and independent right (*divers droites*), as if anything left-of-centre did not exist. Limoges, a Socialist stronghold since 1912, was lost to the right. Many towns run by the left for 70 years since World War II were lost as well. The scale of the Socialists' defeat was historic – and a humiliating personal defeat for the President, two years into his five-year term. To everyone's surprise, not least the UMP's, in the Municipal elections of 23 and 30 March 2014, the UMP did extremely well. This was in part because they were indeed the mainstream opposition, in part because they had a real and often sound and respectable local presence. It was also because of the collapse of the Socialist vote either through defection (to the far left, right or extreme right) or through – and this was decisive – abstention. The Socialists were in a state of shocked disbelief – and widespread recriminations and in-fighting at local level, such as Marseille, made matters even worse.

In an attempt to salvage the situation, the deeply unpopular President took drastic action. On Monday 31 March, he sacked his Prime Minister, Jean-Marc Ayrault, and in his place appointed the most popular minister in the government, the former Interior Minister, Manuel Valls. In opinion polls Valls was the most popular figure from the left. He was a popular figure among right voters too. His style was what people wanted: tough and decisive on crime and security, and well to the right in his party on virtually everything else. One of his problems was therefore to manage the left of the party. Two appointments to his new cabinet, Benoît Hamon and Arnaud Montebourg, should be seen in this light. Both of these represented the left of the Party. Hollande's ex-partner, former presidential candidate Ségolène

Royal, was also back in government. We can make two remarks here. First, the appointment of Hamon and Montebourg only had a limited effect upon controlling the left of the party in the Assembly, 41 of whom failed to endorse Valls' reforms package, a development which would immediately undermine the new Prime Minister, particularly in the myriad of negotiations which would take place throughout 2014 in the run-up to and the passing of the Budget in November 2014. The sudden resignation of this new government in September, which we shall come back to below, would complicate the situation. The second, concerning Ségolène Royal, was seen as welcome – she was an experienced minister from the Bérégovoy and Jospin governments; but her two-year delay from office threw into relief how Hollande had been personally influenced by Valérie Trierweiler, i.e. unable to mobilise Royal's skills until he had split from Trierweiler (Degois 2014).

The tasks were clear: balance the books and get public spending down, make French businesses more competitive, and reinvigorate the Franco-German alliance and France's leadership role in Europe. The main issue, however, was to find 50 billion euros of cuts in government spending, and this last would add to the growing rift within the PS. These things would have been better addressed two years earlier when Hollande was elected. In 2014, unemployment was still rising (up by more than 30,000 in February 2014), the deficit was not going down, and national debt was now 93% of GDP. After two years of virtually no change, apart from tax rises and spending cuts, the economic tasks facing the new government were immense. But perhaps more than anything, Valls had to change the culture and attitudes of the French if reforms were truly to take place; he had to offer a kind of leadership that would rally support that his own President had failed to do. This raises questions about the fundamentals of leadership in the Fifth Republic. Valls heralded a fundamental change in French politics. Seemingly without the French having realised it, the events of April 2014, the local elections, and the appointment of Manuel Valls as Prime Minister, turned the Fifth Republic on its head. The Prime Minister is meant to be a lightning rod, protecting and enhancing the prestige of the President by taking the criticism and unpopularity directed at his government. This has been the case from 1958 up until 2014 (Pompidou 1974). The problem was that Valls was much more popular than Hollande (20% to 60% in April and May 2014 and had been nominated for that reason); if his policies were a success, Hollande would therefore not profit from them. All the applause would be for Valls, and he would soon look more presidential than his

President boss. If he did not succeed, both men would be regarded as failures. In appointing Valls, Hollande played his Joker (and earlier than he would have liked, as following on from the Municipal elections were the European elections in May 2014); but the significance of such a move had profound implications for the nature of the Fifth Republic itself. In the event, the collapsing popularity of the President in September 2014, started seriously to impact upon the new Prime Minister's popularity; worse than this, Valls failed to act as a buffer against the President's popularity which – after a brief reprieve – continued to fall, and the continuing, seemingly interminable, lapse between proposals and action militated against Valls' own popularity. The Responsibility Pact, proposed in January 2014, was the only major proposal given to Valls to push through; and this would have to be incorporated into the budget proposals which – if passed – would not come into force until a year later. By the *rentrée* of 2014, it was clear that Valls was trying to address the situation, in particular his relationship to the scale of reforms required and his longer-term strategy vis-à-vis the PS and its further reform along more social-democratic lines. These initiatives – in view of 2017 or even perhaps 2022 – eclipsed Hollande from the political centre of gravity, an unprecedented event outside periods of 'cohabitation'.

The European elections and the victory of the Front National

The European elections of May 2014 are interesting from our perspective as they capture the state of party politics and public attitudes at this two-year anniversary of the Hollande presidency. They also mark the beginning of a descent towards presidential legitimacy collapse. They were also interesting, perhaps because rather than in spite of their second-order status, in that their symbolic significance was heightened. Because of proportional representation and all the parties representing themselves without alliances, the Euro elections – and the abstentions – capture the state of French politics at this moment of near-political crisis.

There are seven metropolitan regions in France: Ile de France (Paris), North West, West, South West, Centre, South East, East, and one overseas constituency. There were 74 seats to be had (of which the Ile de France which includes Paris has 15 seats, two extra since the last European election in 2009). There were on an average 24 lists per region (Paris had 31), that is 193 in total. This large number reflected the sense of a country in complete flux.

60% of the lists were not from the main parties. There was, for example, Nouvelle donne (New Deal) (*divers gauche*), Féministes pour une Europe Solidaire, le Parti Pirate (for transparency), Europe Citoyenne (Corinne Lepage), Force Vie (Christine Boutin), The Esperanto Party, Cannabis sans frontières and many more, the vast majority of which no one had ever heard of. The polls were equally confusing. 56% of the French were against France giving up the euro (26% for); 44% for continuing EU membership (23% against); although 60% said they were interested in the European elections (with, however, only 35% at the time of the poll intending to vote). There was more poll interest than in 2009 (where turnout, however, was 41%). Since 1979, the decline had been steadily downwards from 61% (apart from an upward +3% blip in 1989). In the weeks before the election, polls gave: Front National 20+%, UMP 20+%, PS 17+%, Alternative (The Centre) 10%, EELV (Greens) 9%, and the Front de Gauche 6%. European elections in France – as elsewhere in the main – are driven by 'national' considerations/attitudes to government. There are two points to note in the case of the 2014 French elections. First, they were national, but in a very negative way. Abstention rates reflected in great part disapproval of national politics rather than indifference to Europe. Second, and paradoxically, they were 'European' in a very anti-European way. As a result, 2014 saw the dramatic rise of the far-right. And this against the background of the developing disapproval/decline in support for the EU, particularly since the '*Non*' in the 2005 Referendum on the Euro Constitution. The 'populist' Front National vote, moreover, also reflected a growing hostility to the legitimacy of the EU itself.

A first point to note is that although the FN was tapping anti-European sentiment, the elections were quintessentially about national politics, and especially about a growing hostility to the political system itself. As regards the national saliency of the FN, we should mention here the unusual pertaining conditions of the French case, in particular the role of the presidential election in the FN's fortunes. In 2002, Jean-Marie Le Pen went through to round two of the presidential election, to everyone's surprise including his own; but after that its fortunes waned. In 2012, however, the new leader, his daughter, Marine Le Pen reached 18% in round one. By 2014, talk began of her possibly going through to round two in 2017. The FN's campaign in the European elections of 2014 should be seen in this light.

As a politico-social phenomenon, most of the FN's support, particularly as regards Europe, were the *laissés pour compte/exclus* of 'Europe', those who felt they had 'lost out' in the process of modernisation/globalisation. The voting map for the FN historically ran across the periphery of the country across the north, down the eastern border, and around along the Mediterranean coast, i.e. it 'captured' a France that was marginal, worried, 'left behind' and seeking leadership and direction. It was, therefore, a very virulent – and disorientated – constituency, reflecting in part a whole country that was disorientated. In 2014 the FN vote increased dramatically across all France's regions. In four of the seven metropolitan regions it came first, and second in the remaining three (in the 'Overseas' region the FN came fourth). Over and above Europe, the election was about the unpopularity of François Hollande and his government; so one characteristic of these elections was that *neither* Europe nor the French executive had ever been as unpopular as they were in 2014. In a CSA poll for BFMTV on 8 May 2014, 51% of respondents said they were worried about Europe ('*inquiets*') and a further 10% were hostile (only 20% said they were happy with the EU). And as for the President, he was clearly the target of respondents' discontent. On Tuesday 6 May, in a renewed effort to increase his ratings, the President gave a one-hour interview on BFMTV and RMC Radio (8.30 am, with J.-J. Bourdin). The following day, in a poll about his credibility on the programme, and whether the changes he claimed were happening, 79% of respondents were unconvinced. And although he subsequently talked about Europe, and that to leave Europe would be 'to leave History' (8 May, the commemoration of WWII), with Bourdin he did not actually mention Europe, reflecting a deeply divided Socialist Party on the issue, and a pro-European undertaking that in rhetorical terms was half-hearted. It is perhaps worth stressing here that abstentions in the European elections reflected this duality: abstention reflected negative attitudes both to Europe and to domestic politics (just over 40% voted (slightly up on 2009), and 58% of Hollande's 2012 vote abstained). We should also note that – as was demonstrated by Hollande's lack of reference to Europe – for the pro-Europeans, there was virtually no one to vote for, no one who spoke clearly to and for them – the only truly pro-Europeans were the Greens and the Centrists, with barely a 15+% constituency between them. Before looking at each of the main parties, let us make several contextual points about the 2014 European election campaign.

First, it began to inform the national scene/political space only from the end of April 2014. Before, it almost only existed in News TV/

discussion programmes. These latter began to focus more specifically from about 15 May, i.e. ten days before the elections, and the main thrust of their interest was in the popularity of the FN and the sense of approaching doom in the PS. Second, as we have mentioned, the immediate context was the Municipal elections of 23/30 March 2014, i.e. less than one month before, where the UMP did well, as did the FN, and the governing PS did historically badly, ending overnight – after two years of Hollande's presidency – almost a century of deep-rooted Municipal Socialism. Third, the campaign had some theatricality, e.g. a street Femen demonstration (agit-prop almost) 'Fascist Epidemic' against the FN in Paris (22 April). This received wide media coverage, and was more like a Kurt Weil production than a political demonstration. And there were all the publicity stunts of all the bizarre parties we have mentioned. Fourth, unlike in, say, the German or UK cases, there was much more in-fighting in the French parties, a lot of it from 'barons' who had lost their National Assembly seats in 2012 or in the Municipals in 2014. This meant that there was not really a class of respected and experienced MEPs as there is elsewhere. In France, MEP places – and their salaries – are often used as political rewards for major party politicians who have lost their seats in the National Assembly. Fifth, the backdrop to some of the in-fighting was the huge dismay and disaffection with politicians amongst the public, which saw parts of the party – fearful for their seats if they had them – begin calls for changes to policy. This was arguably more profound in France than elsewhere apart perhaps from Greece. Sixth, in part a consequence of this, was the dramatic rise in populist rhetoric about corruption and retribution (*'tous pourris'*, *'sortez les sortants'*) that accompanied this election. These elections, perhaps more than any European elections before in France, were a referendum on the President and the government, so that the elections' negative thrust would be dramatically amplified by the proportional representation system. Seventh, as we have mentioned, the 2014 European elections, were like the end of a cycle, not simply that of the 2009–14 Euro elections cycle, but also like the end of a cycle of the Hollande presidency (half way through and touching bottom); the Municipals rout, the change of government and Prime Minister forced upon the President, and the Euro elections acted as a kind of trio of defeats whereby the Hollande presidency had nowhere to go but up; from now, the 2017 presidential election campaign began, but it was no longer certain whether Hollande would even be a candidate. Finally, the European elections threw into high relief the France/Germany problem that the French left in power had exacerbated. J.-C. Junker, the former Luxembourg Prime Minister and contender for the presidency of the European Commission, called for a revival of the Franco-German entente. In one poll at the time, 80% of Germans were happy with their economy/economic performance. This was a staggering contrast with France (20% happy with the EU). But the European elections point to a more sinister aspect of French politics which saw, since 2012, the rise of anti-German feeling throughout 2013. And such attacks came mainly from within the PS, from such figures as Bartolone, Montebourg, even Hollande; the PS likened Merkel to Bismarck, and referred to her 'selfish stubbornness' (*intransigeance égoiste*) (Fr24 TV, 27 April 2013). Hollande's being invited to stay with Angela Markel in her constituency of Stralsund in early May should be seen in this light: an attempt to get the French to take Europe and leadership within it seriously. Let us look at the fortunes of the main parties as the campaign began.

It is true that the rise of right-wing populism was a Europe-wide phenomenon. So from the continental perspective, the French FN was part of a wider phenomenon. In the European Parliament (EP) itself, however, this continent-wide phenomenon was problematic. There were no electoral/manifesto alliances between far-right parties. In order to form an advantageous parliamentary group in the EP, parties need representation from seven countries and 25 MEPs. Given national and ideological differences between these groups, they could not cohere as well as they might; there was still the possibility, however, that the parliamentary groups well to the right of the spectrum could be formed in the aftermath of the elections, giving Marine Le Pen both status and publicity. Over and above everything else, however, the FN should be seen in the context of PS/UMP having no voice or narrative and, in fact, great inconsistency on Europe. Part of the FN's success at the rhetorical level was that there were no pro-Europeans driving the 'pro'-narrative.

Less than two months before the European elections in May 2014, as we have seen, the UMP won an unexpected victory at the Municipal elections. This offered them a boost for the European election campaign itself. They were hoping for a similar '*Vague bleue*'. The success had been partly 'accidental', given the huge abstention of traditionally leftist supporters. The local election successes masked total disarray at the top of the party, in terms of both its leadership and its attitude to Europe. The party was also in a deep financial crisis that would come to a head soon after and see the resignation of the leader J.-F. Copé. The fundamentally problematic issue regarding the UMP in the

European campaign and in the future was its schizophrenic attitude towards Europe (cf. Sarkozy's anti-Europeanism during the 2012 election campaign). This was highly problematic for both the party's direction and policies, as it meant the party had no clear 'voice' let alone a persuasive attractive one. Coming first rather than second to the FN would give the party a major boost. There was a constant problem for the UMP, however, who often lose 10% of their (potential) electorate to the FN and another 10% to the Centre (UDI or Modem) in major elections, and this even more so in a one-round proportional ballot. For the Socialist Party, however, the European elections were a test of Hollande's legitimacy. There had been very little preparation for the European elections. This was accompanied by a sense of dread after the Municipal results and Hollande's unpopularity. The results for both parties were even worse than anticipated. The FN gained 25% of the vote, the UMP 21%, and the PS less than 14%, its lowest ever score.

Like the UMP, the PS did not help its own image with a near-schizophrenic attitude to Europe (and for 'Europe' in places read 'Germany'). We outlined above some of the examples of this anti-German feeling, which contrasted almost comically with Hollande's 8 May declaration to the press near the Arc de Triomphe (there was also a published article in *Le Monde* using same expression, and in a TV interview the Prime Minister also used the expression): that 'to leave Europe is to leave History'. This was, moreover, a provocative declaration given its lack of detail, and the lack of clear commitment to 'Europe' and the EU since 2012. The non-recognition of the issues now pertaining to disaffection within Europe was one of the reasons for disaffection increasing, and this in the context of a widespread sense of Europe's distance from the lives of ordinary people. As regards Germany, there was another issue of even more importance in the European arena. France not only allowed anti-German feeling to develop, but France (and the left particularly) allowed (a reluctant) Germany to become the leader of Europe, and – in its own way – the exemplars of the European project. This severely limited Hollande's political scope for manoeuvre in European policy both then and subsequently through 2014. France's gradual loss of its leadership role in Europe had been happening for a decade but it crystallised at the start of the Hollande presidency and was compounded by rhetorical inconsistency vis-à-vis both Germany and Europe.

The Hollande presidency was now caught in a contradiction of its own making: calling upon the EU to encourage economic growth at the moment it was cutting 50 billion euros from national spending added a sense of absurdity to the French and PS position. It was clear that structural reforms should have been made two years before, before urging Germany to lead growth (cf. Hollande's visit to Merkel the day of his inauguration). 40% of those polled named their dissatisfaction with François Hollande as being the reason for their European vote in May 2014 and/or abstention.

The left in government, when not attacking Europe and Germany, attacked the populism its own rhetoric was encouraging. Manuel Valls both as Minister of the Interior and, from April 2014 as Prime Minister, spent an inordinate amount of time attacking the FN, arguably evidence of the vacuousness of the governing party's real contribution to the European debate. The real threat posed by the far-right, of course, was not its role in the European Parliament, but its impact on domestic politics. Earthquake metaphors, both political and journalistic, had strong currency in the aftermath of May's elections. The most spectacular tremors were those caused by the British and French far-right. Each came first in their national competition, with both gaining a quarter of the national vote. The historical significance of the hitherto insignificant United Kingdom Independence Party (UKIP) was an unprecedented political event – knocking Labour and the governing Conservatives into second and third place respectively (the Liberal Democrats, a partner in the UK governing coalition, were near-annihilated). In France, Marine Le Pen's *'Vague Bleue Marine'* Front National humiliated the centre-right Union for a Popular Movement (UMP) opposition and even more so the ruling Socialists.

Alongside UKIP and the Front National, there were a score of far-right parties who gained seats. Taken together, the 'populist' anti-Europeans took around 140 seats (out of a total of 751). Not all the 'populists' were right wing; populists on the far-left such as Syriza (Greece) and Podemos (Spain) did well (and, in fact, these two parties were not anti-European in many ways). 'Europe' thought the far-right would storm all the gates from every direction. In reality, it was only UKIP and the FN that made significant breaches. As regards Europe itself, the focus of all the worry over these elections was misplaced. The EP has little in terms of parliamentary threats to worry about with the arrival of 140 or so populist anti-Europeans who had nothing coherent to propose, and could barely stop their groups let alone their parties in the EP from falling apart. The real danger lay not here but at the national level. Both the main French political parties were being undermined, because of their own poor rhetoric; their ambivalent discourse on Europe and immigration, for example, simply encouraged the populist vote. The real political consequence of Le Pen's success was its effects upon symbolic politics in France. Her success, therefore, clearly contributed to the collapse of François Hollande's legitimacy. The European elections demonstrated, moreover, that the Front National was now a well-established party at national and local level. Since Marine Le Pen took over the party from her father in 2011, this was her and her team's main effort: to implant the party organisation throughout the country. In the French case, however, we should bear in mind that 25% of 40% meant that only 10% or so of the electorate had voted FN. The real enemies were abstention and indifference – just under 60%.

The summer of 2014

In France, after the European elections of May 2014, and Marine Le Pen's 25% of the vote – to the ruling Socialists' paltry 13.8% – she said very little. She did not need to; between them, the left and the right had opened up a royal road, and one that might now take her through to the second round of the presidential elections in 2017. The new Prime Minister, Manuel Valls, also found his party and parliamentary majority in danger of rebellion. At the moment he and President Hollande began to confront the real issues, the President had become an electoral liability. Also, Hollande was clearly, after two years of doing very little, trying to push Valls towards a reformist agenda, to cut the massive public debt and state spending, and stimulate business, so that business in turn would stimulate the economy. For the left of the party, both were now social democrats at best, social liberals at worst. And yet it is arguable that few of the intended reforms would be adequate to the economic and social challenges ahead. Very little could happen before the detailed budget discussions in November 2014. The government was looking for savings of at least 50 billion euros (a huge amount, yet still regarded as quite inadequate to recovery by most economists), 30 billion of which no one had an accurate idea where it was to come from. In order to fend off its own left, and the unions, and placate its disintegrating constituency, every 'reformist' measure was countered by exceptions, special cases, and special summits between the 'social partners' whose political purpose is similar to Royal Commissions in the UK, to put off any decisive, immediate decisions. Across most of Europe, the economic recovery was fragile; in France, the world's recently fifth, now possibly sixth largest economy, it was virtually non-existent during 2014. And unemployment, at over 10%, was still rocketing.

The summer of 2014 saw the end-point of two particular approaches by Hollande to government and the presidency that had lasted since May 2012: the first, Year I, a more relaxed, normal, anti-Sarkozy style (and the growing sense that it was not working), the second, Year II, an escalating desperation to correct the situation. The *rentrée* of 2014 did not mark a new departure in policy – indeed in a *Le Monde* interview in late August (*Le Monde* 21/8/14) Hollande restated that the policies undertaken would remain (essentially the *pacte de responsabilité* which had still not become law). This was arguably a poor rhetorical and symbolic device: changing Prime Minister in order to do what he had charged his first Prime Minister to do. This questionable steady-as-she-goes approach was seconded by his new Prime Minister, Manuel Valls (and contradicted, predictably by the ever-contestatory Economy Minister, Arnaud Montebourg on 24 August, who called for reflation and growth and precipitated the resignation of the new Valls government). By October 2014, the Employment Minister, François Rebsamen, admitted that the government's policy on unemployment had been a failure. Hollande had made this in his Jean-Jacques Bourdin interview his only priority. What had changed was the sense that everything had gone wrong and the regime itself was now to face a period in which the legitimacy of the President was virtually non-existent, and the President and his government and even the regime were now insecure. In one sense, even the appointment of Valls was a double admission of failure in that he was simply being asked to do what the government appointed two years earlier (of which he was a member) had failed to do.

The right

One of the most remarkable things about the first two and a half years of Hollande's presidency and the aimlessness of his government was the failure of the opposition right to profit from it. This failure tells us a great deal about the nature of the Fifth Republic and bears out our theoretical framework which we shall return to in the next chapter. The right made gains in all by-elections and in the local elections, but the same drivers of the Fifth Republic that were undermining the President and government were undermining the right as well.

In the aftermath of Nicolas Sarkozy's defeat in 2012 and the resignation of his government and the election of a Socialist parliamentary majority to the National Assembly, the right went into opposition, and the ex-President into an apparent – because self-proclaimed – retirement. Sarkozy had said during the campaign that if he lost the presidency he would leave politics for good – an unnecessary hostage to fortune which brought him no advantage, partly because such claims suggested petulance rather than magnanimity; – when de Gaulle said such – if I lose I shall leave – everyone believed him, and it was true (Malraux 1971). Sarkozy's absence meant that the UMP was leaderless. The leader of the party, Jean-François Copé, remained party leader – and saw himself as leader until 2017, and the party's next presidential candidate. Copé, however, rather like Hollande as PS leader when Jospin was Prime Minister (1997–2002), was seen as an administrative leader, a general secretary, rather than an inspirational one. In November 2012, François Fillon, Sarkozy's Prime Minister throughout his presidency, made a bid for the leadership of the party – also with a view to becoming the party's presidential leader. He was an experienced and quite popular Prime Minister, and a figure who might arguably unite the two 'wings' of the party (he having come from the 'social' wing of Gaullism).

The subsequent competition for the leadership of the UMP, however, took up months and saw the party almost wrought asunder. Moreover, it was a competition which was inconclusive, the leadership election itself raising many accusations of fraud. In order to stop the public spectacle of an opposition party in near-civil war, a compromise was reached whereby Copé would keep the leadership, Fillon's team would join the leadership team, and primaries would be held later to determine the party's presidential candidate. Fillon's own popularity – greater than Copé's – fell significantly, so that the expected party and party leadership renewal did not take place. All of this was a mirror of the PS' internal warfare of the 2000s, with a similar lack of policy reflection and renewal, prima donna displays of would-be leaders, and the overall decline of the party in terms of both votes and membership.

Ideologically, the right is more *'disponible'* to the cult of the leader, and the UMP in its Gaullist origins a personalised rally rather than a party like the PS. Nevertheless, the mythical idea, as it were, underpinning the UMP – a rally that grows and grows, like audience applause, until the 'star' must return to the stage for an encore – was ill-suited in the aftermath of Hollande's victory, given that it had recently been ousted from government, and Sarkozy the 'natural' leader had been defeated. The party was now expending all of its energy in a 'non-rally' leadership struggle, and all this in front of the cameras. From Sarkozy's presidential defeat in 2012, the right bickered over leadership issues, while now waiting to see if Sarkozy would make a comeback (making leadership renewal and party direction impossible). From June 2014, however, the situation deteriorated to near-collapse. Three tsunamis hit the party. The first was financial. The party suddenly found it had an inexplicable 80 million euro deficit. A first remark to make is that, if the UMP could not manage its own finances, it seemed unlikely the French would consider it fit to manage the country any better than the incompetent Socialists. Public confidence in the whole political class, therefore, teetered on the edge of collapse.

The second tsunami to hit the UMP was made up of all the scandals that hit the headlines within and around the party in the course of 2014. A lot of the party debt appeared to have come from massive overcharging by a private company, Bygmalion – the French have a hopelessly unfunny compulsion for anglicised puns – used by the party leader J.-F. Copé (and run by close friends of his) for events, campaigns, and so on, particularly for services rendered during the Sarkozy campaign of 2012. Some of Copé's team or the Bygmalion agency were suspected of double invoicing and false accounting, to the tune of about 20 million euros. Copé was also accused of paying four of his assistants 10,000 euros each per month, and this in a party that made an appeal in 2013 to the membership to help pay a 10,000,000 euros 'fine' (non-reimbursement of campaign funds by the state) imposed for what was thought in 2013 to be overspending on the 2012 presidential campaign of a few hundred thousand euros. The party membership raised the money and paid the fine, but in the wake of the party scandal began to leave the party in droves. Because of the Bygmalion scandal, Copé resigned as leader in June 2014, and a triumvirate of former Prime Ministers (Raffarin, Juppé, and Fillon) became caretaker leaders who ordered an inquiry into party finances. Before the inquiry reported, however, the accusations of financial mismanagement, corruption even, rained down on Copé regarding, for example, excessive travel expenses claims for his wife and others. The former Justice Minister and 'Sarkozyiste', Rachida Dati was accused of charging the party 10,000 euros for her annual phone bill, and 13,000 for travel. The fact that she was a supporter of former President Sarkozy said a great deal, because the triumvirate, whose task was to bring probity, was also trying to block Sarkozy's return.

Alongside this set of revelations, came news of further mis-doings. Copé, for example, was reported as paying his wife 5,000 euros pcm, half of his research and administrative allowance allocated by the National Assembly. A hundred MPs were similarly paying family members. More revelations of this type appeared each day. The UK expenses scandal and the public disillusion in its aftermath was nothing now to the generalised and deep disdain the French public had for the whole political class. It is generally held as being true that this corruption is not confined to the right. The Socialist René Dosière (*Le Point* 30/10/14) highlighted the government's own mis-use of financial favours. For example, each government ministry had around fifteen advisors; most of them on average monthly salaries of 12,000 euros. Nine million French people live on less than 1,000 euros per month.

The main scandals, however, involved Sarkozy himself, and he went from accusation to accusation, and in July spent 14 hours in custody. He was questioned over perverting the course of justice (*'trafic d'influence'*), offering favouritism in return for information on one of the financial scandals he was implicated in, the Liliane Bettencourt scandal. These several scandals, one involving an apparent (unproven) gift of millions from Colonel Gaddafi as well as his possible involvement in the Bygmalion affair, seemed to be coming perilously close to him, close enough to cripple his chances for a 2017 comeback. In October 2014, even the personal 'fine' (over and above the 10 million euros non re-imbursement) which the party had paid for him (over 300,000 euros) was being investigated – he repaid it personally upon his election to the party leadership in December 2014.

The third tidal wave was a consequence of the other two, namely, the public settling of scores, although this of course predated them in one sense in that it was linked to the very nature of the republic, the 'war of the chiefs'. The French Socialist Party was unprepared for government in 2012, largely because it had had little policy reflection since Lionel Jospin's defeat in 2002. The subsequent decade was simply a war of personalities at the top (Blier 2008). For the UMP, particularly in the aftermath of Sarkozy's 2012 defeat, it was the same. It mainly took the form of an unending duel between François Fillon and Jean-François Copé in 2012–13. The result was a kind of stalemate, but the fallout was severe public dismay. Sarkozy would have to make a decision as to whether, when, and how to make a return to mainstream politics, given that the leadership of the UMP was now vacant. 'Return' itself, however, would mean becoming the administrative leader of the party over a period of years up until 2017. The second issue was that as, incident after incident, Sarkozy became more embroiled in the mounting series of scandals and judicial investigations; condemnation in any one would possibly bar him from standing in the 2017 election. Sarkozy denied all these allegations, and his supporters saw the secret hand of Hollande and his entourage in these attempts to eliminate Sarkozy from the 2017 race – which, according to polls in 2013 and 2014, he would win, which made the struggle for leadership of the right even more intense. Who would be the candidate for the UMP started to matter more given that, by mid-2014 polls began to indicate that Marine Le Pen, not a PS candidate, would be the other candidate in round two of the 2017 presidential election (and therefore, the logic went, the UMP would win).

The overall result of this was two-fold. First, there was no properly organised, effective, or even particularly credible mainstream opposition to the Socialist government in the two years following Hollande's election. The second consequence was that the 'rhetorical opposition', as it were, was provided by and benefited greatly the Front National. In some ways the rise and rise of the Front National was seen as helpful to the PS and ministers, in particular Manuel Valls, as both Interior and Prime Minister; in both the Municipal and European election campaign he focused upon the danger of the rise of the Front National more than anything else. Such incongruous fear – for since François Mitterrand in 1986, encouraging the Front had been the clear intention of the PS, in order to split the right – is a dubious political, and moral strategy, particularly given that according to the polls, the left was likely, as we have seen, to see its candidate eliminated in round one in 2017; even more surprisingly, according to polls in September 2014, if the left's candidate in round two was François Hollande, Marine Le Pen would be elected President of the Republic.

Endgame?

The whole political class, therefore, was, by the summer of 2014, held in public disdain and derision. The only party profiting from all this was the far right National Front. The issue was compounded by an overwhelming public disconnect from the political class' sense of privilege and '*suffisance*', a sense of self-satisfaction amongst many politicians at both national and town hall level. By half way through Hollande's presidency, there was a generalised sense that the whole political class was as arrogant as it was ineffective as it was corrupt. This was not the reality, but it faced a mounting tide of populist outrage. And this brings us to the real significance of all of this incompetence and lack of accountability which we shall analyse more systematically in the next chapter. It is systemic, and the republic is arguably dysfunctional. The personalisation of politics and the associated coteries, sycophancy, back-stabbing, and permanent intra-party strife seemed to take over the functioning of the Fifth Republic. All the parties lost support. By mid-2014, the atmosphere was not just one of a *fin de règne*, but sometimes of a *fin de régime*, as the Fifth Republic slid towards crisis.

It was hoped that the new Valls government and a bold *rentrée* of 2014 would improve the political situation. It was about to get even worse. Arnaud Montebourg provoked the government's resignation at the end of August by publicly criticising his own government's policy (and Germany's), and adopting a scornful tone towards the President. The following day the new Education Minister, Benoît Hamon added his support. On 25 August, Valls decided to offer the government's resignation so 'Valls II' was created. The withdrawal of the left from government – Aurélia Filippetti, the Culture Minister also resigned – would make Valls' passage of the budget more difficult as the '*frondeurs*', the left in the Assembly, would become more hostile to the budget proposals, particularly during the amendment process and, from October 2014, they had the support, not only of the ex-ministers but also of Hollande's historic rival, Martine Aubry. The Greens refused to join Valls' new government. A more 'modernising' Economy Minister, Emmanuel Macron, replaced Montebourg. The left-leaning Christiane Taubira remained in government at the Justice Ministry. The problem for the new government was that the unemployment figures were up once again (27 August), and the economy had stopped growing altogether. And again France would miss its EU deficit targets.

There was an immediate scandal when one newly-appointed Junior Minister, Thomas Thévenoud, had to resign because of personal tax irregularities; and then in this sullen atmosphere, came the Exocet (secretly published in Germany to create maximum surprise) of Valérie Trierweiler's book on her relationship with President Hollande, which amounted to a character assassination. It immediately became a bestseller, going into reprint after 200,000 copies sold in the first week. By the end of September, it had sold nearly half-a-million copies, by November 600,000, and it was then translated into 12 languages with Trierweiler accompanying book launches in the UK, Italy and elsewhere. Between 1–6 September social media carried 8,000 related messages/tweets per minute. The effect of all of this on Hollande was extremely serious. His rating fell to 11%; and contrary to his official line of not commenting on his private life felt obliged to defend himself at a press conference after a NATO meeting on 5 September and an interview with the *Nouvel Observateur* magazine (11 September

2014); in both he concentrated upon countering her suggestion that he did not care about the poor. This was because Trierweiler had 'exposed' his character, in particular a kind of sneering at poor people, and a cold, obsessive, calculating side that seemed a complete contradiction to the received view of him. 62% of the French wanted him to resign (*Figaro Magazine* 11/9/14). The role of 'character' in the political process had come full circle. Let us examine this in the next chapter from a more theoretical perspective.

6
Conclusion: Character and Performance in French Presidentialism

In this chapter we shall appraise the 'character', the performed persona of François Hollande and its role in the exercise of Fifth Republic presidential leadership. We shall use the frameworks we identified in Chapter 3 and the presidential activity we identified in Chapters 4 and 5 to analyse Hollande's presidential performance, and how the Hollande presidency conforms to and/or deviates from a developing presidential style, identity, and function in the institutional political configuration of the Fifth Republic. We shall then draw a series of conclusions relating to presidential performance, and to a more comprehensive theoretical understanding of leadership in the Fifth Republic.

'France' and 'the French'

A first qualitative point to note from Chapter 3 is that the dramatic manner of de Gaulle's coming to power in 1958 conferred upon the presidency specific characteristics (Tenzer 1998). We also noted that its dramatic and providential quality (each is indispensable to the other) is something that is embedded in French history and culture and, therefore, is a political and rhetorical resource that is recognised as being part of the fabric of political life, for better or worse (Hoffman 1967). We say for better or worse because, generally speaking although not exclusively, the dramatic arrival of leaders or the exercise of their power and office has historically been part of a non-republican, arguably undemocratic tradition, and republics have attempted to screen out this political resource from the exercise of power within the political institutions. This was particularly true of the Fourth Republic (1946–58) which through its constitutional organisation and practice marginalised this aspect of political life (Gaïti 1998). In so doing, however, it had the shadow of de Gaulle over it, almost as its anti-thesis, and on several occasions, in particular during the Algerian crisis of May–June 1958 (Pickles 1962; Williams 1972; Williams and Harrison 1960) the shadow 'materialised'.

A second qualitative point we can make about the origins and nature of the Fifth Republic presidency, and which had inordinate influence upon de Gaulle's presidency and that of all his successors was the wide-spread observation that he brought strong leadership or 'presidential' leadership to the heart of the republican form and to democratic prac-tice – with the caveat that, for some, the Fifth Republic was neither republican nor democratic (Mitterrand 1964); it became gradually more so, that is, more rationally democratic after him, given the some-what arbitrary nature of his rule and the less arbitrary nature of his suc-cessors. This is a correct analysis (Chapsal and Lancelot 1975), but is inadequate to a complete understanding of the Fifth Republic because it makes too light of the fundamental and permanent quality that de Gaulle brought to the new republic. It was not that he brought strong leadership to France, although he did, but the real quality he brought was the idea of the 'self', the persona and character of the President and presidential performance as central to political practice, and the heightened capacity of leaders to 'embody' and 'give voice to' the political process and elements/moments within it, and to bring muta-bility to political ideas and sets of ideas.

The persona of the President possesses a range of qualities such as the ability to conflate these 'sets' such as republicanism and personal-ism by 'embodying' and 'performing' in rhetoric, intention, or action, the politics of the regime (non-presidential leaders can also do this but to a lesser degree). The consequences of this notion of 'presidential self' (rather than that of 'strong leadership', for example) cannot be overes-timated. Highly personalised leadership in a cultural and institutional context such as this has a series of important effects. We said above that politics became more democratic after de Gaulle. In one sense this is true, in another he himself practised a form of plebiscitary demo-cracy within the republic that was highly influential and would remain in various forms, not just through the use of the referendum which was never subsequently used in such a plebiscitary way – although on his return to political activity in September 2014, Nicolas Sarkozy implied that if returned to power, he would use the referendum in this way – but through the form of the political relationship practised. By this we mean that through his style of rule, use of the referendum, presidential elections, and indeed legislative elections, his press confer-

should point out that these speeches, for all the candidates, are also directed at the general public – Hollande adopted a much more emotional register which contrasted with his overall 'normal' persona, giving it a certain ambivalence which, retrospectively, lent an air of artificiality to the persona, in particular the Le Bourget speech – very left-wing, very 'Mitterrandian' circa 1971 – given that the implied radical policies never came to fruition, and the leftist populism was given no further 'voice' after the elections.

A second fundamental feature of this personalised form of leadership, and this especially in the French case, is another imagined but highly consequential relationship, and which is linked to the posited intimacy, but is actually preponderant, namely, the President/leader's relationship to 'France'. This is where the French President's legitimacy truly lies and distinguishes itself from many other democratic systems. The French President has a vision of France, and the role of election is to authorise the exercise or fulfilment of that vision. And this becomes the case even for Presidents (Mitterrand 1981; Hollande 2012) who are seen as having won through their adversary (Giscard and Sarkozy) having lost. The nature of the office immediately brings this exigency – an envisioning quality – into play. One of the characteristics of vision is that the envisioner/leader can 'see' before others, or can see things or solutions they cannot see. This means they have a Cassandra-like quality of pre-existing wisdom and knowledge. Authority to act comes into being through democratic election, but the popular nature of the office is not its essential feature.

The election itself is a form of legitimation of presidential action in the realisation or pursuit of the vision. This (imagined) relationship posits, as we have seen in Chapter 3, a highly-charged emotional relationship of devotion to France by all the French, with a special extra quality of intensity by the President given his representing and 'imagining' that France. Just as this France is not entirely 'democratic', nor is it simply a France as represented in mainstream nationalism; it has a fragile, cherished, perhaps even 'feminine' quality because of France's history, both vulnerable and triumphant. It was, therefore, a highly emotional *'certaine idée de la France'* that de Gaulle enacted but also bequeathed to the office as a rhetorical imperative. The interlocutor himself need not be grand in the de Gaulle manner; immediately with Pompidou, a less grandiose style emerged, and as society developed, real changes in attitudes to rhetoric, for example, took place (they had begun to change significantly during de Gaulle's presidency with the cultural changes of the 1960s), but the essential thing to bear in mind is that the 'self' and display of emotion of de Gaulle did not leave the parameters of the presidency in 1969, simply others entered adding a further range of types; and although no one could truly 'follow' de Gaulle, the traits of his character remained as political resources. To put it another way, no one could follow de Gaulle, so they followed him.

For Hollande, this latter aspect of the presidential relationship, namely, the semi-mystical relationship to France, was initially screened out from his persona and his rhetoric. As his relationship with public opinion began to deteriorate, there is a clear correlation with his attempts to invigorate the privileged presidential relationship with 'France'. He does this, not only through reference (to France and to himself), but also by his growing initiatives in foreign policy in order to heighten the international dimension of the presidency; but the main consequence of this was the dramatic increase in emphasis – in direct contrast to his original intention – upon the omnipotence of the French presidency and upon increased self-referencing, upon his ability to reflect France's interests, take almost any decision unilaterally, and 'incarnate' these elements of the French presidency. His behaviour over the Syrian crisis in August 2013, as we have seen, was a quintessential expression of this, in particular the inordinate self-referencing in his TV interview of 15 September. We can say, therefore, that the mismanagement of these two related relationships, with the French and with France, each fundamental to the presidential persona, created enormous difficulties for and stresses within the presidency; one might even say they caused a systemic dysfunction of the presidency.

Action, fortune, and politics as saga

Linked to these two relationships is the idea of the President as a man of action. This is fundamental to the idea of the presidency in France. It is almost its central logic. It is not, as we have said, election which gives legitimacy; this predates election. Election simply provides – and is essential to the conferring of – authority to act. In Gaullist terms, the hero arrives because the elites cannot undertake the proper action to revive the country, the hero re-establishes the authority of the state (*redressement*), does not give in to *fatalité*, and does this by using personal *volonté*, and so on. Although reflecting Gaullist doctrine, this notion of the President as a man of will and action has informed the French presidency in different forms ever since, and often (e.g. Chirac's failing in 1995 to act upon his campaign notion of *la fracture sociale*) inaction triggers major public disaffection. With his reputation as a 'Hyperpresident', Sarkozy pushed this notion to extremes, but it was not against the spirit of the presidency which mediates the presidency as both reflective and activist in a Barrèsian manner; in its best expression the hero is both a philosopher and a warrior. In this sense, de Gaulle was the perfect hero.

Over and above this, as we argued in Chapter 1, the move in 2000 from the seven to the five-year presidential term had unforeseen consequences, precipitating the presidency into a less imperial and more prime ministerial rhythm, but an even more activist role. This also coincided with the further personalisation of politics with the advent of modern celebrity politics, and the *'peopolisation'* of politics (encouraged by Sarkozy before he became President) which thrust political figures into the limelight and encouraged the idea of constant activity and 'presence' and adding further complexity to and contradiction within the presidency. It is clear that François Hollande seriously underestimated this aspect of contemporary political communication, having been misled into seeing it only as a deviation by Sarkozy from a desired presidential norm.

Also linked to the nature of action in the presidency is the idea of individual fortune, *fortuna*. This was partly based upon the 'adventure' of de Gaulle's life, and later by the very 'individuated' nature of the presidency itself which encourages individualism and personalisation. This has created the idea of long individual journeys to power (e.g. de Gaulle, Mitterrand, Chirac, Sarkozy) and, conversely, precipitous falls (de Gaulle 1969, Mitterrand 1968–69, Pompidou 1968, Chaban-Delmas 1974, Giscard 1981, Chirac 1988, Sarkozy and Balladur 1995, Jospin 2002, and so on). This means that the 'fortunes' of the Presidents and other leaders and their political lives are like a 'Saga' or a narrated tale. This idea of biography as narrative is extremely important. It begins, of course, with de Gaulle and, as we saw in Chapter 3, has chivalric connotations of desert crossings, trials, setbacks, quests, and so on. But all the leaders have a personal saga, shared with or understood by different audiences. For Mitterrand it was the war and mysteries about his allegiances (to Vichy and the Resistance (Péan 2011)), the successful Fourth Republic career, then his own desert crossing and then conversion to Socialism, followed by his own monarchical exercise of power (Bell 2005; Lacouture and Rotman 2000); for Pompidou his brilliance, his 'philosophy' and his special relationship with de Gaulle (Frerejean 2007; Rials 1977; Pompidou 1974); Giscard his Kennedy-style pretentions and his attempts at changing the political landscape (Giscard d'Estaing 1976, 1984); Chirac his long road to power and many defeats, and his tenacity (Derai and Guez 2001; Desjardins 1995; Macé-Scaron and Taillandier 2002).

The most recent example of saga (which blended older 'journey' and newer celebrity politics ideas) was Sarkozy's trajectory. His Icarus-like falls (after the 1995 election, the 1999 European elections, and his defeat in 2012) contrasted with his triumphs – from young mayor of Neuilly up to the heights of power, his character and temperament, his relationships, his ambition, even his taking his sons to the US for a holiday after he split from Cécilia so the media saw him looking after his family, his adolescent *'c'est du sérieux'* remark about Carla, and so on; all of these were known by wide swathes of the public, as was his *'Je vous aime'* farewell to his supporters in the wake of his 2012 defeat. Sarkozy's personal saga produced his own widely-read books and newspaper columns and commentaries on politics and ideas (Sarkozy 2001, 2006, 2007). There were also dozens of books on him, often saga-like in themselves or else inordinately fixated on his character or psychology (*inter alia*, Colombani 2008; Douglas 2010; Friedman 2005; Gambotti 2007; Hefez 2008; Lambron 2008; Nay 2007; Plenel 2011; Reza 2007; Rayski 2010). There were even thinly-disguised novels (Domain 2006) and a film (*The Conquest* (2011)). His life was a mix of political drama and celebrity politics, and this became the context and justification of his return to frontline politics in 2014 (Guénolé 2013). The only French President not to have or not to have fashioned his own trajectory-as-saga is François Hollande. It is difficult to be certain of the effect of this, and he was elected in part because the French had been somewhat over-exposed to Sarkozy's life as President. Nevertheless, this meant that as soon as the 'normal' label was seen to be inadequate and that this, it was assumed, reflected his world view and character, there was nothing to 'read'. There was no 'story' he could draw upon to redress his image. It is true that there had been some 'accounts' of him (Bachy 2001, 2005; Pfaadt 2012), collections of interviews (Hollande 2006, 2009) and a biographical study after his election (Pouget 2012), but his public identity, such as it was, was defined essentially by the two, later three women associated with him – Royal, Trierweiler, and Gayet; but without a deeper story, this identity fell, immediately the gossip began, into saucy seaside-postcard mode. And unlike all the other Presidents, he was the only 'accidental' President – had benefited from the Strauss-Kahn scandal and Sarkozy's unpopularity, unlike all the others whose life's 'quest' had been the conquest of the presidency. His relationship with Trierweiler and her capriciousness lent him a slightly hen-pecked image at the start of his mandate, and the Closergate scandal turned him into a figure of fun. Significantly, the Trierweiler book of September 2014 was a frontal attack upon his assumed good qualities: funny, calm, 'sympa', modest, and respectful. All five of these qualities were overturned by the Trierweiler book, so that it was as if the private, the 'real' character of this little-known man had been 'discovered': cold, mean-spirited, hypocritical, indecisive, sarcastic about the poor, obsessive, and a snob (Trierweiler 2014). Quite a list. From this point of view, Trierweiler's book, although poorly written and self-righteous, was rhetorically a *tour de force*.

François Hollande and presidential character traits

We should see character traits in relation to the 'ups and downs' that are built into the system as individual narratives and linked to the question of popularity. Popularity is subject to great volatility and this has increased more or less sequentially as the republic has developed. For Sarkozy and Hollande, the rhythm seemed to reach a negative trough of almost instant unpopularity. This in turn raises the question of 'time' and we will come back to this. Let us first turn to the different types of character traits we identified in Chapter 3.

Characterial capital traits. i.e. what is expected: competence, good/ happy to be President, reflective, and with a sense of direction. It is the case, as we have seen, that Hollande was barely perceived as possessing any of these traits, not because he might not have them, but because he was unknown. Whether he possessed these traits would, therefore, only be attributed when confronted with an issue – which was usually a difficult situation which militated against attribution. What was 'known' was that he was normal, simple, morally righteous, '*sympa*', and affable. As we have seen in Chapters 4 and 5, he was rapidly (certainly by Year II) perceived as possessing none of these character traits either, except perhaps the last two, and these were undermined severely by Trierweiler's book. Of the other traits: competence, good/happy to be President, reflective, and with a sense of direction; none of these traits was conferred for any length of time, the sense of direction was very poorly communicated by his entourage, and the Closergate affair seemed to question whether, temperamentally, psychologically, he actually wanted to be President.

Generic capital traits. Being 'presidential'. An early indication of this poorly grasped symbolism was Hollande's official photo which deviated deliberately from his predecessors' (Chirac's official photo was also taken outside but he filled the picture). Hollande's photo was banal in the extreme, taken at the bottom of the Elysée garden, the President standing in the shade to one side, cut off at the bottom of the photo strangely at half-thigh level. Most of the photo is shaded grass, with the Elysée overexposed in sunlight at the very far end of the lawn. The President is standing unnaturally, his white shirt cuffs far too prominent against the dark suit and the shade, and – perhaps semiologically telling from a psychoanalytical point of view – he looks almost as if he is leaving the picture; and his pose and look, and dyed black hair saw him immediately depicted on social media as a 'Playmobil' man; hundreds of parodies of the photo immediately appeared on the Web.

To be presidential, moreover, a President needs to be seen as in control without being seen to be controlling, and as if alone, in the sense of being above the fray. The unending series of mistakes and seemingly ineffective government activity in the first year – the rain, the tweet, going on holiday, the *'pigeons'* and the *'poussins'*, the Cahuzac debacle, the rising unemployment, the *Manif pour tous* undermining the claim to the *'apaisement'* of French society; then, in the second, Syria and Leonarda, Closergate, zero growth, the major electoral defeats, and so on, up until Trierweiler's book, saw Hollande's popularity fall to around 13% and accompanied by, very importantly, the widespread view that he was not 'presidential'. In an attempt to counter this, he quite early on reverted to greater observance of presidential protocol. He gave up the highly-publicised travelling by train, and the more casual interviews, and made greater use of the majesty of the Elysée Palace, a greater emphasis upon foreign policy initiatives and the international stage more generally. Possibly because such gravitas was not part of his makeup, such efforts were partial, in part because, as we have said, stepping 'up' is more difficult than stepping 'down'. Moreover, the general protocolary mistakes continued; the overuse of humour and *'petites blagues'* (especially in Year I), the further drenching, for example, at the war commemorations on the Île de Sein (25 August 2014), almost 'sacrificial' in its imagery, widely circulated in the media and on social media as symbolic of the catastrophic *rentrée* of 2014 (and about which he was asked mockingly at his September press conference), his tie continuing always to slide to the right, rather cheap-looking shoes of which he seemed only to possess one pair, the ponderous yet halting speech. In fact, one could argue that Hollande possessed no generic traits – except that he was the President, he held the office, and had been elected by a majority of voters – and then made a series of efforts to create or retrieve presidential stature. 'I am the President of the Republic' became a recurring phrase in the course of 2014. There was, moreover, a general sense that President Hollande ill-understood his own presidency. In a TV and radio interview with Jean-Jacques Bourdin (6/5/14), he argued that his only task was to reduce unemployment (something government ministers are respons- ible for, and something he and the government had failed to do). He then argued this would be his only task and that he had nothing to lose (*je n'ai rien à perdre*). He added that he had not been elected because of a sparkling manifesto but because of Nicolas Sarkozy's unpopularity. All of this, almost confessional admission of presidential inadequacy, suggested either desperation or incomprehension, in an almost wilful undermining of his own status.

A quality or character trait associated with the generic traits of office in the Fifth Republic is what we might call 'imperium' often expressed in the form of humiliation. This has been a feature of presidential behaviour since the beginning, in particular in the form of prime min- isterial sackings, which have appeared arbitrary, even capricious, but have always had as their function the (re)assertion of presidential dominion. De Gaulle's sacking of Pompidou, Pompidou's sacking of Chaban-Delmas, Giscard's sacking of Chirac (although making his position untenable is more accurate in this case), Mitterrand's sacking of Rocard were all acts of this kind. Hollande, who had painstakingly created his cabinet as a finely balanced synthesis of party, allies, gender, and close colleagues, did not want to disturb this equilibrium. And yet Arnaud Montebourg, the Economy Minister (and a rival in the primaries) made a continual stream of comments and complaints, often about the Prime Minister and sometimes about the President himself. Hollande's failure to impose himself appeared like a real weak- ness. The only person he did sack was the Environment Minister, Delphine Batho, for criticising her budget allocation. Her sacking, however, was seen as cowardly – she could be sacrificed because she had no power base. In the end, Montebourg was effectively sacked, but by the new Prime Minister not the President in September 2014 when Valls offered the resignation of his whole government because of Montebourg's outspokenness.

Regarding Valls, as Hollande's Prime Minister from April 2014, it is worth stressing that he was the first of what we might call a 'popularly nominated' Prime Minister in the Fifth Republic, that is to say, a Prime Minister chosen because of his public popularity. The nearest compar- ators, Jacques Chaban-Delmas (1969) and Michel Rocard (1988) were both popular in public opinion before their nomination, although were not imposed upon the President, and both were sacked, in part because of their popularity. Valls is the only Prime Minister of the Fifth Republic appointed in response to public opinion and presidential unpopularity, appointed in order to try and enhance the President's image by means of his popularity, and create a dynamic in government reforms. This, however, was an inversion of the presidential logic of the Fifth Republic whereby the Prime Minister, always less popular than the President, was '*dispensable*'. The only cases where this symbolism did not apply were in the '*cohabitations*' of 1986, 1993, and 1997. In all these cases the Prime Minister failed to win the following presidential election, and in the 1986–88 and 1997–2002 cases, it was the sitting President who won. Altering this general 'logic', that of the Prime Minister's clear subordination to the President, introduced uncertainty into the regime, particularly given Hollande's deep unpopularity. In one sense, the system partially reasserted itself in that Valls' own popularity as Prime Minister began to fall after his appointment, in part because his essential task was to do no more than implement Hollande's policies (in particular the interminable Responsibility Pact).

A further aspect of a kind of inverted imperium, given the pomp surrounding the presidency, is when the President himself is humiliated. This too is built into the system. De Gaulle suffered it first when he lost his referendum in 1969 (or perhaps when he was forced to a second round in 1965, or seen as out-of-touch in 1968); Mitterrand in 1968 when he was brushed aside by the May events; again in 1986 when he lost his majority; *idem* Chirac in 1997. Hollande's humiliations, as we have seen in Chapters 4 and 5 seemed almost constant, almost daily. Hollande gave press conferences in January 2014 just after the Closergate scandal broke and another in September 2014 after the publication of Trierweiler's book. It is striking how by the time of the September press conference how exhausted, depressed, and awkward he seemed, as if the revelations in the book had demolished his character, demolished his ability to perform.

Cultural character traits. These are essentially all the chivalric traits that de Gaulle brought to the presidency through the prism of his 'legendary' life: a quest, lonely certainty, isolation, courage, vision, trials and tribulations, return, triumph (and rejection). In order to possess these a leader needs a past and/or a narrative, a saga, as we have suggested. President Hollande clearly possessed none of these traits. It is true that no one could claim a legend like de Gaulle's, and the world of 2014 was not the same as 1958 but, as we have seen, even Sarkozy was able to allude to a 'story' of his own with its triumphs and adversity.

Hollande's 'saga' begins, in fact, with his presidency and might just have relevance if he made it through to the presidential elections of 2017.

Real traits. i.e. traits that are real or assumed to be so; the assumed 'real' character. Initially, cheerfulness was a marked trait of the President which gradually came to be seen as an optimistic disposition out of touch with the actual deteriorating situation, to the point where, combined with perceived inaction, procrastination, and indecisiveness, 'blind optimism' becomes a 'real' trait. Being 'anti-Sarkozy' was also akin to a real trait, both in his disdain and his actions (undoing his reforms and behaving in an opposite way). Down-to-earth and unpretentious were two more traits he possessed as he took office. In the course of the first two years, Hollande lost all the real/ascribed traits he had. Then, with the revelations of Trieweiler's book, he gained several traits that were extremely negative (nasty, cold, etc.). It is worth pointing out that although Mme Trierweiler had a 70% disapproval rating herself, even as late as September 2014, 600,000 people bought her book, and polls tended – while disapproving of her – to believe the things that she wrote in the book as being true.

New traits. i.e. traits brought to the accumulated, path-dependent clusters of received traits. In François Hollande's case the obvious new trait in 2012 was normality itself. As the first year unfolded, however, there were attempts to replace this with a more presidential style and discourse. This was not, however, a 'Prince Hal' moment where the normal President steps up to kingship. He did not make this transition as he assumed the presidency in May 2012, the moment when Prince Hal becomes Henry V. He did attempt a version of a conversion of sorts in his January 2014 press conference (the 'Closergate' conference) where he put it on record that he was a social-democrat (rather than a socialist) with all that this entailed for policy elaboration (we shall come back to this left dichotomy below). This 'transition', however, meant very little to those outside the political class, and to the extent that it had substance, Hollande had always been a social-democrat. To the public if it signified anything it was that he was a moderate. This obscure 'new' trait, however, was overshadowed by the Closergate affair which was more defining of a perceived 'character', moving as it did away from the political-doctrinal to the private-intimate.

By the beginning of Year II, Hollande had moved to highly personalised rhetoric and to ostentatious displays (the press conferences and interviews generally moved back to the Elysée Palace, and the 'tone' changed significantly). But a characteristic of opinion by the end of the first year was a strong sense that nothing that was claimed or promised was true or achieved. The classic illustration of this was, as we have seen, the promise that unemployment would fall by the end of 2013. We shall return to this at the end of the chapter. In fact, all of Hollande's pronouncements during the first two years: e.g. 14 July in Paris, 31 August at Chalôns, the 13 November press conference, 12 March 2013 speech at Dijon, all became more and more personalised (e.g. in his Fr2. 28 March 2013 TV interview he mentioned only himself, his Prime Minister for example not once), and especially his press conference after the European Council in December (10/12/13). After the Fr2 interview, 66% of respondents said they were unconvinced by any of the President's arguments, and 56% said his presidency would end a failure (*The Independent* 20/3/13), and the following day figures revealed that public spending had hit a new high, and France would miss its EU deficit reduction target. Almost from the start of his presidency and throughout Hollande seemed like a character struggling against a permanent gale, incessantly battered by neverending, horizontal wind and rain. A further feature of virtually all of Hollande's major press conferences, interviews, and major speeches, was that his poll rating fell slightly further after each one of them, in spite of or because of the growing personalisation of his discourse. A contributory factor to the negative responses was that in the absence of action and results, Hollande's speeches became declarations of intent: what he or the government were going to do rather than what they were doing or had done. The classic case of this was the 'launching' of the 'Responsibility Pact' on 1 January 2014. By September still no significant legislation had been passed (and in December 2014, the Economy Minister, Emmanuel Macron, said it was a failure (*Radio Classique* 2/12/14)). Nearly all of Hollande's announcements had this deferred quality. The general point, however, is that the assumption of kingship, if it is to happen, probably needs to take place at the moment of coronation, the performative, ritual, and symbolic moment of the conferring of kingship.

A path-dependent tree of traits

Each President comes into a developing emotional/characterical matrix, some parts of it incompatible, some contradictory, of more or less accepted types and styles informing the presidency; a kind of path-dependent family tree of traits. If we use the term a little loosely here to include style, dispositions, and even 'operating methods', we can say that a presidential culture or cultures has developed with types of Presidents being added to, each of them adapting to predecessors and to circumstance, and to evolutions in culture and society. We looked at this matrix of traits in greater detail in Chapter 3. Here we can make several observations. One of the first qualities ascribed to the first President was that he had a character which made the new republic 'work', even though it was one that was uncharacteristic of republicanism, and was generally 'romantic', 'providential', and grandiose. Pompidou brought a certain managerialism, political realism, and a kind of naturalness which both complemented and contrasted with his former boss. Giscard extended the President's character forward and widened it, responding to the modern, and bringing in a more Atlanticist, and therefore less dramatic, Gaullist style. But he also introduced – in spite of or perhaps because of the economic crisis that ended the 'Thirty Glorious Years' – a fiscal and economic mastery and preoccupation which took France, quite successfully albeit in crisis-management mode, through the 1970s. And he complemented this orientation by appointing as his (second) Prime Minister the man he himself called 'France's best Economist', Raymond Barre. Giscard's modern, technocratic style co-existed with a more monarchical one reminiscent of his predecessors, and we have argued elsewhere (Gaffney 2012) that this blend of traits became highly problematic for the 'persona' of Giscard d'Estaing. Mitterrand was treated by the left as almost a providential hero – a contradiction in terms on the left – and brought the left to power as if it was part of its – and his – destiny. He also, through his own behaviour, made the presidential left regal. Unlike Giscard, the contradiction in Mitterrand (leader of the left and monarchical) actually did work, and he 'reigned' unquestioned by his own party until very close to the end of his two seven-year terms. One of the consequences, however, was that French socialism itself failed to renew and re-invigorate itself because he, almost literally, stole its voice. Chirac changed the high regal nature of the presidency, bringing qualities of unpretentiousness, vigour, and an occasional 'Gaullist' style (there was also a sense that he was more cultured than he appeared or projected himself). He also brought, as had Mitterrand, echoes of subterfuge and probably corruption. Sarkozy, like Giscard, was more Atlanticist, and would probably have pushed France more in this direction if the 2008 crisis had not pushed economic liberalism off the agenda. Moreover, Sarkozy's retreat into a more Gaullist tradition was in part possible because he had already demonstrated this ability when Chirac's Minister of Finance (he protected French firms from the worst aspects of international competition). This is a further reason for Hollande's mistaking Sarkozy's 'character' as being mono-linear. Sarkozy had, in fact, a range of paradoxical character traits – volatile, affectionate, sentimental, repentant, and so on, which made him more formidable.

What then did Hollande bring to the matrix of traits? He added normal almost as a way of being, a mode of operation but, as we have seen, it was relatively quickly abandoned but not replaced by anything truly decisive for the reasons we have given. He also came into office with the trait of the desire to appease, to reconcile (*apaiser*) which has a strong palliative, succourable quality. The 'cleaving' developments (the '*pigeons*' and the '*poussins*') began almost immediately and the first year ended in the deeply socially divisive *Manif pour tous* protest movement, withdrawing from Hollande one of his remaining claims to a caring exemplarity. The trait of exemplarity was further undermined by the (unsubstantiated) rumours – at the same time as Trierweiler's book – of a '*cabinet noir*' at the Elysée (*L'Express* 26/11/14), a secret operation designed to wreck Sarkozy's political career.

He was reputed to have a good sense of humour, and other Presidents, particularly de Gaulle (Jullian 2000) and Mitterrand, were reputed to have great wit; but theirs – and in an age where 'asides' were reported rather than caught on microphones and mobiles – were, or rather were reputed to be, witty, ironic, and intellectual. Hollande, on the other hand, was more of 'a funny man' and a mimic, a form of humour which did not lend itself to the generic character traits of the presidency. And, as far as character was concerned, Trierweiler's book challenged all the received views on Hollande's 'nicer' traits. It is from this point of view that the Trierweiler book was so damaging. By replacing his received traits with a series of their opposites – obsessive, cruel, mean, uncaring – Trierweiler seriously damaged Hollande's reputation because the President's 'character' lies, as we have argued throughout, at the heart of the Fifth Republic. Her claims were clearly questionable, given her 'woman scorned' status and the kiss-'n-tell nature of the revelations, but they had resonance, partly because his 'character' by late 2014 was so fragile and vulnerable, partly because the public tended simply to believe she was closer to the truth than were the hitherto received traits, several of which had already been undermined; her character depiction was plausible. Her attack was also effective because of her use of the rhetorical device of assumption-revelation; he appears like this, but he is actually the opposite (e.g. he claims to care about the poor but mocks them); he pretends to be this but is actually its negation (e.g. he appears easy-going but is actually driven and obsessive), and so on. Her rhetorical assault was also effective because the French presidency is, as we have argued, about the relation between the imagined private and the displayed public. She offered a difficult (and privileged) reading of the imagined private character. Her attack was also powerful because, although she was herself unpopular, there was widespread sympathy for the very sudden position of public humiliation and rejection she found herself in in January 2014. Finally, as the book sales demonstrated, in spite of an element of public disapproval for celebrity politics and *'peopolisation'*, the spectacle of an unpopular (and misbehaving) President getting his comeuppance from his embittered Ex, and all the intimate gossip that went with it, was clearly irresistible to a large portion of the reading public.

Celebrity and privacy

From around the beginning of the new millennium, 'celebrity politics' fully joined the mainstream of personalised politics in France, and has been growing in strength ever since, blurring the lines between the public and private and between politicians and the new celebrity culture. This means that in spite of lip-service to the right to privacy (strongly protected in French law), the private lives of politicians are the constant topics of the new media, along with those of media celebrities more generally. There had been media precedents in figures like Françoise Giroud, Bernard Tapie and Bernard Kouchner, and there had long been the association – much more so than in the rest of Europe – of celebrities with politics: Johnny Hallyday, Alain Delon, Yves Montand, Simone Signoret, Brigitte Bardot, Renaud, and many others made the interface of politics and celebrity a reality. Sarkozy, however, in the ten years before he was President, was the first major politician to truly exploit this relationship to the media and 'fame' more generally, entering into systematic – and friendly and *'toujours disponible'* relations with journalists and the world of celebrity culture. Politicians were not, therefore, simply exposed to celebrity politics but exploited it, organising themselves with advisors, press officers, and communications teams (*la com'*). As the 2000s developed, social media, the tweetosphere, texting, and the ability to film and record almost anything and everything with mobile phones, changed the nature of political exchange. Sarkozy himself, even as President, was rarely seen without his mobile phone to his ear, Hollande constantly seen to be texting (and we are led to believe from Trierweiler's book that it was often to her, even after they had separated (26 texts in one day)). Tweeting had become near-universal by the mid-2010s. It is arguable that most politicians only came gradually – like the general public – to grasp the import of these changes.

In the context of French presidentialism, this collision of the public and the private would have profound effects upon the political process, both in terms of daily politics and at the symbolic level upon the notion of kingship itself and that of the King's Two Bodies; the monarchical semi-sacred response to the separation of secular and state power in which the monarch blended 'earthly' and 'transcendental' status in order to maintain authority and legitimacy. Celebrity gossip was folded into the culture of presidentialism. At the 'daily' level, because of a lack of awareness of the new media's constant influence and an early refusal by Hollande to use communications advisors, the presidency – and government – were subject to being constantly caught on the back foot, with gaffes (*couacs*), and a general incoherence and confusion. Moreover, both practically and symbolically, the excruciating exposure of Hollande's private life in the Closergate affair, which followed well over a year of a very 'public private life' with Valérie Trierweiler, followed in turn by her book's revelations in September 2014, exposed the President to public ridicule, but more than this exposed and undermined the 'characterial' base that the Fifth Republic is established upon.

After the Closergate revelations at the beginning of 2014, Hollande was able – with the approval of most French journalists and politicians (and the utter disbelief of foreign correspondents and publics) – to 'hide' behind his claim to privacy ('private issues are dealt with in private', he said at the January conference, and the French agreed). By the time of the Trierweiler book, as we saw in Chapter 5, this tactic had been abandoned, as had the idea that the French were not interested in such tittle-tattle. Her accusations were so disparaging that the President broke his protective protocol, even defending himself at a press conference at the NATO summit on 7 September (itself an inappropriate place for a 'domestic' conference, particularly over such a personal issue), then several days later in an interview with *Le Nouvel Observateur* (11/9/14). His responses were an indication of how serious was the damage to his reputation and therefore presidential status caused by the best-seller. This meant that 'the trivial' (here, an account of a relationship) had become politically consequent and had entered the daily practice of the exercise of the presidency – what he wore, whether he made any Freudian slips, the way he spoke, his interventions (announcements, press conferences), his non-interventions or delays, his mixing of 'high' (Syria) and 'low' (Leonarda) politics, his high profile unpopularity (and that, incidentally, of his ex-partner Trierweiler – if she had been popular the damage would have been far worse), the rising popularity of his other ex-partner, Royal, his being regularly drenched on official visits, his hot awkwardness sitting with Obama, and rather comical height and shape contrasted when standing between the tall graceful Obamas (his own ex-partner, scheduled to go with him, still recovering from her hospitalisation because of the nervous collapse caused by the Closergate scandal), his halting speech, and so on; all these gained inordinate traction in the political process. France seemed unique in displaying the dynamic and destructive interplay of the trivial and 'the consequent' (military interventions, the economy, taxation, European policy) to the point where the trivial became itself inordinately consequent.

The self and embodiment

We have argued here and in Chapter 3 that de Gaulle's fundamental contribution to the norms of the Fifth Republic was the bringing of 'self' to the political process in a concerted and formative way. Once this was established, the persona of the President became imbued with his physical presence. Perhaps a paradoxical confirmation of this was the painful spectacle of both Pompidou and Mitterrand at the end of their presidencies when they were clearly ill and fragile – the earthly body trying to 'carry' the transcendental one (and the public sympathy for each at this time, 1973–74 and 1994–95 was enormous). Since 1958, the physical presence/body of the President as 'representing' the republic/France has been normative. Even Hollande used his physical self very early on when using the immediacy of his post-inaugural trip to Berlin to meet Angela Merkel; he gave the clear impression that he (a man) was going to 'sort her (a woman) out', as it were. This was not to be the case, and in fact his plane, struck by lightning, had to turn back... He used a similar corporal presence and in a similar way after the ringing defeat of the European elections of May 2014. He went on television (sitting in front of the bookshelves Mitterrand used in his official photograph), affirming that he was immediately going to the European summit, but once again with the intention, quite aggressively, to 'sort Europe out'. Such 'pre-meeting' assertions are political hostages to fortune as they inordinately raise expectations and, in each case, produced no results, further undermining the President's longer-term credibility. The consequence of interventions such as these was that Hollande who had projected his personality as being all Sarkozy was not, very soon, and with increasing insistence, began to display similar traits in an attempt to create 'new' traits and re-invigorate the generic traits of the office.

We have also argued in our analysis that the 'operating self' of the leader, the use of the presidential persona, has another major function in Fifth Republic political culture, namely, the mediation and some-times conflation of narratives and 'isms', often seen as incompatible. It is true that it is not only individuals who can affect such discursive mutability. Narratives and ideologies themselves do this (Freeden 1996), or lend themselves to such mutability; a case in point is the movement of 'nationalism' from being a leftist notion to a rightist one (and back and forth) from 1789 to today with momentary twentieth-century conflations in the ideas of, paradoxically, Charles Péguy and Maurice Barrès and later the Resistance and the French Communist Party. But individuals can blend and merge discourses. As regards the Fifth Republic, de Gaulle was paradigmatic by interweaving republican-ism and the role of the providential leader. But once the precedent is set, and depending upon the relative mutability of doctrine and nar-rative themselves, the practice becomes normative. Mitterrand was also a classic case of this, blending – and later usurping – personal leader-ship and socialism. Mitterrand's treatment by the PS as a kind of de Gaulle figure meant that in the longer term socialism happened to be whatever Mitterrand was thinking – or not. His grip upon the voice of the party became such that no real reflection upon the nature of modern French socialism was possible until he stepped down in 1995. Others also brought blends of ideas: Giscard, a technocratic modernism alongside a monarchical style; Sarkozy a 'just do it' style and a claim to European leadership. Hollande, on the other hand, brought little to blend with his 'socialism', apart from – declared in his January 2014 press conference – a certain technocratic style and provenance, and a commitment to social-democracy. As we have seen, such was purely for internal party consumption and quite irrelevant to most French observers who would have been in some difficulty knowing what each signified, let alone what a comparison would mean. Although, as regards internal effects, such distinctions would be consequential given that the Le Bourget campaign would later be interpreted by the left of the party as evidence of Hollande's betrayal of socialism's promise –

hence the disillusionment and, from late 2012 onwards, the hostility and opposition of *les frondeurs* and the justification for Filippetti, Hamon, and Montebourg leaving the government in 2014.

The normal, the chivalric, and the Sixth Republic

This brings us to a question we have not addressed throughout our analysis because we have concentrated upon what happened rather than what might have happened. But we would do well here to put the question: could normal, a normal self, a normal character, a normal President have worked? The French did, after all, vote for this normal President knowing that he claimed that quality. And there was a rhetoric implicit in 'normal' which was that it was not normal, i.e. was a panacea for Sarkozy's divisiveness. One also thinks of other leaders who might have filled such a role, a Pierre Mendès France, for example, or an Antoine Pinay. How might Raymond Barre or Michel Rocard have fared as President? Do such posit a northern European type, compatible with or antithetical to the prevailing Fifth Republic paradigm? One thinks also of the majority of Centrist candidates in Fifth Republic France from Jean Lecanuet to François Bayrou. It is impossible to tell given that none of them won, but all these candidates do reflect major, perhaps even majority, tendencies and 'types' in European, particularly northern European political cultures. France, moreover, is much more than it used to be an '*État de droit*', where process rather than dramatic events is the rule. The electorate too has evolved. Do people really explicitly believe these days, even in France, in providential leaders?

The media is less reverential and more inquisitive, and now of course, 24/7. And France itself with its presidency is no longer the European or global power it was in de Gaulle's time. The speed with which recent Presidents have become unpopular, Chirac in 1995, then Sarkozy, and Hollande, would also imply that there is a strong misalignment between what is expected and presidential popularity. And in the case of all the Presidents since Giscard, the power of the presidency to bring decisive change, prosperity, and so on has been questionable. All these issues raise the question of whether all of these things could or would better be done 'normally'. Having said all this, it is clear that the active deployment of such a register in Hollande's presidency moved from bad to worse, and this raises the issue we raised in Chapter 3, namely, the chivalric nature of the French presidency and the public recognition of its very special status and the character traits it demands and encourages. And when associated with morality and claims to morality, 'normal' also triggers other traits – integrity, honesty, and so on, which become factors which have to be managed and are vulnerable. Normal is itself a moral claim, but it claims no rhetoric (except that it will be more than normal in its adequacy); perhaps character needs a rhetoric that implies or constructs the morality of the persona, rather than simply claims it, otherwise character has little resistance to exposure if anything negative happens, such as the Cahuzac scandal or the Trierweiler book. And such events can have important and sometimes dramatic political consequences.

Was Hollande's 'weakness', namely, his claim to a 'normal' presidency, an implicit (or explicit?) attempt to domesticate the chivalric within presidential identity? We said in Chapter 1 that the response to poor personal leadership was often the offer of an alternative personal leadership rather than its being called into question as a principle; and the rising popularity of Marine Le Pen after 2012, the return to frontline politics of Nicolas Sarkozy in 2014, and the surge in popularity of Alain Juppé, and of others (Manuel Valls, Emmanuel Macron ...) should be seen in this context, namely, that the danger of putting 'strong' romantic, providential, or rally leadership back outside the established institutions would not necessarily see the end of the phenomenon or a decrease in its virulence. Whichever is the case, the role of character is consequential. As regards the chivalric nature of the presidency, or rather the chivalric elements it contains, this brings us to the idea of a France without a presidency, or at least a presidency of this nature. If Hollande were deliberately trying to 'domesticate' the presidency – even without being fully aware of this, in his case it clearly was not a success, but it raises the question of whether a different kind of domestication might have been or might be a success.

It was clear that the political class and many observers believed that the Fifth Republic, if it outlived the Algerian conflict would not outlive de Gaulle's presidency. The idea of and proposals for a Sixth Republic soon emerged (Duverger 1961; Cotta 1974), and it was clear that the 'run' that Gaston Defferre, an SFIO 'baron', made for the presidency in 1964 (*L'Express* '*Monsieur X*') was a bid for a new kind of presidency (Defferre 1965) along American, or for others German or Italian lines; in whichever case, one in which the President's influence and powers were rationalised and reduced, and parliament's and government's increased. A great deal of the discussion since then has been of this nature. Both the Convention for a Sixth Republic set up by Montebourg and others in 2001, and the call for a Sixth Republic by Mélenchon and others (e.g. Eva Joly, François Bayrou) over the last decade had as their main target the 'personal power' (a very pejorative term in French political vocabulary) of the Fifth Republic. The dilemma has always been how to transcend the Fifth Republic without recreating the Fourth.

A first problem here is that, in spite of the ideological, moral, and emotional hostility to the nature of the Fifth Republic's presidency (its arbitrariness), the near-totality of both proscription and prescription is constitutional. But there is clearly something very limiting about this widespread view. One need only read the constitution of the Fifth Republic (*Conseil constitutionnel* 2014) and follow the debates of the summer of 1958 (*Anneé politique 1958* 1959) to see that the constitution advocated by the Sixth Republic's supporters (although there are significant variations, of course) is not that dissimilar from the Fifth's (and this more parliamentary interpretation was the view of people as diametrically opposed as Guy Mollet (who helped elaborate the 1958 constitution) and Michel Debré (who wrote the initial draft)). For them, the constitution as voted was much more like the UK's parliamentary political structure than like the French regime as it became. What we mean by this reference to a reading of the constitution, or rather what lies behind it, is that it is not just a constitutional question but a cultural and performative question. The reason French politics is 'presidential' is not because of the constitution but because of the manner of its emergence and the performative leadership of its first President. It is also as it is because de Gaulle's performance in the 1958 crisis and beyond was 'recognised', and was legitimated by popular approval (by two referendums and two legislative elections in both 1958 and 1962, as well as the referendums on Algeria). French politics is also as it is because all of the Presidents who followed de Gaulle, although for the most part de-dramatising his style, subscribed to his view of the presidency and to presidential pre-eminence. In many ways, the proposals for a Sixth Republic are sensible and laudable, e.g. an end to the dominance of a political elite perpetually renewed from the upper civil service, and the search for a less dysfunctional and undemocratic arbitrary presidency. But all of these questions, because of the lawyers (e.g. Montebourg, Joly) who ask them, are questions about constitutional law. The question that has not been calibrated into the proposals for a Sixth Republic is the strong providential tradition in French culture, and the notion of the rally (*rassemblement*). It does not necessarily mean that screening out presidential pre-eminence and celebrity politics from the political institutions would screen them out of French political life more generally. It is also true that most of the supporters of a Sixth Republic are on the left – Ecologists, Socialists, Left Front. The calls for a Sixth Republic fell silent while Mitterrand presided and the Socialists governed. Hollande's highly problematic presidency has brought the issue back to the debate. On his return to frontline politics in September 2014, even Nicolas Sarkozy said he did not believe in providential leaders, but the 'romantic leadership' we have identified and analysed here is a deep and consequential one within French political culture.

This question of character and notions of 'normal' as normative raise the further question of the President as 'human'. We have looked at the notion of the President, like a monarch, mediating the sacred and the profane. At a practical level this raises the question of the fallibility of the President. Could Hollande have reversed his fortunes after having made several fundamental mistakes? Is weakness or having been mistaken – both opposites of infallibility – permissible? De Gaulle in April 1961 in his televised and radio broadcast '*Françaises, Français, aidez-moi!*' speech against a military putsch showed the President in need, and it increased his popularity (De Gaulle 1970a). His arrogant attitude to social unrest in 1963 decreased it. Did his being made to go to a second ballot in 1965 – to his own great surprise – enhance or diminish his reputation? In 1968, his image took a serious blow because his reputation as 'a seer' was tarnished. Giscard's struggles with the financial crisis did less to harm his reputation than the farcical 'Bokassa Diamonds Affair' (Becker 1998; Frears 1981). Mitterrand's having to abandon Alain Savary's educational reforms in 1984, after massive street protests, diminished his regal status. Chirac's presidential status was seriously diminished by his mistaken parliamentary dissolution in 1997. Sarkozy's only half-hearted confessional *mea culpa* over his brash presidential style probably cost him the 2012 election (my own view is that a more 'Oprah'-style *mea culpa* would have won it). So the question of weakness or mistakes probably depends, in part, upon the perceived ethical dimension of character identified in each mistake (mistake and repentance as an 'event'). In the case of Hollande, it is arguable that the 'false start' of normalcy at the start of his five-year term, was in great part responsible for the fact that very soon the 'fallibility' of his character and activity became virtually a daily occurrence, and 'being wrong' or 'making mistakes' drew 'normal' towards 'mediocre'.

It is also arguable that, although 'unsuccessful' as a characterial strategy, President Hollande's 'normal' persona meant that, along with its inadequacy, the symbolism of the presidency entered new territory.

The fact that a particular character is seen to have been inappropriate re-opens the question of what today might be or might not be appropriate, now or in the future. It also throws up further questions about character in past Presidents. It is true that a stylistic shift begins with Jacques Chirac, and Hollande was a friend and admirer of Chirac; even his official photo, taken in the Elysée garden is the nearest to Chirac's photo. In this way – more ordinary for more ordinary times? – Chirac, Sarkozy, and Hollande are comparable. This brings us back to our question as to whether there are indeed now elements of 'normal' in the presidency in a way there were not before Chirac.

We have already argued that the apparently trivial – the things that happen to normal and ordinary people – is in a dynamic and unusual relationship with the celebrity politics of the presidency; but it co-exists with more Gaullist expectations and protocols, still very dominant in the French presidency, even under Hollande, not only because of the presidency's legitimacy, but also because of its constitutional and acquired scope, its history, and its symbolism. This, no doubt, is where the Gaullist Settlement meets *'peopolisation'* and the two interact with one another. It is clearly the case from our analysis, moreover, that the latter may enhance the presidency but also exposes it to a series of stresses and a rhythm that has imposed a new series of constraints. Whichever is the case, the two interact strongly with one another, changing each other and dynamising the presidency and its performative effects.

Mitterrand and French socialism

Within the framework of the analysis that we set ourselves here, we have not dealt in depth with the question of the relationship of the presidency to party politics. It is, however, crucial, and has been extremely well researched (Knapp 2004). We can assert here that both the practical and the symbolic relationship of the President to his political party are central. De Gaulle set the tone with the UNR, a rally of opinion around himself. Pompidou also gained the allegiance and *de facto* leadership of the Gaullist Party. Giscard's presidency suffered from the rally politics detonated by Chirac around himself when he transformed the Gaullist Party into the RPR. Giscard tried to counter this belatedly in 1978 with the UDF. Mitterrand, far more incongruously for a party of the left, did the same with the PS from 1971, and this to the point where he partially paralysed the PS as a modern social democratic party after he gained the presidency. Sarkozy – typically –

had a tempestuous relationship with his party until 2004 when it became 'his' (and again in 2014). François Hollande is the only French President who did not enjoy the devoted loyalty of his party, and even though he was leader of the PS for over a decade, he was always seen as a kind of caretaker leader (and had no 'faction' of his own as did Mauroy, Jospin, Rocard, Fabius, and Aubry – and it was Aubry as party leader who oversaw many of the candidate selections for the 2012 legislatives). From as early as December 2012, the party began to react critically to the President, and the *frondeurs*, whose numbers rose and fell from around 30 to sometimes nearer 50, undermined Hollande's status; some of them claimed a kind of greater authenticity than he, claiming their closer proximity to the policies for which he and they were elected. Such 'independence' seems to have a clearly negative effect upon the President's authority, and every President before him had the rally style allegiance of his party, arguably a prerequisite to presidential authority. The Hollande presidency showed that the French Socialist Party faced a series of serious questions, not only regarding its relationship to public policy, which was (invariably) a *presidential* manifesto but, just as importantly, its relationship to the presidency itself. When the political party does not behave like a personalist rally it withdraws legitimacy from the President.

How can we explain the serious divisions which were taking place within the French PS by the autumn of 2014? One of the effects of the in-fighting within the party at the moment 'Valls II' began its programme of reform from the autumn of 2014 was the public spectacle of the governing party in disarray. The polemics between the Prime Minister's camp and in particular the party leader, Aubry, and the recently resigned ministers Filippetti, Hamon, and Montebourg were rhetorically violent – words such as 'danger to the republic' (Hamon) and 'disgust' (Valls) being used. It is clear that the *frondeurs* were manoeuvring for pole position within the party. Valls too, by suggesting the party change its name and move further towards the centre of the political spectrum (*L'Obs* 23/10/14), was also (under the constraints of being unable to truly develop his own narrative for fear of precipitating a crisis between himself and the President) trying actively to provoke a dynamic shift in opinion towards himself and his longer-term plans. In the media, this division was generally represented as a clash between a 'left of government' and an ideological left that we characterised earlier as 'leftist emotionalism'.

These developments, however, were surface phenomena of a much more profound issue linked to French socialism on the one hand and the presidency on the other. The received representation of the divisions within French socialism was real but inadequate as an explanation. It is true two essential and paradoxical strains of thought have opposed one another in French socialism since the party's creation in 1905 (itself the reconciliation of many other strains). A first point we need to make is that the rhetoric associated with these two 'sides' ('discursive strains') of French socialism were distinct (to simplify, 'social democracy' and 'socialism'). They can be grouped into two clusters, perhaps even two ideologies (in Freeden's sense (Freeden 1996)), but they interact, cross over, mix with other associated ideologies and discourses (leftist and other) and can exist, particularly rhetorically (in terms of enthymeme rather than logic) on *either* side of the divide we mentioned above (pragmatism and lyrical emotionalism) and, most importantly, can exist within one person: and when that person is a leader or contender for leadership, can give voice to (or withdraw voice from) either and both of those ideologies/rhetorics. Usually, they are represented within the party and have been for over a century – by two 'voices', one maximalist/morally intransigent and one practical/morally suasive (arguably reflecting an earlier Jacobin/Girondin division). Let us go back to the beginning to see where they come from and why they remain unresolved in the PS today.

There were several strains of thought in nineteenth-century French socialism. The ideas of Sorel, Proudhon, Blanqui, Allemane, Saint-Simon, Marx, the *possibilistes*, and others; and in the twentieth-century Marxism in particular, and Leninism, Trotskyism, and later Stalinism *inter alia* to the left of the SFIO and Léon Blum in particular within it, as well as anarchist thought to the left and left republicanism to its right; these were all extremely influential. From 1905, however, two ideologies, two discourses, were bound together by the new party's operating paradigm: the more maximalist, *ouvriériste*, thought and rhetoric of Jules Guesde, and the more pragmatic parliamentary socialism of Jean Jaurès (Mexandeau 2005) who abandoned the idea of class struggle circa 1900. Both were informed by Marxism (of a relatively simple, conceptually restricted kind (Mexandeau 2007; Rioux 2008)); and French socialism kept its Marxian, millenarian, and often insurrectionary register (often through reference to moments like the Commune of 1871) throughout the twentieth century, unlike most other socialist and social democratic parties. The 'Jauresian synthesis' was an attempt to bring all the strains of socialism together. The insurrectionary rhetoric remained. This was partly due to the Russian Revolution of 1917, then to the SFIO's having as its closest neighbour from 1920 to circa 1980, the French Communist Party (PCF), an avowedly Marxist breakaway from the SFIO at the 1920 Tours congress (we say 'breakaway' as in its initial division it took a majority of the party with it into the Third International, although a majority of those soon left, many of whom re-joined the SFIO (Bell and Criddle 1994)). The PCF's Marxism was also rather simplistic although it, much more so, was informed and intellectually 'irrigated' by a host of highly intellectual members and fellow travellers throughout the 1920–80 period.

In the 1930s, within the SFIO, Léon Blum tried once again to synthesise the two strains within French socialism (as well as respond to a strong Trotskyite element in the party), and this both before and after the 1936 Popular Front which brought the left to power, and Blum to the premiership (Blum 1945, 1946, 1946a). His essential distinction was between the 'exercise of power' and the 'conquest of power', the first, essentially, being parliamentary government, as a pre-requisite or precursor of true socialism, the second a more rhetorical and uncompromising socialism, closer to the PCF. What is interesting for our purposes were both the ideational and rhetorical/emotional elements of these attempts at reconciliation. In the post-war period, the PCF became a mass party with a plethora of major intellectuals involved. The SFIO was a junior partner in both membership and ideas. Although both had been compromised by the war – the PCF by the Hitler-Stalin pact and the SFIO by most of its MPs having voted for Pétain in 1940 (only 80 voted against) – the PCF emerged from the war as having been the main component of the internal Resistance to Nazism (in part because the PCF's internal structure and discipline was better able than the SFIO to resist German attempts at disrupting the organisations). In the aftermath of the Liberation, there was a short-lived struggle for the control of the Socialist Party between a 'modern' SFIO (led by Daniel Mayer) and a still rhetorically Marxian but practically social-democratic, parliamentary 'Molletism'. Under Guy Mollet, the SFIO became one of the main coalition governing parties, entering into almost all the coalitions, following one another in rapid succession throughout the Fourth Republic (1946–58). Its two intellectually impressive though secondary ideological/discursive strains were its 'statism' as expressed by Jules Moch and its socially inclusive municipal socialism. When the Fifth Republic was established, the SFIO, like the PCF (and virtually everyone else), was swept aside by the Gaullist tide – first in 1958, then more decisively in 1962 (though not at local level cf. the Municipal elections of March 1959). At national level, however, the new system saw the eclipse of the left (the PCF were reduced to ten seats from 150 in the National Assembly). For the SFIO, a decade and a half of participation in coalition governments came to an end, and paradigmatically it is without a doubt that the SFIO had little grasp of the nature and operating principles of the new regime (even though Mollet had swung his party around to supporting de Gaulle in 1958 rather than see a military coup take place). Its one positive response to the conditions of the new regime was to begin electoral alliances with the PCF to increase its presence in the National Assembly, but its thrust was based upon an assumed return at some point to the practices and opportunities provided by the previous regime. This was a first and potentially fatal interpretation of the longer-term fortunes of the new regime (Bauchard 1986; Bell and Criddle 1988, 2014; Dray 2008; Giret and Pellegrin 2001; Leclerc 2006).

Just before the fall of the Fourth Republic, and in two phases (opposition to SFIO/government policy in Algeria, and opposition to de Gaulle), a now newer version of French socialism emerged: younger, idealistic, radical, intellectually-informed. By the mid-1960s it had become the 'second left', *la deuxième gauche* (it would re-join the new PS in 1974). It revived socialist ideology – and would inform ideological developments within the party too (e.g. an equally young and intellectual CERES, set up by Guy Mollet himself). The *deuxième gauche* brought together notions of a wide coalition of *'forces vives'*: the young, the unions, associations, students, advocates of *'autogestion'* (self-management), and a commitment to a new moral leftism – significantly influenced more by the thought of the left radical Pierre Mendès France (Mendès France 1962, 1968) who joined the new PSA, later PSU, in 1960, rather than any thinkers from traditional socialism, the *première gauche*. On the right and to the right of the SFIO too there was organisational change and intellectual development (in fact, the least evolving part of the left in terms of ideas and initiatives was the SFIO itself, led from 1946 to 1969 by Guy Mollet). To the right of the party, and even from within it, there were attempts to make the left respond to the new political exigencies of the Fifth Republic (Defferre 1965; Club Jean Moulin 1965); many new political clubs developed in order to try to influence the parties – and propose a presidential regime but one that was more modern, less authoritarian, more incorporating of France's parliamentary tradition, with a proper separation of powers, a coherent legislative programme, a response to the developing bipolarisation of the political system, and so on. Each of these wings of left republicanism, the PSU and the FDS (which was trying to develop the Defferre/Club strategy and modernise the centre left) was incapable on their own of rallying opinion and the parties to anything like a credible opposition to Gaullism. Neither could the dwindling and almost ideologically bereft SFIO, even in alliance with the PCF. No combination of alliances seemed able to counter the grip of the UDR upon the political life of the new regime.

What happened next transformed the potential for the left in the Fifth Republic. François Mitterrand was the first mainstream politician (ironically, given that he had opposed de Gaulle in 1958) to understand how the Fifth Republic worked. He transformed the left – over a period of years in two phases (1965–71, 1971–81) by making it first accept him as its representative (1965 presidential election), rather than as its voice; then from 1971 (leader of the party, the renamed *Parti socialiste*) as its voice, even incarnation and embodiment. In this, Mitterrand's was not an attempt to modify the Fifth Republic but to use its emphasis upon 'self' as incarnation. 1968 was a moment where this strategy was thrown off course, as was the whole political class, by an almost spontaneous, culture-changing burst of ideas and activity from a coalescence of leftist strands (anarchism, situationism, Sartrean Marxism/Existentialism); an uprising that engulfed the country in 1968 and swamped the traditional left. Having said that, many from the *'génération '68'* would flock to the new Mitterrand-led PS from the early 1970s onwards.

Mitterrand pitched his rhetoric well to the left (his Epinay speech in 1971 when he took the leadership of the party was insurrectionary – a revival of socialist discourse that would be folded into the new party) in order eventually to gather all the left's discourses together: the *première gauche* (SFIO, Marxism, Municipal socialism, the new SFIO generation, CERES, the Poperenists), as well as on the right, Defferre, the Left radicals (MRG/PRG), his own CIR followers, even some leftist Gaullists, and from the early 1970s the *deuxième gauche*. A major point to note here is that in spite of the range of rhetorics informing these strains within socialism, all of them were ultimately parliamentary republican. Mitterrand allowed/accepted all these voices, his own pre-eminently, recapitulating them until, by 1981, they were 'his', and his voice, their voice. The now presidential voice/s of socialism gathered into a millenarian rally around him (even the least personally committed like CERES and the *deuxième gauche*). As we argued in Chapter 3 he then dominated socialism's discourse and, as President, drew the whole of socialism's discourse towards a 'Mitterrandian' Gaullism, a non-Marxist republicanism, and himself as the 'performer' of these. This shift was also greatly helped by the collapse of Marxism in the 1980s.

This is the ideational and rhetorical background to the post-2012 rhetorical climate (Cotta 2012): Mitterrand embodied French socialism but allowed both its maximalist and its parliamentary discourse, its lyricism and its pragmatism, to flourish and interact. What we need to bear in mind in order to understand what was happening to the PS in the mid-2010s, both before and after Hollande's gaining the presidency, are three 'legacies' of Mitterrandism. First, although the nature of Epinay 1971 (when Mitterrand took the party leadership) began a process of acute personalisation which we shall come back to, an essential feature of that personalisation was his reciprocal acceptance and encouragement of all socialism's voices; millenarianism, left-Catholicism, Marxism/s, social democracy, insurrectionism, 'break with capitalism' socialism, non-communist syndicalism, *deuxième gauche*, incrementalism, Delorism, Jaurès, Blum, Mendès, Gramsci, republicanism – every leftist discourse and rhetoric flowed into the socialist 'discursive space' and became rhetorical resources; with the exception of Molletism which was written out of French socialism's history – ostensibly because of Mollet's reputation being compromised by his premiership during the Algerian war (Mitterrand's own record was similarly compromised), but actually because it could claim no lyricism – the essential quality of this new socialism.

The second legacy was that every single ideational and discursive strand that recognised itself in the (re)unification of French socialism also recognised 'governmentalism' as the mode and the aim of their involvement. The maximalist culture of refusal and necessary strife was always there rhetorically, but had been dominated strategically from the very start. For Jaurès and for Blum the task had always been to justify compromise and governmentalism (even though Jaurès never governed). This is what in part makes the *'frondeur'* initiative of 2013–14, and 'principled' departure of the three leftist ministers in September 2014 ultimately incongruous politically, although not rhetorically. In the long period of socialist government (1981–86, 1988–93) not one minister resigned in this way, except Michel Rocard in 1985 over the change in the electoral system, a 'principled' departure, in the name of the Fifth Republic rather than socialism. Within the entire range of rhetorical registers within socialism, the left populism of Montebourg etc. was one of the best adapted to personal leadership, a radical principled register of 'purism', and in some cases an almost millenarian or migratory notion of (but as if temporarily thwarted) promise. This form of left populism is in the fabric of French socialist discourse and it was the register used by the *frondeurs* and by

Montebourg and others. It makes a claim to purism; it is 'true' and uncorrupted, and follows the true path. This justifies its dissidence, because the ruling clique has betrayed this, has gone from the true path. It is, nevertheless, part of the overall discourse of socialist governmentalism. This is reminiscent of the divisions in the party at the Rennes conference of 1990. Here too the clashes were between factions, all of whom were in government. This brings us to the third legacy of Mitterrandism after rhetorical inclusion and governmentalism, namely, the personalisation Mitterrand operationalised in French socialism.

From 1971, the fundamentally Gaullist idea of a personalised rally around Mitterrand accelerated; this in great part because the PS had accepted the presidentialism of the Fifth Republic. It was able to do this partly because it organised *its own* rhetoric and ideas around him. The idea, for example, of the *rassemblement populaire* or *rassemblement d'idées* already existed in socialism; it only had to be adapted. Moreover, the personalist rally around Mitterrand – though all-embracing and devotional – was never utterly admitted to by the party to itself (even today). It could not because socialism is embedded in an impersonalism. The mantra, for example, was always *La Ligne d'Epinay*, as if this meant something other than allegiance to Mitterrand, or that the allegiance was just the consequence. There was always the illusion that it meant ostensibly the Union of the Left (with the PCF), but it remained both after its breakdown in 1977 and the departure of PCF ministers from government in 1984. In 1979 after the failed legislative elections of 1978, the *deuxième gauche*, aided by the municipal left, i.e. Rocard aided by Mauroy, challenged Mitterrand at the Metz conference, but he beat off the challenge (partially through an alliance with CERES) and went on to beat Giscard in 1981 and bring the PS to power (and with an absolute majority, a feat that was considered impossible for the left, even for the Gaullists, apart from June 1968). It is not without significance therefore that Rocard's resignation in 1985 was from the man who was Mitterrand's only personal challenger in the history of the PS. Such personalisation of ideas was facilitated not just by the Fifth Republic and Mitterrand's personalist initiative, but – and this is partly why Mitterrand was able to do what he did: socialism has always had a tradition of leaders representing its ideas or strands within it (similar to, say, G.D.H Cole, Nye Bevan, Jennie Lee, Tony Crosland, or Tony Benn in the UK). Jaurès and Blum were iconic (and Mitterrand often depicted as their *héritier*) (Mollet, Prime Minister, Deputy Prime Minister, and leader of the party for 23 years, airbrushed out of history).

Moreover, from 1971, *all* party factions became acutely personalised; in fact much doctrinal debate and factionalism and *courants* activity became functions of the personal promotion of faction leaders (even strictly doctrinal factions like CERES became personal fiefdoms); and as we have argued became ultimately debilitating to party development. We can also add that within certain disagreements, on the basic issues, solutions, and policies, even ideology – on defence, education, health, and so on, there was no disagreement within the party or between Aubry, Hollande, Valls, Montebourg, and so on. All are governmentalists. The breaks, accusations, resignations, conflicts, and so on are disguised personal strategies designed for gaining advantage within or in relation to the party and, more importantly, win the PS candidacy for the presidency. From 1971 to the present, all party activity has been organised around such personalisation, 2014 being no exception; the cacophony of leadership voices and counter voices in 2014 was in direct contrast to Mitterrand's univocalism, and this because, lyrically, Hollande not only offered no narrative to the party or the country, he also, prosaically, did not control the party itself nor the myriad voices within it.

A final point to note is that after 1971, even though a myriad of rhetorics bloomed – *première gauche, deuxième gauche*, CERES, municipal socialism, *Delorisme*, and so on, they could all be gathered around the two original rhetorical clusters of (Guesdist) maximalism and (Jauresian) pragmatism, now highly personalised, but a dualism, as we have seen, that corresponds to the Fifth Republic's own rhetorical dualism. The Aubry, Montebourg, and *frondeur* rhetoric on the one hand and the Hollande, Valls, Macron rhetoric on the other should be seen in this light (a would-be maximalism v. a pragmatic rationalism). We can add that success usually comes to the PS (1981, 2012) when it blends the two discursive strains; but the question arises whether this oldest and newest of the party's rhetorical divisions still functions, particularly given that – for all the reasons we have elaborated – the political parties no longer structure the social and ideological debate, having reorientated themselves to personalised purpose, which as Hollande's presidency has demonstrated is itself dysfunctional.

François Hollande, time, and performance

Another issue which has emerged from our analysis is the relationship of the President with time and sequencing. This has clearly become a major issue in the 24/7 media world. The first temporal clash of Hollande's presidency was the highly publicised yet 'normal' going on holiday immediately after the legislative elections. This was clearly done to slow the tempo of 'political time' and impose a new 'Hollande' rhythm upon Sarkozy's frenetic pace. Sarkozy's hyperactivity had, however, masked the underlying changing tempo of politics; and the fact that the notion of crisis had been central to the campaign, the failure to impose one or several decisive domestic initiatives before going away was a symbolic gesture of *inaction*, which would become the *leitmotif* of Hollande's presidency. Regarding time, the immediacy of his unpopularity was related to this inaction. One of many illustrations of this was the temporal hostage to fortune, the *Pacte de Responsabilité*, announced in January 2014 and still not applied a year later. The announcement was made to domesticate time, to offer 'a plan' and a project, but its slow application turned time to disadvantage, and pushed 'crisis' time towards ordinary political, legislative time. This clashing of political and mediatic time is one of the problems of modern governance. In a highly personalised system the leader/President becomes the main site where these two meet. Hollande's central mis-use of time, turning political time into mediatic time and adding a wild prediction, was the 'inversion of the unemployment curve' (*l'inversion de la courbe du chomâge*) made a year (over a year, in fact) before the fatal date of the end of 2013, a King Canute gesture of predictable outcome and based on no evidence, only a kind of 'buying time' until the date when the sceptical public were proved right. In fact, this buying time aspect was nearer to Hollande's real reasoning for there had been a growing sense of irritation at the President's constant optimism and assertions that things were already getting much better, or just about to, when it was clear they were not. He clearly calculated that giving himself over a year's respite would halt the criticisms of inaction. This, what we have called 'sequencing the self', was extremely problematic for President Hollande.

What of the 'actual performance' of François Hollande? He suffered in part from his 'look'. He was quite short, growing slightly overweight during his presidency (having been much thinner during the campaign). He also had a somewhat halting and ponderous public discourse. In this, however, he was not alone as a less than riveting speaker. Sarkozy was quite a good speaker, but took unknowing liberties with the French language itself, all this noticed not just by the media but by the culturally sensitive French themselves, sometimes aghast at Sarkozy's poor grasp of grammar (Calvet and Véronis 2008). Chirac was a notoriously awkward public speaker. Mitterrand was compelling. Pompidou and Giscard were average speakers (the latter aristocratic, 'plummy' sounding). And de Gaulle was de Gaulle. All of Hollande's press conferences and TV interviews saw his audience drop steadily. He rarely captured attention in what he said, how he said it, or how he looked. And in his press conference in the wake of Trierweiler's book in September 2014, he appeared and sounded (*'c'est pas facile'* uttered numerous times ...) a somewhat plaintive, wounded figure. These small, performative issues taken individually do not seem to amount to much, but as elements in the overall performance of a presidential character and presidential image, these gestures, images, and elements of performance are, as we have seen, of profound significance.

The international and the domestic in Hollande's presidency

We said in Chapter 1 that the French presidency was almost designed for foreign policy initiatives; and, constitutionally, the President has sweeping powers as we saw over the decision to intervene in Mali, and the near-intervention in Syria in 2013. Generally, however, Hollande's tendency to give press conferences or make announcements about domestic issues, as in the case of the September 2014 NATO summit, even very personal issues, while representing France abroad, was a recurring and major mistake in terms of presidential status. Nevertheless, his international action and image, in part given France's world importance, was satisfactory in his first two years or so. However, from our perspective, it is clear that a foreign policy profile for a French President is necessary but not sufficient. As we saw in Chapters 2 and 4, Hollande undertook a scheduled series of five international meetings and summits immediately after his inauguration. This contrasted with the absence of a similar and immediate dynamism in the domestic arena. Such a combination is arguably even worse than 'necessary but not sufficient' given that the contrast between the two threw the paucity of domestic initiatives into higher relief; and Hollande's very deliberate slowing of the tempo of political activity, so that it became clear that no reforms would begin until the autumn at the very least, began a fast downward spiral of popularity that would become relentless. International initiatives can be impressive (e.g. Hollande's impromptu stop-over to meet with Putin in December 2014 to address the Ukrainian crisis), but if they are not accompanied by a presidential or governmental thrust of equal intensity at the domestic level they are counter-productive. Such scenarios, given the personalised nature of the presidency, appear like *personal* evasions.

A further disadvantage to presidential foreign policy initiatives was the fact that given the involvement of the presidency now in all matters – not his initial intention – the contrasts (e.g. Syria/Leonarda, US State visit/public separation from Ms Trierweiler, etc.), it became increasingly the case that Hollande's international activity became a substitute for his falling domestic popularity, and yet the presence of domestic issues (e.g. Leonarda, Trierweiler's book, particularly its English translation launch in London in November 2014) *alongside* the international tended to ridicule the President (and France...) even more. And the more he used the international stage, the more he personalised the presidential function – the most blatant being his 15 September 2013 TV interview on Syria which we analysed in Chapter 5 – and therefore the more he was seen as disconnected from the domestic. Hollande's relative political eclipse by September 2014 and the presence of an active and forceful Prime Minister altered this situation, arguably returning the configuration of institutional power back to what Hollande – and perhaps Michel Debré – had originally intended.

The presidency and character

Just before the 2012 presidential election (*Le Point* 26/2/12), when polled, a majority of respondents in France (as anywhere) named the cost of living (*pouvoir d'achat*), the economic crisis (*la crise*), and unemployment (*le chômage*), as their greatest concerns. The same poll said Hollande would bring change (65%), but that he inspired confidence in only 31%. When asked if he was of presidential stature, only 16% agreed. In many ways, the two sets of questions are more related than they appear. The answers regarding the cost of living are obviously people's main preoccupation, but the low 'stature' of Hollande's presidential image tells us something about the nature of the presidency, and the subsequent fortunes of President Hollande. (And we can add that the monthly *Figaro Baromètre* on the popularity of a range of politicians, especially the President, is a permanent fixture in the French media, and is cited endlessly on TV and on radio.) Presidential performance is in a permanent and critical relation to public perceptions. The Fifth Republic frames political relationships between the presidency and 'the French' and 'France', and these are active elements of political rhetoric. The dramatic advent of the Fifth Republic, de Gaulle's choices, and the configuration of the institutions made the presidency the central actor in the republic. This political configuration drew upon the actors within it and upon the culturally informed history of leadership in France in a very singular way, refashioning both the political parties and also 'opinion', and introducing into political exchange the idea of envisioning leadership and a set of imagined yet very important relationships. The fundamental characteristic of de Gaulle's republic was the introduction of presidential character into the political process. This remains its defining characteristic today.

Bibliography

Bibliographical note

Given the range of sources for this study, only an indicative bibliography is given. We have not included journal articles or book chapters unless cited. In the text, the source texts – e.g. for presidentialism or the founding of the Fifth Republic – were so many we have included only the main sources; a complete bibliography is given below. We have also used extensively the quarterly journal *Sondages: Revue française de l'opinion publique* (Paris: Chancelier), IFOP's webpages, SOFRES' annual *L'État de l'Opinion* (Paris: Seuil), the journal *Revue française de science politique* and *Le Monde, Le Figaro, Libération, L'Express, Le Point* and *Le Nouvel observateur/L'Obs*, as well as the news programmes BFMTV, iTélé, Fr2, and LCP.

Alter, A. and Cherchève, P. (2007) *La Gauche et le Sexe: Ségolène, François, Dominique, Olivier, Arlette et les autres...* (Paris: Danger Public).

Amar, C. (2013) *Jusqu'ici tout va mal* (Paris: Grasset).

Amar, C. and Chemin, A. (2002) *Jospin & Cie. Histoire de la gauche plurielle, 1993–2002* (Paris: Seuil).

Amar, C. and Hassoux, D. (2005) *Ségolène et François* (Paris: Privé).

Anderson, B. (2006) *Imagined Communities* (London: Verso).

Andolfatto, D. (2005) *PCF: de la mutation à la liquidation* (Paris: Éditions du Rocher).

André, A. and Rissouli, K. (2009) *Hold-uPS, arnaques et trahisons* (Paris: Archipoche).

André, A. and Rissouli, K. (2012) *L'homme qui ne devait pas être président* (Paris: A. Michel).

Andrews, W.G. (1982) *Presidential Government in Gaullist France* (Albany: Suny Press).

Angeli, C. *et al.* (1969) *Les héritiers du général* (Paris: Denoël).

Année politique, économique et sociale en France (1945–) (Paris: PUF/Éditions du Moniteur).

Ariès, P. (2005) *Misère du sakozysme: Cette droite qui n'aime pas la France* (Lyon: Parangon/Vs).

Artufel, C. and Duroux, M. (2006) *Nicolas Sarkozy et la communication* (Paris: Éditions Pepper).

Association française de science politique (1960) *Le référendum de septembre et les élections de novembre 1958* (Paris: Presses de la fondation nationale des sciences politiques).

Astruc, V. (2013) *Florange, la tragédie de la gauche* (Paris: Plon).

Audigier, F. and Bavarez, N. (1998) *De Gaulle et le RPF 1947–1955* (Paris: A. Colin).

Bachelay, G. (2007) *Désert d'avenir? Le Parti socialiste, 1983–2007* (Paris: Bruno Leprince).

Bachy, F. (2001) *François Hollande: un destin tranquille* (Paris: Plon).

Bachy, F. (2005) *L'énigme Hollande* (Paris: Plon).

Bacqué, R. (2002) *Chirac ou le démon du pouvoir* (Paris: Albin Michel).

Bacqué, R. and Chemin, A. (2007) *La femme fatale* (Paris: Albin Michel).

Ballet, M. (2014) *Émotions et élections: les campagnes présidentielles françaises, 1981–2012* (Bry-sur-Marne: INA, impr).

Baniafouna, C. (2012) *Présidentielle 2012: et maintenant, la guerre dans les urnes!* (Paris: L'Harmattan).

Barthes, R. (1957) *Mythologies* (Paris: Seuil).

Bartolone, C. (2007) *Une élection 'imperdable'* (Paris: L'Archipel).

Bassi, M. (2004) *Cinq présidents à armes égales* (Paris: J.C. Lattès).

Bauchard, P. (1986) *La guerre des deux roses* (Paris: Grasset).

Baumel, L. (2007) *Rénover le Parti socialiste: Un défi impossible?* (Paris: Bruno Leprince).

Baumel, L. (2013) *La malédiction des gouvernants: François Hollande peut-il être réélu?* (Lormont: Le Bord de l'eau).

Beau, N. (2013) *Papa Hollande au Mali: chronique d'un fiasco annoncé* (Paris: Balland).

Becker, J.-J. (1988) *Histoire politique de la France depuis 1945* (Paris: Armand Colin).

Becker, J.-J. (1998) *Crises et alternances 1974–1995* (Paris: Seuil).

Bell, D.S. (2000) *Presidential Power in Fifth Republic France* (Oxford: Berg).

Bell, D.S. (2005) *François Mitterrand* (Cambridge: Polity).

Bell, D.S. and Criddle, B. (1988) *The French Socialist Party*, 2nd edn (Oxford: Clarendon Press).

Bell, D.S. and Criddle, B. (1994) *The French Communist Party in the Fifth Republic* (Oxford: Clarendon Press).

Bell, D.S. and Criddle, B. (2014) *Exceptional Socialists: The Case of the French Socialist Party* (Basingstoke: Palgrave).

Bell, D.S. and Gaffney, J. (eds) (2013) *The Presidents of the French Fifth Republic* (Basingstoke: Palgrave).

Benoist, J.-M. (1979) *Chronique de la décomposition du PCF* (Paris: La Table Ronde).

Benoist, L. (1977) *Signes, symboles et mythes* (Paris: Presses universitaires de France).

Bercoff, A. (2013) *Moi, Président...* (Paris: First Editions).

Berenson, E., Duclert, V. and Prochasson, C. (eds) (2011) *The French Republic: History, Values, Debates* (Ithaca, NY: Cornell University Press).

Berger, P. and Luckmann, T. (1991[1959]) *The Social Construction of Reality* (London: Penguin).

Berstein, S. (1989) *La France de l'expansion I. La République gaullienne 1958–1969* (Paris: Seuil).

Berstein, S. (2001) *Histoire du gaullisme* (Paris: Perrin).

Berstein, S. and Milza, P. (1991) *Histoire de la France au XXe siècle: 1945–1958* (Brussels: Complexe).

Berstein, S. and Milza, P. (1994) *Histoire de la France au XXe siècle de 1974 à nos jours* (Brussels: Complexe).

Berstein, S., Rémond, R. and Sirinelli, J.-F. (eds) (2003) *Les années Giscard: Institutions et pratiques 1974–1978* (Paris: Fayard).

Berstein, S. and Rioux, J.-P. (1995) *La France de l'expansion 2. L'apogée Pompidou (1969–1974)* (Paris: Seuil).

Berstein, S. and Rioux, J.-P. (2000) *The Pompidou Years, 1969–1974* (Cambridge: Cambridge University Press).

Berstein, S. and Sirinelli, J.-F. (eds) (2007) *Les années Giscard. Les réformes de société* (Paris: Armand Colin).

Bertolus, J.-J. and Bredin, F. (2011) *Tir à vue, 1965–2012: la folle histoire des prés identielles* (Paris: Fayard).

Bertrand, D. *et al.* (2007) *Parler pour gagner* (Paris: Presses de Sciences Po).

Binet, L. (2012) *Rien ne se passe comme prévu* (Paris: Grasset).

Blier, J.-M. (2008) *Le combat des chefs* (Paris: Éditions du Rocher).

Blum, L. (1955–72) 'Notes sur la doctrine' (1946) and 'Discours au XXXVIIIe congrès' (1946a) in *L'Oeuvre 1943–1947* (Paris: Albin Michel).

Blum, L. (1945) *A l'echelle humaine* (Paris: Gallimard).

Boniface, P. (2012) *Le monde selon Sarkozy* (Paris: J.-C. Gawsewitch).

Bottici, C. (2007) *A Philosophy of Political Myth* (Cambridge: Cambridge University Press).

Bouilhaguet, A. and Jakubyszyn, C. (2012) *La Frondeuse* (Paris: Éd du Moment).

Bourdieu, P. (1984) *Distinction* (London: Routledge).

Bourmaud, F.-X. (2010) *PS, la bataille des ego* (Paris: L'Archipel).

Branca, E. and Folch, A. (2008) *Histoire sècrete de la droite, 1958–2008* (Paris: Plon).

Bréchon, P. (ed.) (1994) *Le discours politique en France: Evolution des idées partisanes* (Paris: La Documentation française).

Bréchon, P. (ed.) (2001) *Les partis politiques français* (Paris: La Documentation française).

Bréchon, P. (ed.) (2002) *Les élections présidentielles en France* (Paris: La Documentation française).

Bréchon, P. (2013) *Les élections présidentielles sous la Ve République* (Paris: La Documentation française).

Bréchon, P., Laurent, A. and Perrineau, P. (eds) (2000) *Les cultures politiques des Français* (Paris: Presses de Sciences Po).

Bugat, S. (2012) *Le président Hollande: ses équipes, ses réseaux, ses projets* (Paris: L'Archipel).

Butler, B. (1990) *Gender Trouble: Feminism and the Subversion of Identity* (London: Routledge).

Butler, J. and Scott, J.W. (eds) (1992) *Feminists Theorize the Political* (London: Routledge).

Cabana, A. and Rosencher, A. (2012) *Entre deux feux* (Paris: Grasset).

Calvet, L.-J. and Véronis, J. (2008) *Les mots de Nicolas Sarkozy* (Paris: Seuil).

Cambadélis, J.-C. (2007) *Parti pris: Chroniques de la présidentielle chez les socialistes* (Paris: Plon).

Capitant, R. (1971) *Ecrits politiques 1960–1970* (Paris: Flammarion).

Capitant, R. (1972) *Démocratie et participation* (Paris: Bordas).

Carter, E. (2011) *The Extreme Right in Western Europe: Success or Failure?* (Manchester: Manchester University Press).

Cathala, J. and Prédall, J.-B. (2002) *Nous nous sommes tant haïs. 1997–2002. Voyage au centre de la droite* (Paris: Seuil).

Cayrol, R. (2000) *Sondages, mode d'emploi* (Paris: Presses de Sciences Po).

Centre de Recherches Politiques de Sciences Po (Paris) (2013) *Elections 2012: les électorats, les enjeux et les votes* (Paris: Presses de Sciences Po).

Cerny, P.G. (1980) *The Politics of Grandeur: Ideological Aspects of de Gaulle's Foreign Policy* (Cambridge: Cambridge University Press).

Chafer, T. and Godin, E. (eds) (2006) *The French Exception* (Oxford: Berghahn).

Chagnollaud, D. and Quermonne, J-L. (1996) *La Vᵉ République 1 – Le régime politique* (Paris: Fayard).

Chalaby, J.K. (2002) *The de Gaulle Presidency and the Media: Statism and Public Communications* (Basingstoke: Palgrave).

Chandernagor, A. (1967) *Un parlement, pour quoi faire?* (Paris: Gallimard).

Chapsal, J. and Lancelot, A. (1975) *La vie politique en France depuis 1940* (Paris: Presses universitaires de France).

Charaudeau, P. (2008) *Entre populisme et peopolisme: comment Sarkozy a gagné!* (Paris: Vuibert).

Charbonneau, N. and Guimier, L. (2006) *Le roi est mort? Vive le roi! Enquête au cœur de notre monarchie républicaine* (Paris: Michalon).

Charlot, J. (1970) *Le phénomène gaulliste* (Paris: Fayard).

Charlot, J. (ed.) (1971) *Les Français et de Gaulle* (Paris: Plon).

Charlot, J. (1983) *Le Gaullisme d'opposition, 1946–1958* (Paris: Fayard).

Charlot, J. (1994) *La Politique en France* (Paris: Fallois).

Charpier, F. (2006) *Nicolas Sarkozy: Enquête sur un homme de pouvoir* (Paris: Presses de la Cité).

Charteris-Black, J. (2005) *Politicians and Rhetoric* (Basingstoke: Palgrave).

Chatain, J. (1987) *Les affaires de M. Le Pen* (Paris: Messidor).

Chavelet, E. and Grépinet, M. (2011) *Élysée 2012: les hommes de l'ombre* (Paris: R. Laffont).

Chevallier, J.-J., Carcassonne, G. and Duhamel, O. (2002) *La Vᵉ République 1958–2002: Histoire des institutions et des régimes politiques de la France* (Paris: Armand Colin).

Chevènement, J.-P. (1980) *Le Projet Socialiste* (Paris: Parti Socialiste).

Chevrier, M. and Gusse, I. (eds) (2010) *La France depuis de Gaulle: la Ve République en perspective* (Montréal: Les Presses universitaires de Montréal).

Chirac, B. (2001) *Conversation* (Paris: Plon).

Chombeau, C. (2007) *Le Pen, fille et père* (Paris: Panama).

Clerc, C. (2006) *Tigres et tigresses: Histoire intime des couples présidentiels sous la Vᵉ République* (Paris: Plon).

Clerc, C. (2014) *Tout est fichu!: les coups de blues du général* (Paris: Albin Michel).

Club Jean Moulin (1965) *Un parti pour la gauche* (Paris: Seuil).

Cole, A. François Mitterrand: From Republican Contender to President of all the French, in Gaffney, J. (1989a) *The French Presidential Elections of 1988* (Aldershot: Dartmouth).

Cole, A. (1998) *French Politics and Society* (Hemel Hempstead: Prentice-Hall).

Cole, A. (2008) *Governing and Governance in France* (Cambridge: Cambridge University Press).

Cole, A., Le Galès, P. and Levy, J. (eds) (2005) *Developments in French Politics* (Basingstoke: Palgrave Macmillan).

Colombani, J.-M. (2008) *Un Américain à Paris* (Paris: Plon).

Conseil constitutionnel (2014) *Texte intégral de la Constitution du 4 octobre 1958 en vigueur* (Paris: Conseil constitutionnel).

Corner, J. (2000) Mediated Persona and Political Culture: Dimensions of Structure and Process. *European Journal of Cultural Studies*, 3, 3, pp. 386–402.

Corner, J and Pels, D. (eds) (2003) *The Media and the Restyling of Politics* (London: Sage).

Cotta, M. (1974) *La VIᵉ République* (Paris: Flammarion).

Cotta, M. (1995) *Les secrets d'une victoire* (Paris: Flammarion).

Cotta, M. (2012) *Le rose et le gris: prélude au quinquennat de François Hollande* (Paris: Fayard).

Cotteret, J.-M. and Moreau, R. (1969) *Recherches sur le vocabulaire du général de Gaulle* (Paris: Armand Colin).

Cotteret, J.-M., Emeri, C., Gerstlé, J. and Moreau, R. (1976) *Giscard d'Estaing, Mitterrand: 54,774 mots pour convaincre* (Paris: Presses universitaires de France).

Courage, S. (2012) *L'Ex* (Paris: Éd du Moment).

Courcol, C. and Masure, T. (2007) *Ségolène Royal: Les coulisses d'une défaite* (Paris: L'Archipel).

Crousnilhon, M. de (2012) *De Gaulle, le général-président* (Toulon: Presses du Midi).

Daniel, J.-M. and Sterdyniak, H. (2012) *Présidence Sarkozy: quel bilan?* (Bordeaux: Éd. Prométhée).

De Gaulle, C. (1954, 1956, 1959, 1970, 1971) *Mémoires*, 5 vols (Paris: Plon).

De Gaulle, C. (1970a) *Discours et messages*, 5 vols (Paris: Plon).

De Gaulle, C. (1990, 1994 and 1999) *Le Fil de l'épée et autres écrits* (Paris: Plon).

De la Gorce, P.-M. (1999) *De Gaulle* (Paris: Perrin).

De Sutter, P. (2007) *Ces fous qui nous gouvernent: Comment la psychologie permet de comprendre les hommes politiques* (Paris: Les Arènes).

Debré, J.-L. (1974) *Les idées constitutionnelles du général de Gaulle* (Paris: Pichon).

Debré, M. (1972) *Une certaine idée de la France* (Paris: Fayard).

Debû-Bridel, J. (1970) *De Gaulle contestataire* (Paris: Plon).

Defferre, G. (1965) *Un nouvel horizon* (Paris: Gallimard).

Degois, F. (2014) *Quelle histoire! Ségolène Royal et François Hollande* (Paris: Plon).

Delais, B. (2012) *Elle et lui ou la chronique d'un mariage forcé* (Paris: J.C. Lattès).

Delapierre, F. (2012) *Quelle histoire! Chronique(s) du Front de gauche* (Paris: Bruno Leprince).

Deloire, C. and Dubois, C. (2006) *Sexus politicus* (Paris: Albin Michel).

Déloye, Y., Haroche, C. and Ihl, O. (1996) *Le protocole ou la mise en forme de l'ordre politique* (Paris: L'Harmattan).

Delwit, P. (2014) *Les partis politiques en France* (Bruxelles: Éd. de l'Université de Bruxelles).

Dély, R. (2008) *La guerre des ex* (Paris: les Éd. du Moment).

Denquin, J.-M. (1988) *1958: la genèse de la Ve République* (Paris: Presses universitaires de France).

Derai, Y. and Guez, L. (2001) *Appelez-moi Jacques: Enquête sur un 'président sympa'* (Paris: Calmann-Lévy).

Desjardins, T. (1978) *François Mitterrand: un socialiste gaullien* (Paris: Hachette).

Desjardins, T. (1995) *L'homme qui n'aime pas les dîners en ville* (Paris: Édition No. 1).

Domain, V. (2006) *Entre le coeur et la raison* (Paris: Fayard).

Donegani, J.-M. and Sadoun, M. (1998) *La Vᵉ République: Naissance et mort* (Paris: Gallimard).

Douglas, P. (2010) *Sarko Folie's* (Paris: Éditions du Rocher).

Drake, H. and Gaffney, J. (eds) (1996) *The Language of Political Leadership in Contemporary France* (Aldershot: Dartmouth).

Drake, P. and Higgins, M. (2012) Lights, Camera, Election: Celebrity, Performance and the 2010 UK General Election Leadership Debates. *British Journal of Politics and International Relations*, 14, 3, pp. 375–391.

Dray, J. (2008) *Et maintenant?* (Paris: Le Cherche Midi).

Dreyfus, F.-G. (1982) *De Gaulle et le gaullisme* (Paris: Presses universitaires de France).

Duhamel, A. (2006) *Les prétendants 2007* (Paris: Plon).

Duhamel, A. (2009) *La marche consulaire* (Paris: Plon).

Duhamel, O. (1993) *La gauche et la Ve République* (Paris: Quadrige).

Duhamel, O. (1993) *Le pouvoir politique en France* (Paris: Seuil).

Duhamel, O. (2008, 3rd ed.) *Le Quinquennat* (Paris: Presses de Sciences Po).

Dupin, E. (2012) *La victoire empoisonnée* (Paris: Éd. du Seuil).

Duverger, M. (1961) *La VIe République et le régime présidentiel* (Paris: Fayard).

Duverger, M. (1974) *La monarchie républicaine* (Paris: Laffont).

Duverger, M. (1978) *Échec au roi* (Paris: Albin Michel).

Edelman, M. (1964) *The Symbolic Uses of Politics* (Urbana: University of Illinois Press).

Edelman, M. (1988) *Constructing the Political Spectacle* (Chicago: University of Chicago Press).

Elgie, R. (ed.) (1996) *Electing the French President: The 1995 Presidential Election* (Basingstoke: Palgrave).

Elgie, R. (2003) *Political Institutions in Contemporary France* (Oxford: Oxford University Press).

Estier, C. (2012) *François Hollande, journal d'une victoire* (Paris: Cherche midi).

Evans, J. and Ivaldi, G. (2013) *The 2012 French Presidential Elections: The Inevitable Alternation* (Basingstoke: Palgrave).

Evin, G. (2012) *'Je n'aime pas les riches': enquête sur Hollande, la gauche et l'argent* (Paris: les Éd. du Moment).

Faligot, R. and Guisnel, J. (eds) (2007) *Histoire secrète de la Ve République* (Paris: La Découverte).

Favier, P. and Martin-Roland, M. (1990–99) *La Décennie Mitterrand*, 4 vols: I: *Les ruptures*, 1990; II: *Les épreuves*, 1991; III: *Les défis*, 1996; IV: *Les déchirements*, 1999 (Paris: Seuil).

Ferniot, J. (1965) *De Gaulle et le 13 mai* (Paris: Plon).

Fieschi, C. (2004) *Fascism, Populism and the French Fifth Republic: In the Shadow of Democracy* (Manchester: Manchester University Press).

Finlayson, A. (2002) Elements of the Blairite Image of Leadership. *Parliamentary Affairs*, 55, 3, pp. 586–599.

Fleurdorge, D. (2001) *Les rituels du président de la République* (Paris: Presses universitaires de France).

Flood, C. and Bell, L. (eds) (1997) *Political Ideologies in Contemporary France* (London: Pinter).

Fondation Copernic (2013) *Un an après l'élection de François Hollande: tableau d'un glissement néolibéral* (Paris: Syllepse).

Fondation nationale des sciences politiques (1970) *L'élection présidentielle des 5 et 19 décembre 1965* (Paris: Armand Colin).

Fondation nationale des sciences politiques (1971) *Les élections législatives de mars 1967* (Paris: Armand Colin).

Frears, J.R. (1981) *France in the Giscard Presidency* (London: Allen and Unwin).

Freeden, M. (1996) *Ideologies and Political Theory: A Conceptual Approach* (Oxford: Clarendon Press).

Frerejean, A. (2007) *C'était Georges Pompidou* (Paris: Fayard).

Freud, S. (2002) *The Psychopathology of Everyday Life* (Harmondsworth: Penguin).

Friedman, J.-P. (2005) *Dans la peau de Sarko* (Paris: Éditions Michalon).

Gaetner, G. (2007) *L'Art de retourner sa veste: La trahison en politique* (Paris: Éditions du Rocher).

Gaffney, J. (1989) *The French Left and the Fifth Republic: The Discourses of Socialism and Communism in Contemporary France* (Basingstoke: Macmillan).

Gaffney, J. (1989a) *The French Presidential Elections of 1988* (Aldershot: Dartmouth).

Gaffney, J. (2001) Imagined Relationships: Political Leadership in Contemporary Democracies. *Parliamentary Affairs*, 54, 1, pp. 120–133.

Gaffney, J. (ed.) (2004) *The French Presidential and Legislative Elections of 2002* (Aldershot: Dartmouth).

Gaffney, J. (2012) *Political Leadership in France: From Charles de Gaulle to Nicolas Sarkozy* (Basingstoke: Palgrave).

Gaffney, J. (2012a) Leadership and Style in the French Fifth Republic: Nicolas Sarkozy's Presidency in Historical and Cultural Perspective. *Journal of French Politics*, 10, 4, pp. 345–363.

Gaffney, J. (2012b) Presidents Behaving Badly: Leadership and Governance in France, in Helms, L. (ed.) *Poor Leadership and Bad Governance: Reassessing Presidents and Prime Ministers in North America, Europe and Japan* (Cheltenham: Edward Elgar).

Gaffney, J. (2014) Political Leadership and the Politics of Performance: France, Syria and the Chemical Weapons Crisis of 2013. *Journal of French Politics*, 12, 1, pp. 218–234.

Gaffney, J. (2014a) Performative Political Leadership, in t'Hart, P. and Rhodes, R. *The Oxford Handbook of Political Leadership* (Oxford: Oxford University Press).

Gaffney, J. and Holmes, D. (eds) (2011) *Stardom in Postwar France* (London: Berghahn).

Gaffney, J. and Kolinsky, E. (eds) (1991) *Political Culture in France and Germany* (London: Routledge).

Gaffney, J. and Milne, L. (eds) (1997) *French Presidentialism and the Election of 1995* (Aldershot: Ashgate).

Gaïti, B. (1998) *De Gaulle, prophète de la cinquième république* (Paris: Presses de Sciences Po).

Galliano, L. (2007) *Les élections presidentielles et législatives de 2007* (Toulouse: Presses de l'université des sciences sociales de Toulouse).

Gambotti, C. (2007) *Sarkozy: La Métamorphose 1999–2007* (Toulouse: Éditions Privat).

Garaud, M.-F. (2006) *La fête des fous: Qui a tué la Ve République?* (Paris: Plon).

Garrigues, J. (2012) *Les Hommes Providentiels: Histoire d'une fascination française* (Paris: Seuil).

Gary, R. (2000) *Ode à l'homme qui fut la France* (Paris: Gallimard).

Gauvin, F. (2012) *Bayrou, Hollande, Joly, Le Pen, Mélenchon, Sarkozy, leur philosophie* (Meaux: Germina).

Gibson, R., Nixon, P. and Ward, S. (eds) (2003) *Political Parties and the Internet: Net Gain?* (London: Routledge).

Giesbert, F.-O. (1990) *Le Président* (Paris: Seuil).

Giesbert, F.-O. (2006) *La tragédie du président* (Paris: Flammarion).

Gildea, R. (1996) *France since 1945* (Oxford: Oxford University Press).

Girard, P. (1999) *Ces Don Juan qui nous gouvernent* (Paris: Éditions 1).

Giret, V. and Pellegrin, B. (2001) *Vingt ans de pouvoir 1981–2001* (Paris: Seuil).

Giscard d'Estaing, V. (1976) *Démocratie française* (Paris: Fayard).

Giscard d'Estaing, V. (1984) *Deux Français sur trois* (Paris: Flammarion).

Giscard d'Estaing, V. (1988, 1991, 2006) *Le pouvoir et la vie*, 3 vols (Paris: Compagnie 12).

Giscard d'Estaing, V. (2009) *La Princesse et le Président* (Paris: Éd. De Fallois).

Goguel, F. (ed.) (1965) *Le référendum d'octobre et les élections de novembre 1962* (Paris: Armand Colin).

Goodliffe, G. (2012) *The Resurgence of the Radical Right in France: From Boulangisme to the Front National* (Cambridge: Cambridge University Press).

Graham, B.D. (1993) *Representation and Party Politics* (Oxford: Blackwell).

Grunberg, G., Mayer, N. and Sniderman, P.M. (2002) *La démocratie à l'épreuve. Une nouvelle approche de l'opinion des Français* (Paris: Presses de Sciences Po).

Guénolé, T. (2013) *Nicolas Sarkozy, chronique d'un retour impossible?* (Paris: First).

Guilledoux, F.-J. (2006) *Tous candidats! Le poids des petits dans la présidentielle 2007* (Paris: Fayard).

Hamon, L. (1958) *De Gaulle dans la république* (Paris: Plon).

Hay, C. (1998) Punctuated Evolution and the Uneven Temporality of Institutional Change. *11th Conference of Europeanists*, 26–28 February.

Hayward, J.E.S. (1983) *Governing France: The One and Indivisible Republic*, 2nd edn (London: Weidenfeld & Nicolson).

Hayward, J.E.S. (ed.) (1993) *De Gaulle to Mitterrand: Presidential Power in France* (London: Hurst).

Hazareesingh, S. (1994) *Political Traditions in Modern France* (Oxford: Oxford University Press).

Hazareesingh, S. (2012) *In the Shadow of the General: Modern France and the Myth of De Gaulle* (Oxford: Oxford University Press).

Hees, J.L. (2007) *Sarkozy Président! Journal d'une élection* (Paris: Éditions du Rocher).

Hefez, S. (2008) *La Sarkose obsessionnelle* (Paris: Hachette).

Helms, L. (2012) (ed.) *Poor Leadership and Bad Governance: Reassessing Presidents and Prime Ministers in North America, Europe and Japan* (Cheltenham: Edward Elgar).

Herman, T. (2008) *Au fil des discours: La rhétorique de Charles de Gaulle (1940–1945)* (Limoges: Lambert-Lucas).

Hewlett, N. (2003) *Democracy in Modern France* (London: Continuum).

Hewlett, N. (2011) *The Sarkozy Phenomenon* (Exeter: Societas).

Hoffman, S. (1967) Heroic Leadership: The Case of Modern France, in Edinger L.J. *Political Leadership in Industrial Societies* (New York: Wiley & Sons).

Hoffman, S., Kindleberger, C.P., Wylie, L.W., Pitts, J.R., Duroselle, J.-B. and Goguel, F. (1963) *In Search of France* (New York: Harper Row).

Hollande, F. (2006) *Devoirs de vérité: dialogue avec Edwy Plenel* (Paris: Stock).

Hollande, F. (2009) *Droit d'inventaires* (Paris: Seuil).

Hollande, F. (2011) *Le rêve français: discours et entretien, 2009–2011* (Toulouse: Privat).

Hollande, F. (2012) *Discours du Bourget: et autres discours de la campagne présiden-tielle* (Paris: L'Harmattan).

Hugues, T. and Dard, B. (2007) *Élections 2007: Les chiffres qui font débat, les réponses des candidats* (Neuilly-sur-Seine: Michel Lafon).

Institut Charles de Gaulle (1981) *Bibliographie internationale sur Charles de Gaulle* (Paris: Plon).

Institut Charles de Gaulle (1983) *Approches de la philosophie politique du général de Gaulle* (Paris: Cujas).

Institut Charles de Gaulle (1990) *Nouvelle bibliographie internationale sur Charles de Gaulle: 1980–1990* (Paris: Plon).

Jaigu, C. (2009) *Sarkozy, du Fouquet's à Gaza* (Paris: Laffont).

Jeudy, B. and Vigogne, L. (2007) *Nicolas Sarkozy: De Neuilly à l'Élysée* (Paris: L'Archipel).

Johnson, R.W. (1981) *The Long March of the French Left* (London: Macmillan).

Jouan, H. (2012) *Le petit Hollande illustré par l'exemple* (Paris: Nouveau monde éd).

Jullian, M. (ed.) (2000) *De Gaulle, traits d'esprit* (Paris: La Cherche Midi).

Kane, J. (2001) *The Politics of Moral Capital* (Cambridge: Cambridge University Press).

Karlin, É. (2014) *Le président qui voulait vivre ses vies* (Paris: Fayard).

Knapp, A. (2004) *Parties and the Party System in France: A Disconnected Democracy?* (Basingstoke: Palgrave).

Knapp, A. (2006) *The Government and Politics of France. Fifth Edition* (London: Routledge).

Kohrs Campbell, K. and Hall Jamieson, K. (2010) *Presidents Creating the Presidency: Deeds Done in Words* (Chicago: The University of Chicago Press).

Krotz, U. and Schildt, J. (2013) *Shaping Europe: France, Germany, and Embedded Bilateralism from the Elysee Treaty to Twenty-First Century Politics* (Oxford: Oxford University Press).

Labbé, D. and Monière, D. (2013) *La campagne présidentielle de 2012: votez pour moi!* (Paris: L'Harmattan).

Laborde, C. (2008) *Critical Republicanism* (Oxford: Oxford University Press).

Lachaise, B. *et al.* (2011) *Les Élections législatives de novembre 1958: Une Rupture?* (Bordeaux: Presses universitaires de Bordeaux).

Lacouture, J. (1984–86) *De Gaulle*, 3 vols (Paris: Seuil).

Lacouture, J. (1998) *Mitterrand*, 2 vols (Paris: Seuil).

Lacouture, J. and Rotman, P. (2000) *Mitterrand: Le roman du pouvoir* (Paris: Seuil).

Lafay, D. (2012) *Tout un programme: présidentielle 2012, ils éclairent le débat* (Lyon: Acteurs de l'économie).

Lambron, M. (2006) *Mignonne, allons voir ...* (Paris: Grasset).

Lambron, M. (2008) *Et bien, dansez maintenant ...* (Paris: Grasset).

Le Brazidec, G. (2000) *René Capitant et Carl Schmitt: Crise et réforme du parlemen-tarisme* (Paris: L'Harmattan).

Le Monde (1978) *Les élections législatives de mars 1978* (Paris: Dossiers et documents).

Le Monde (1995) *Élection présidentielle, 23 avril et 7 mai 1995* (Paris: Dossiers et documents).

Leclerc, G. (2006) *La guerre des deux roses* (Paris: La Table Ronde).

Leclerc, G. and Muracciole, F. (1996) *Lionel Jospin, L'héritier rebelle* (Paris: J.C. Lattès).

Leclerc, G. and Muracciole, F. (2001) *Jospin, L'énigme du conquérant* (Paris: J.C. Lattès).

Lévy, C. (2006) *L'une enchante, l'autre pas* (Paris: Calmann-Lévy).

Lewis-Beck, M. (ed.) (2000) *How France Votes* (London: Chatham House).

Lewis-Beck, M., Nadeau, R. and Bélanger, E. (2012) *French Presidential Elections* (New York: Palgrave).

Lienemann, M.-N. and Cohen, P. (2007) *Au revoir, Royal* (Paris: Perrin).

Longhi, J. and Sarfati, G-E. (eds) (2014) *Les discours institutionnels en confrontation: contribution à l'analyse des discours institutionnels et politiques* (Paris: L'Harmattan).

Lucas, R. and Mourgue, M. (2011) *Martine Aubry: les secrets d'une ambition* (Paris: L'Archipel).

Maarek, P.-J. (2013) *Présidentielle 2012: une communication politique bien singulière* (Paris: L'Harmattan).

Maarek, P.-J. (2014) *Communication et marketing de l'homme politique* (Paris: Lexis Nexis).

Macé-Scaron, J. and Taillandier, F. (2002) *Pour ou contre Jacques Chirac* (Paris: Bayard).

Madjar, R. (1995) *L'Autre Chirac* (Paris: Lafon).

Maier, C. (2001) *Le Général de Gaulle à la lumière de Jacques Lacan* (Paris: L'Harmattan).

Maitrot, J.-C. and Sicault, J.-D. (1969) *Les conférences de presse du général de Gaulle* (Paris: Presses universitaires de France).

Mallet, S. (1965) *Le Gaullisme et la Gauche* (Paris: Seuil).

Malouines, M.-E. (2012) *François Hollande ou La force du gentil* (Paris: J.C. Lattès).

Malouines, M.-E. and Meeus, C. (2006) *La Madone et le Culbuto* (Paris: Fayard).

Malraux, A. (1971) *Les chênes qu'on abat ...* (Paris: Gallimard).

Manow, P. (2010) *In the King's Shadow* (Cambridge: Polity).

Mantoux, A. (2003) *Nicolas Sarkozy: L'instinct du pouvoir* (Paris: Éditions Générales First).

Marcowitz, R., Miard-Delacroix, H. and Fondation Charles de Gaulle (eds) (2012) *50 ans de relations franco-allemandes* (Paris: Nouveau Monde).

Martin, J. (2013) *Politics and Rhetoric* (London: Routledge).

Mary, N. (2013) *Les intellectuels et les figures politiques charismatiques: De Gaulle, Mendès France, Mitterrand* (Paris: Les Indes savantes).

Mascret, A. and Jeanvoine, A.-L. (2007) *Ce qu'on ne vous a pas dit sur Ségolène Royal, Nicolas Sarkozy, François Bayrou, Jean-Marie Le Pen, Nicolas Hulot, Jacques Chirac, José Bové, Arlette Laguiller ...* (Paris: ViaMedias).

Massot, J. (1986) *La Présidence de la République en France: vingt ans d'élection au suffrage universel 1965–1985* (Paris: La Documentation française).

Mayaffre, D. (2012) *Le discours présidentiel sous la Ve république: Chirac, Mitterrand, Giscard, Pompidou, de Gaulle* (Paris: Presses de Sciences Po).

Mayer, N. (2002) *Ces Français qui votent Le Pen* (Paris: Flammarion).

Mayer, N. and Perrineau, P. (1992) *Les comportements politiques* (Paris: Armand Colin).

Mayer, N. and Perrineau, P. (1996) *Le Front National à découvert* (Paris: Presses de Sciences Po).

Mazeau, J. (2007) *Merci Madame Royal* (Paris: Hors Commerce).

Mendès France, P. (1962) *La république moderne* (Paris: Gallimard).

Mendès France, P. (1968) *Pour préparer l'avenir* (Paris: Denoël).

Mendras, H. with Cole, A. (1991) *Social Change in Modern France: Towards a Cultural Anthropology of the Fifth Republic* (Cambridge: Cambridge University Press).

Mergier, A. *et al.* (2005) *Le jour où la France a dit non: Comprendre le référendum du 29 mai 2005* (Paris: Fondation Jean-Jaurès/Plon).

Messenger, J. (2006) *Les gestes des politiques* (Paris: Flammarion).

Mexandeau, L. (2005) *Histoire du parti socialiste 1905–2005* (Paris: Tallandier).

Mexandeau, L. (2007) *Discours des deux méthodes de Jean Jaurès et Jules Guesde* (Paris: Édition: 1).

Michel, R. (2011) *François Hollande, l'inattendu* (Paris: L'Archipel).

Mitterrand, F. (1964) *Le coup d'état permanent* (Paris: Plon).

Mitterrand, F. (1969) *Ma part de vérité: de la rupture à l'unité* (Paris: Fayard).

Mollet, G. (1962) *13 mai 1958, 13 mai 1962* (Paris: Plon).

Mollet, G. (1973) *15 ans après. La constitution de 1958* (Paris: Albin Michel).

Montoya, R. and Anger, V. (2004) *Scandales à l'Elysée* (Paris: Rozan-Laffont).

Morelle, C. (1998) *De Gaulle, le gaullisme et les gaullistes* (Paris: Armand Colin).

Muzet, D. (2007) *La croyance et la conviction: Les nouvelles armes du politique* (La Tour d'Aigues: L'Aube).

Nay, C. (2007) *Un pouvoir nommé désir* (Paris: Grasset).

Nel, N. (1995) *Mai 1981, Mitterrand président* (Paris: La Documentation française).

Neumann, L. (2012) *Les dessous de la campagne* (Paris: Fayard).

Nick, C. (1998) *Résurrection* (Paris: Fayard).

Nicolet, C. (1982) *L'Idée républicaine en France* (Paris: Gallimard).

Noir, V. (2005) *Nicolas Sarkozy, le destin de Brutus* (Paris: Denoël).

Noir, V. (2007) *Putsch au PS* (Paris: Denoël).

Nora, P. (1984) *Les lieux de mémoire* (Paris: Gallimard).

Ottenheimer, G. (2007) *Le sacre de Nicolas: Petits et grands secrets d'une victoire* (Paris: Seuil).

Parker, A. and Kosofsky Sedgwick, E. (eds) (1995) *Performativity and Performance.* (London: Routledge).

Parti de gauche (2012) *Où est le changement? Les 100 premiers jours de François Hollande* (Paris: Bruno Leprince).

Pascal, J. and Potier, F. (2012) *L'élection présidentielle en France* (Paris: Lexis Nexis).

Péan, P. (2011) *Une jeunesse française: François Mitterrand, 1934–1947* (Paris: Pluriel)

Perrier, J.-C. (2000) *De Gaulle vu par les écrivains* (Paris: La Table Ronde).

Perrineau, P. (ed.) (2013) *Le vote normal: les élections présidentielle et législatives d'avril-mai-juin 2012* (Paris: Presses de Sciences Po).

Perrineau, P. (2014) *La France au Front: essai sur l'avenir du Front national* (Paris: Fayard).

Perrineau, P. and Rouban, L. (eds) (2011) *La solitude de l'isoloir: les vrais enjeux de 2012* (Paris: Éd. Autrement).

Perrineau, P. and Ysmal, C. (eds) (1993) *Le vote sanction: les élections législatives des 21 et 28 mars 1993* (Paris: Département Études Politiques du Figaro and Fondation nationale des sciences politiques).

Perrineau, P. and Ysmal, C. (eds) (1995) *Le vote de crise: L'élection présidentielle de 1995* (Paris: Presses de Sciences Po).

Perrineau, P. and Ysmal, C. (eds) (1998) *Le vote surprise: les élections législatives des 25 mai et 1ᵉʳ juin 1997* (Paris: Presses de Sciences Po).

Perrineau, P. and Ysmal, C. (eds) (2003) *Le vote de tous les refus: Les élections présidentielles et législatives de 2002* (Paris: Presses de Sciences Po).

Peyrefitte, A. (1994, 1996, 2000) *C'était de Gaulle*, 3 vols (Paris: de Fallois/Fayard).

Pfaadt, L. (2012) *François Hollande de A à Z* (Saint-Victor-d'Epine: City éd).

Pickles, D. (1958) *France, the Fourth Republic* (London: Methuen).

Pickles, D. (1962) *The Fifth French Republic* (London: Methuen).

Pierson, P. (2000) Increasing Returns, Path Dependence, and the Study of Politics. *American Political Science Review*, 94, 2, June, pp. 251–267.

Pingaud, D. (2002) *L'impossible défaite* (Paris: Seuil).

Pingaud, D. (2013) *L'homme sans com'* (Paris: Seuil).

Plenel, E. (2011) *Le Président de trop* (Paris: Don Quichotte éditions).

Pompidou, G. (1974) *Le nœud gordien* (Paris: Plon).

Portelli, H. (1987) *La Vᵉ République* (Paris: Grasset).

Pouget, C. (2012) *François Hollande: de la Corrèze à l'Élysée* (Paris: L'Archipel).

Quermonne, J.-L. (1980) *Le gouvernement de la France sous la Vᵉ République* (Paris: Dalloz).

Raffy, S. (2012) *Le Président: François Hollande, itinéraire secret* (Paris: Pluriel).

Ramsay, R.L. (2003) *French Women in Politics* (New York: Berghahn Books).

Raymond, G. (1994) *France During the Socialist Years* (Aldershot: Dartmouth).

Rayski, B. (2010) *L'Homme que vous aimez haïr* (Paris: Grasset).

Reinhard, P. (2004) *Après Chirac: Le bal des prétendants a déjà commencé* (Paris: Éditions Générales First).

Rémond, R. (1982) *Les droites en France* (Paris: Aubier Montaigne).

Rémond, R. (1983) *1958: Le retour de de Gaulle* (Brussels: Complexe).

Rémond, R. (2005) *Les droites aujourd'hui* (Paris: Audibert).

Revault d'Allonnes, D. (2012) *Petits meurtres entre camarades: enquête secrète au coeur du PS* (Paris: R. Laffont).

Revel, J.-F. (1988[1959]) *Le Style du général* (Bruxelles: Editions Complexe).

Reza, Y. (2007) *L'aube le soir ou la nuit* (Paris: Flammarion).

Rials, S. (1977) *Les idées politiques du Président Georges Pompidou* (Paris: Presses universitaires de France).

Rimbaud, C. (1997) *Traversées du désert* (Paris: Albin Michel).

Rioux, J.-P. (1983) *La France de la Quatrième République 2. L'expansion et l'impuissance 1952–1958* (Paris: Seuil).

Rioux J.-P. (2008) *Jean Jaurès* (Paris: Perrin).

Robert, D. (1997) *Pendant les 'affaires' les affaires continuent* (Paris: Éditions Stock).

Rocard, M. (2012) *Mes points sur les i: propos sur la présidentielle et la crise* (Paris: O. Jacob).

Roche, J. (1971) *Le style des candidats à la présidence de la République, 1965, 1969* (Toulouse: Privat).

Royal, S. (2009) *Entretiens avec Françoise Degois: Femme Debout* (Paris: Denoël).

Sabatier, G. and Ragueneau, P. (1994) *Le Dictionnaire du Gaullisme* (Paris: Albin Michel).

Saint-Iran, J. (2005) *Villepin vu du Quai, Les cent semaines* (Paris: Privé).

Sarkozy, N. (2001) *Libre* (Paris: Laffont).

Sarkozy, N. (2006) *Témoignage* (Paris: XO).

Sarkozy, N. (2007) *Ensemble* (Paris: XO).

Saussez, T. (2013) *Les deux corps du Président* (Paris: R. Laffont).

Schemla, E. (1993) *Edith Cresson: la femme piégée* (Paris: Flammarion).

Schwartzenberg, R.-G. (2011) *L'État Spectacle* (Paris: Plon).

Séguéla, J. and Saussez, T. (2007) *La prise de l'Elysée: Les campagnes présidentielles de la Vᵉ République* (Paris: Plon).

Seligmann, F. (2006) *Les socialistes au pouvoir Tome II. 1981–1995* (Paris: Éditions Michalon).

Seznec, B. (1994) *Séguin* (Paris: Grasset).

Shépard, Z. (2010) *Absolument debordée* (Paris: Albin Michel).

Siegfried, A. (1958) *De la IVᵉ à la Vᵉ république* (Paris: Grasset).

Sinclair, A. (1997) *Deux ou trois choses que je sais d'eux* (Paris: Grasset).

Sirinelli, J.-F. (1992) *Histoire des droites en France*, 3 vols (Paris: Gallimard).

Sirius (H. Beuve-Méry) (1958) *Le suicide de la IVe République* (Paris: Le Cerf).

Street, J. (2004) Celebrity Politicians: Popular Culture and Political Representation. *British Journal of Politics and International Relations*, 6, 4, pp. 435–452.

Street, J. (2012) Do Celebrity Politics and Celebrity Politicians Matter? *British Journal of Politics and International Relations*, 14, 3, pp. 346–356.

t'Hart, P. (2010) *Understanding Public Leadership* (Basingstoke: Palgrave).

Tandonnet, M. (2013) *Histoire des présidents de la République: vingt-quatre hommes et la France* (Paris: Perrin).

Tenzer, N. (1998) *Le face cachée du gaullisme* (Paris: Hachette).

Thevenon, G. and Jal, J.-P. (2014) *Les partis politiques: vie politique française* (Lyon: Chronique sociale).

Thody, P. (1989) *French Caesarism: From Napoleon to Charles De Gaulle* (Basingstoke: Macmillan).

Thody, P. (1998) *The Fifth French Republic: Presidents, Politics and Personalities* (London: Routledge).

Tiberj, V. (2013) *Des votes et des voix: de Mitterrand à Hollande* (Nîmes: Champ social).

Todd, E. (2008) *Après la démocratie* (Paris: Gallimard).

Touchard, J. *et al.* (1960) *Le Référendum de Septembre et les élections de Novembre 1958* (Paris: Pressses de la Fondation des Sciences politiques).

Touchard, J. (1978) *Le Gaullisme 1940–1969* (Paris: Seuil).

Touret, D. (1994) *L'élection présidentielle, au coeur des institutions de la Vᵉ République* (Paris: Les Éditions d'Organisation).

Trierweiler, V. (2014) *Merci pour ce moment* (Paris: Arènes).

Vallaud-Belkacem, N. (2012) *Raison de plus!* (Paris: Fayard).

Vallon, L. (1969) *L'anti-de Gaulle* (Paris: Seuil).

Viansson-Ponté, P. (1970–71) *Histoire de la République gaullienne*, 2 vols (Paris: Fayard).

Visot, M. and Lachèvre, C. (2014) *Les sales gosses de la République* (Neuilly-sur-Seine: Lafon).

Vivier, J-L. (2013) *Ontologie de la droite et de la gauche en politique* (Paris: L'Harmattan).

Weber, M. (1964) *The Theory of Economic and Social Organisation* (New York: Free Press).

Weber, M. (2004) *The Vocation Lectures* (Indianapolis: Hackett Publishing Co. Inc.).

Weber, P. (2010) *La Reine Carla* (Monaco: Rocher).

Weil, S. (1962) *Selected Essays: 1934–1943* (Oxford: Oxford University Press).

Wheeler, M. (2012) The Democratic Worth of Celebrity Politics in an Era of Late Modernity. *British Journal of Politics and International Relations*, 14, 3, pp. 407–422.

Wilcox, L. (1996) Edith Cresson: Victim of Her Own Image, in Drake, H. and Gaffney, J. (1996) *The Language of Leadership in Contemporary France* (Aldershot: Dartmouth).

Williams, P. M. (1970) *French Politicians and Elections, 1951–1969* (Cambridge: Cambridge University Press).

Williams, P.M. (1970a) *Wars, Plots and Scandals in Post-War France* (Cambridge: Cambridge University Press).

Williams, P.M. (1972) *Crisis and Compromise* (London: Longmans).

Williams, P.M. and Harrison, M. (1960) *De Gaulle's Republic* (London: Longmans).

Winock, M. (1993) *Histoire de l'extrême droite en France* (Paris: Seuil).

Winock, M. (2007) *La Mêlée présidentielle* (Paris: Flammarion).

Wodak, R. (2009) *The Discourse of Politics in Action* (Basingstoke: Palgrave).

Wodak, R. *et al.* (eds) (2013) *Right-Wing Populism in Europe: Politics and Discourse* (London: Bloomsbury).

Wright, V. (1978) *The Government and Politics of France* (London: Routledge).

Zarka, J.-C. (2009) *Institutions politiques françaises*. 5e édition (Paris: Ellipses).

Index

194 *Index*

Printed and bound by CPI Group (UK) Ltd, Croydon, CR0 4YY